PSYCHOPATHOLOGY

AND POLITICS

PSYCHOPATHOLOGY

AND POLITICS

by Harold D. Lasswell

With a

new Introduction

by Fred I. Greenstein

THE UNIVERSITY OF CHICAGO PRESS
Chicago and London

THE UNIVERSITY OF CHICAGO PRESS 60637
THE UNIVERSITY OF CHICAGO PRESS, LTD., LONDON
Copyright © 1930, 1977 by The University of Chicago
Copyright © 1960 by The Viking Press, Inc.
All rights reserved. Published 1930
Phoenix Edition 1977
Printed in the United States of America
ISBN: 0-226-46922-0

86 85 84 83 82 81 2 3 4 5 6

"Afterthoughts" by Harold D. Lasswell reprinted here by
arrangement with The Viking Press, Inc.

CONTENTS

INTRODUCTION

The reappearance in print of Harold Dwight Lasswell's 1930 classic, *Psychopathology and Politics*, is a major intellectual occasion.[1] Like many of the other influential contributions to social science literature that emerged from the University of Chicago during the 1920s and 1930s,[2] this work was well in advance of its time. In two respects, the times have caught up to *Psychopathology and Politics*. First, the years since 1930 have been replete with political events and phenomena that defy complete explanation without following Lasswell's precedent of utilizing contemporary clinical psychology. Examples range from the trajectory of German National Socialism, which was barely underway at the time Lasswell wrote, to the forced resignation in 1974 of that conspicuously enigmatic, emotionally-driven individual, President Richard M. Nixon. The popular analogies that circulated during Nixon's final period in office comparing the White House with Hitler's bunker, and stressing parallels between the two leaders' personal self-destructiveness and lack of contact with reality were polemical oversimplifications. But the comparisons were not wholly

[1] Readers familiar with only the 1960 Viking Press edition will not know (except by inference from textual references to them) that the book originally contained a bibliographical and a methodological appendix, both of which are included in this edition. Readers familiar with only the 1930 original edition and the 1950 edition will discover in this printing the "Afterthoughts" composed by Lasswell for the 1960 edition.

[2] For a discussion of how political science fit into the larger pattern of social science innovation at the University of Chicago during this period, see Barry D. Karl's biography of Charles E. Merriam, the intellectual mentor of Lasswell and many of the other leading University of Chicago political scientists who worked in Merriam's department: *Charles E. Merriam and the Study of Politics* (Chicago: University of Chicago Press, 1974).

without substance. Second, both scholars and lay political observers have increasingly heeded Lasswell's plea for study and analysis of the public significance of political actors' "private" worlds.

To be a classic, a book must not only be a pioneer in its field, but must also be of continuing value. Beginning with the very vividness of its title, *Psychopathology and Politics* arrests the reader's attention and conveys an immediate resonance with perceptions of at least a segment of political behavior—namely, events, like those referred to above, that seem inexplicable if one attends only their environmental context and sees political psychology only as rational action. In terms of Sir Francis Bacon's well-known classification of books, this work falls in the third and highest class of those "few to be chewed and digested." Even readers who treat the book as one merely "to be tasted" or as one to be rapidly "swallowed" will, however, be stimulated by the dramatic impact of the exposition and by Lasswell's numerous bold, forceful assertions about politics and the psyche. For example:

Political science without biography is a form of taxidermy.

Political man [displaces] private motives . . . on to public objects [subjecting the former to] rationalization in terms of public interest.

Political movements derive their vitality from the displacement of private affects upon public objects.

Political crises are complicated by the concurrent reactivation of . . . primitive impulses.

Political symbols are particularly adapted to serve as targets for displaced affect because of their ambiguity of reference, in relation to individual experience, and because of their general circulation.

The political methods of coercion, exhortation and discussion assume that the role of politics is to solve conflicts when they have happened. The ideal of a politics of prevention is to obviate conflict by the . . . reduction of the tension level of society by effective methods of which discussion will be but one.

A collection of admirable quotations does not automatically produce a book of enduring significance. It is upon a Baconian slow digestion that the full significance of this book as an integrated, closely interwoven, fundamentally original presentation becomes fully evident. Such a reading of *Psychopathology and Politics* is immeasurably helped if one recognizes key qualifications that Lasswell asserts in a fashion sufficiently elliptical to put the rapid reader in danger of missing them, and of focusing instead on what may appear to be merely oracular assertions and schematic clinical case studies that dwell on psychosexual sources of political orientation and behavior. The reader should recognize that in spite of its title, the book is in fact only incidentally about the political behavior of "mentally disturbed individuals." Rather, for reasons I will summarize shortly, clinical case materials are presented both as a way of familiarizing the reader with a psychodynamic conception of personality and as a way of providing an instructive, but illustrative, target of opportunity for exploratory inquiry. It is additionally important to recognize that the bulk of the book is a hypothetical analytic formulation, deliberately pressed to its extreme. In the final chapters Lasswell explicitly recognizes that the empirical standing of the formulation and of the illustrative data presented in the previous chapters is tenuous, but that both the conceptual tools and the research procedures for moving from hypothesis to sound empirical knowledge are available. This is the meaning of Lasswell's caveat in the final paragraph of his preface. "The first part of the book proceeds in a rather dogmatic fashion" which "tends to obscure the highly unsatisfactory nature" of the clinical psychology of the day. "The later chapters [chapters 11 and 12] are given over to the critical and constructive discussion of these matters, and should fully indicate the highly provisional, though potentially significant, character of the whole."

Indicating finer divisions of the book, Lasswell provides a more detailed set of guide posts in the last paragraph of chapter 1. The first three chapters, as well as portions of chapter 5, "sketch the psychopathological standpoint in its historical setting." In chapter 4, Lasswell reviews "the current criteria" for distinguishing "political types." The first part of this discussion makes a fundamental distinction between a general and a specialized definition of *politics* that Lasswell has employed consistently in his writings. This definition has eluded some of his readers, resulting in their subsequent confusion about Lasswell's meaning of everyday terms like *politics* and *political man*. In the famous concluding passage of chapter 5 Lasswell resumes his remarks on psychological typology. Following his discussion of classification, Lasswell presents "selected life-history material" (chapters 6 through 9), discusses "the bearing of personality studies on general political theory" (chapter 10 and portions of chapter 13), and "criticize[s] existing methods of study" (the above mentioned "non-dogmatic" eleventh and twelfth chapters).

Proceeding chapter by chapter with occasional reference to Lasswell's subsequent writings and to the work of others who have drawn upon the distinctions and suggestions that Lasswell set forth in 1930, let me now briefly note certain analytic usages, transitions, and connections that unify this book and account for why it continues to provide a fundamental guide for the study of personality and politics.

In chapters 1 and 2 Lasswell explains why the first term in the title of his book does not confine his concerns to psychopathological political participants, but rather refers to a methodology for studying the normal as well as the abnormal using what might be called extreme case analysis. He argues that the patterns of symptomatology which lead to psychiatric treatment involve manifestations in boldly exaggerated, and hence more readily observable, forms of personality trends that are widespread in nonpatient populations. The ego-defensive symptoms and character structures of normal individuals are muted and hence less visible than the sharply delineated psychological portraits revealed by "the clinical caricature" of severe pathology. One can employ control group data from "normal" individuals who have been involved in politics and who underwent psychotherapy for didactic reasons in connection with their own professional training or out of intellectual curiosity, thus extending one's inferences to the general population.

Lasswell also notes that psychiatric archives are the richest available contemporary sources of comprehensive life history and psychodynamic data on individuals. Such records contain numerous observations by diverse, clinically sensitive diagnosticians, as well as other observations in connection with the patient's behavior before and during treatment. Furthermore, psychiatric archives incorporate highly personal data relevant to psychological functioning that usually are unavailable to orthodox biographers. In addition medical procedure imposes certain demands upon the clinician—demands that make his observations and modes of conceptualization especially valuable to the political scientist. The clinician must view his patient holistically, examining how personality facets that academic psychologists often study in isolation relate to one another in functioning individuals. The clinician must repeatedly make decisions based on predictions—decisions such as whether to commit or release an institutionalized patient or what kind of therapy to pursue. Thus clinical approaches, despite their methodological imperfection, seem suited for a discipline in which scholars seek to explain and predict the behavior of individuals in actual situations—namely, the various arenas of politics.

Chapters 2 and 3 contain simplified summaries of the work of Freud and other clinicians whose concerns extended in directions different from Freud's. Though Lasswell frequently lets it be known that he is not a true believer in any personality theory, he also stresses two Freudian innovations—certain key aspects of the psychoanalytic theory of mental functioning and an aspect of psychoanalytic clinical procedure—which he feels are fundamental innovations in the study of humankind.

The aspects of mental functioning as conceived in psychoanalysis that interest Lasswell are based on the assumption that of the memories an individual acquires, a substantial, if variable, portion become laden (usually early in life) with emotionally unacceptable connotations. These cognitions, feelings, and impulses are therefore driven from conscious awareness by the exercise of psychodynamic energy, much as a muscle under severe stress undergoes a spasm and contracts rigidly to protect itself. But just as muscle spasms have side effects (such as pain or physical malfunctions), so do repressions. Psychic energy is consumed by forcing thoughts to remain unconscious. Once they have been repressed, unconscious impulses continue to retain their dynamic charge and seek an outlet. Denied direct expression, they receive indirect expression in a wide range of phenomena, including clinical symptoms, parapraxes (such as slips of the tongue and accident proneness), dreams, and—most fundamental from the standpoint of political analysis—rationalizations. Rationalizations are conscious reasons that individuals give for behavior which, unbeknownst to them (except in fleeting moments, or after psychotherapy or other consciousness expanding experiences), is an outlet for unconscious needs rather than the result of the reasons the individual consciously perceives. Lasswell illustrates rationalization and anticipates his discussion of free association as the antidote to rationalization in the illustration (page 20) of an experimental subject who, in the course of obeying a posthypnotic suggestion, invents a false reason (rationalization) for an act he has just performed and then slowly comes to realize that the act has quite different, unconscious roots.

When the "return of the repressed" thought occurs constructively in psychotherapy, rather than through one of the many disguised outlets described above, this normally is the outcome of the clinical procedure which Lasswell views as the second major Freudian innovation, free association. Lasswell considers this skill to be of such fundamental value that he urges it be widely learned, especially by people in responsible positions, in order to reduce the prevalence of irrational "acting out" social and political behavior.

Psychoanalysts continue to rely upon encouraging patients to learn to use free association—the procedure of moving spontaneously from thought to thought, while verbalizing one's chain of mental processes, no matter how improbable the sequence of associations that emerges. Through free association the patient is able to explore the preconscious borderline between conscious motivations and repressed, unconscious preoccupations, gradually recovering the original repressed memories and achieving catharsis, thus imprisoned no longer by his psychological past.[3]

---

[3] Academic psychologists tend to be skeptical of psychoanalytic theory and therapy, but a literature subjecting both components of psychoanalysis to empirical testing has gradually evolved. Since the time Lasswell wrote, there has been greater emphasis within contemporary psychoanalysis on the slow attrition of, or adaptation to, entrenched character structures than on flashes of insight derived from free association as a direct, immediate source of symptom remission.

The psychodynamic view of the mind and the procedure
of free association are the main components of Freud's contribution upon which Lasswell depends for his analysis of
personality and politics. As he explains in the 1960 "Afterthoughts," in 1930 he was aware not only of the diverse
viewpoints among the psychoanalysts of that era, but also
of the innovations (such as ego psychology) that were on
the horizon. His purpose was to sensitize readers to an
approach, not to promulgate a dogma. In fact, in chapter 5,
when Lasswell summarizes Jung and Adler's disagreements
with Freud, he treats these not as heresies but as constructive additions to the scope of orthodox psychoanalytic theory,
and equally in need of the systematic empirical research
he calls for in chapters 11 and 12.

As I have already suggested, chapter 4, "Criteria for
Political Types," is of critical importance to the reader who
seeks full understanding of this book. It is divided neatly
into two parts—a discussion of the criteria for identifying
phenomena that can usefully be labeled *political* and a discussion of the criteria for constructing psychological typologies. Careful study of the first section will make clear why
so many of Lasswell's critics have misunderstood some of
his pronouncements about the nature of political motivation
and of political processes generally. On pages 42–45
Lasswell introduces a "functional" definition of the term
political, distinguishing this from an *"institutional"* (or, as
he put it in some of his later writings, a *"conventional"*)
definition. Each definition produces different criteria for
identifying politicians. Since Lasswell's definition is functional, but standard usage is ordinarily institutional, the
population to which Lasswell refers when he speaks of
"political man" is not comparable, say, to the population of
delegates to an American presidential nominating conven-

tion, some of whom undoubtedly are Lasswellian political types, but others of whom certainly are not.[4]

Lasswell's definition of *functional politics and politicians* not only excludes many individuals who in everyday discourse might be referred to as political or governmental actors, but who in fact merely carry out mechanical tasks, or engage in activities that are essentially gregarious or status enhancing; his definition also *includes* some individuals who happen to be "institutionally" labeled otherwise by their society, for example, bankers, lawyers, or clergymen. The specific criterion for identifying a society's functional politicians (political men) and their subtypes is provisionally stated by Lasswell in *Psychopathology and Politics* as participation in the defense and extension of "communal enterprises" and "the settlement of disputes."[5] His later writings stress the use of power, in the sense of either being responsible for, or wanting to be responsible for, the making of those social decisions that are enforced by sanctions.

Out of this seeming semantic impurity comes analytic

[4] In later writings such as *Power and Personality* (New York: W. W. Norton & Co., 1948), Lasswell suggested that "damaged self esteem" is a probable cause of power needs. The attempt by Paul Sniderman in his valuable study *Personality and Democratic Politics* (Berkeley: University of California Press, 1975) to test Lasswell's hypothesis using a population of delegates to a 1956 United States party convention is the illustration of an inappropriate comparison group alluded to in the text. Sniderman is aware of Lasswell's specialized meaning, but argues that implicit in Lasswell's formulation is the hypothesis that institutional politicians *tend* to be low in self esteem. I find nothing in Lasswell's writings to sustain Sniderman's contention.

[5] In his many writings Lasswell has consistently defined politics functionally except when he specifies that he is using the institutional definition. This applies to his general body of political theory as well as his personality-and-politics formulations. For a bibliography of Lasswell's writing as of the late 1960s see the festschrift edited by Arnold A. Rogow, *Politics, Personality, and Social Science in the Twentieth Century: Essays in Honor of Harold D. Lasswell* (Chicago: University of Chicago Press, 1969), pp. 407-46.

purity. Lasswell most clearly stated the scientific purpose for using such a definition in the first chapter of his 1948 book, *Power and Personality*. Politicians, as functionally defined, may well have certain common psychological properties, although this has to be ascertained empirically. The congeries of status seekers, time servers, and sinecure holders who happen to be called politicians, because of their institutional positions, represent a set of social roles far too diverse for one, even in principle, to expect them to exhibit psychological properties distinguishing them from other population groups.[6]

In the famous concluding passage of chapter 5 of *Psychopathology and Politics* Lasswell describes a generic political type—political man—who undergoes private life experiences that generate repression of inner impulses which then are displaced onto the public arena and rationalized in terms of his conception of the public interest. His often cited notation for this process is p } d } r = P, the letters referring

[6] Years later Browning and Jacob demonstrated empirically that while institutional politicians were not psychologically distinct in their motivation, functional politicians *were*. See Rufus P. Browning and Herbert Jacob, "Power Motivation and the Political Personality," *Public Opinion Quarterly* 28 (1964) : 75-90, and the summary of Browning's further work in Fred I. Greenstein, *Personality and Politics: Problems of Evidence, Inference, and Conceptualization*, rev. ed. (New York: W. W. Norton & Co., 1975), pp. 131-33. For another empirical study drawing on *Psychopathology and Politics*, see the ingenious set of observations on mental hospital patients by Brent M. Rutherford, "Psychopathology, Decision-Making, and Political Involvement," *Journal of Conflict Resolution* 10 (1966) : 387-407. Both articles are reprinted with analytic introductions in Fred I. Greenstein and Michael Lerner, eds., *A Source Book for the Study of Personality and Politics* (Atlantic Highlands, N.J.: Humanities Press, 1971). Additional work directed toward empirical tests of Lasswell's hypotheses included Fred I. Greenstein, "Private Disorder and the Public Order: A Proposal for Collaboration between Psychoanalysts and Political Scientists," *Psychoanalytic Quarterly* 37 (1968) : 261-81, reprinted in Greenstein and Lerner, *A Source Book*, and Larry R. Baas and Steven R. Brown, "Generating Rules for Intensive Analysis: The Study of Transformations," *Psychiatry* 36 (1973) : 172-83. For a recent expansion on the typological discussion in *Psychopathology and Politics*, see A. F. Davies, *Politics as Work* (Melbourne: Melbourne Politics Monograph, 1973).

to "private," "displacement," "rationalization," and "political man," and the brackets indicating transformation. This passage can best be understood as an extension of the second section of chapter 4, where Lasswell presents a three-step process of formulating types. In the first step "nuclear" defining characteristics are identified (for example "political man" is identified by his interest in wielding power). In the second step, adult correlates of this central characteristic are identified. Finally, in the third step, life history research, from childhood through adulthood, reveals the experiences that form an individual's psychological disposition; these constitute the "developmental profiles."

In this section of chapter 4 Lasswell also distinguishes classes of individuals within the general category political man—agitators, who seek power rewards by appealing through oratory or writing to large populations; administrators, who coordinate political activities; and theorists, who elaborate the ideational explanations and justifications of politics. Individuals may represent pure versions of one of these types or mixtures of typological qualities; in any event each subtype of political man has a nuclear defining characteristic and is open to analysis in terms of its typical correlates (Lasswell's "co-relational" classification) and its antecedents (developmental profile).[7]

In *Power and Personality* (1948) and later writings, Lasswell advanced developmental and correlational hypotheses about the determinants of the p } d } r = P sequence. He suggested that political men are typically individuals seeking to compensate for an unconscious sense of damaged self-esteem resulting from earlier experiences in which re-

[7] For a later discussion of classification of political types see Lasswell's "A Note on 'Types' of Political Personality: Nuclear, Co-Relational, Developmental," *Journal of Social Issues* 24 (July, 1968) : 81-91, reprinted with an interpretive introduction in Greenstein and Lerner, *A Source Book*.

wards and sanctions were intermixed in such a way that, though the individual did not become emotionally incapacitated as the result of the sanctions, he was left with an insecurity that was vented in a compulsion to exercise power, leading him to justify power aspirations by rationalizing them into efforts to enhance public welfare. In that work Lasswell went on to formulate an idea that is briefly suggested in the last two paragraphs of chapter 8 of *Psychopathology and Politics;* a conception of a character structure in which power needs are subordinated to a full spectrum of goals and in which there is a willingness to share power, the democratic character.

The case studies of individual agitators, administrators, and theorists (cases A, B, C, D, etc.) in chapters 5 through 9 of *Psychopathology and Politics* do not in fact include any democratic characters. And, to my knowledge, Lasswell has never presented a case study or biographical account of an individual he considered to fit this category. Nevertheless, in later writings—most notably in a long essay on this topic —he discussed the qualities and hypothetical developmental profiles of such individuals.[8] He has, however, commented that even within the subset of institutional political leaders for whom power is an intrinsic rather than an instrumental value, power-seeking perforce must have a moderate rather than exceedingly high psychic marginal utility. Otherwise, there will emerge a type of individual who is simply unable to engage in the cooperative acts necessary to achieve and hold high positions, at least in complex industrial societies.[9]

Chapter 10 of *Psychopathology and Politics* extends the

[8] Harold D. Lasswell, "The Democratic Character," in *The Political Writings of Harold D. Lasswell* (Glencoe, Ill.: The Free Press, 1951), pp. 465-524.

[9] Harold D. Lasswell, "The Selective Effect of Personality on Political Participation," in Richard Christie and Maria Jahada, eds., *Studies in the Scope*

discussion of individual and typological political psychology into a sweeping exposition of a broad socio-political theory, with prescriptive as well as descriptive components. Lasswell's formulation in chapter 10 can be usefully thought of as an anaylsis of the implications for political systems of a situation in which a high proportion of institutional political leaders and their followers are prone to displace unconscious affect and rationalize the displaced affect in terms of the public interest. Given such a state of affairs, it follows that normal processes of political exchange will often escalate into destructive conflict rather than devolving into processes of conflict resolution and cumulative social problem solving.

The political arena is the most likely place for the displacement of private psychic disturbance, both because of the visibility of public political discourse and conflict and because the symbols used in political conflict are vague and therefore (like other ambiguous stimuli such as the ink blots used in projective tests) readily serve as the objects onto which unconscious affect is displaced. To the same degree that such psychodynamic politics of rationalization occur, Lasswell concludes that the normal adversary processes associated with democratic discourse and conflict are likely to produce the opposite of their intended effect. Rather than conflict politics, a kind of collective psychotherapy, via comprehensive study of the human condition, is needed to solve

---

and Method of "The Authoritarian Personality" (Glencoe, Ill.: The Free Press, 1954), p. 224. In this essay Lasswell again makes it clear that he seeks a state of affairs in which democratic characters lead the institutionally defined political process. Thus, in functional terms, leaders would no longer be political men. As he puts it (p. 210) in a reference to the impulse of infants to dominate their environments, "all men are born politicians and some never outgrow it."

collective problems. Highly skilled policy scientists, whose multidisciplinary training and psychoanalytically achieved self-knowledge enables them to reason rather than rationalize, are needed as guides to whom citizens can turn for policy advice.[10] With such insight, citizens would *transcend* conflicts by understanding their determinants. The parallel between this method of problem solving at the political level of society and the free association technique used by individuals facing personal dilemmas should be obvious.

There is seemingly an analogue to a Platonic philosopher-king in Lasswell's image of an omnicompetent, interdisciplinary social scientist–policy advisor. But Lasswell explicitly warns against a technocracy, ruled by such social therapists. Rather, he foresees the same relationship at the social level as that which occurs in principle in the psychoanalytic relationship between patient and therapist. The therapist does not dominate the patient, but rather serves as a vehicle for the patient's private achievement of self-fulfillment.

In chapters 11 and 12, where Lasswell moves from "dogma" to critical and constructive discussion, he notes the unproven and often automatically self-confirming status of the propositions that had emerged from the various schools of psychodynamic psychology and psychotherapy at that time. He then goes on to advance a research procedure for monitoring and classifying the correlates of change that occur during psychoanalytic therapy. (Appendix B provides the sketch of an interview schedule that might be used in such an inquiry.) In writings published later in the 1930s Lasswell reported on research he had conducted along these lines; for example, polygraph data were correlated

---

[10] Hence Lasswell's frequent emphasis on the importance of a "policy science" approach to political inquiry that is prescriptive as well as descriptive.

with psychiatric interview content.[11] As he explains in footnote 19 of the 1960 "Afterthoughts" essay, he collected a
great quantity of such data, but the records were inadver-
tently destroyed and in subsequent years his other interests
and commitments kept him from returning to the research
endeavor recommended in the two penultimate chapters of
the book.[12]

The final chapter, "The State as a Manifold of Events,"
extends Lasswell's macrotheoretical formulation, constructing empirical theory and engaging in conceptual clarification bearing on various recurrent concerns about the relationship between individual behavior and social process. By
way of conclusion, he furnishes a terse abstract of the entire
book.

The foregoing is offered as a guide, albeit overly con-
densed, meant to encourage readers to extract the full implications of Lasswell's still challenging formulation. Why
close reading of this work and action on its implications is
even more in order now than in 1930 is suggested in the
final passage of the "Afterthoughts," written a decade-and-
a-half into the nuclear era. "As the discrepancy grows"
between the rate of man's "mastery of self" and the rate of
his "command of nature" the tenure of the human species
becomes less and less certain. "We can live and kill and
die . . . [or] we can live and nurture and create." There is

[11] For example, see Harold D. Lasswell, "Certain Prognostic Changes during
Trial (Psychoanalytic) Interviews," *Psychoanalytic Review* 23 (1936) : 240-47.
[12] Among Lasswell's other rare comments on his career as a student of personality and politics is the interview with him published in the October 1968
issue of *Psychology Today* in which he alludes to his continuing activity as a
lay psychoanalyst ("I have always kept one or two politicians in analysis all
during their professional life."). Also see his interview with political scientists
David Kemp and Graham Little, *Melbourne Journal of Politics* 4 (1971):
41-54.

no reason for confidence that the second alternative will prevail. Lasswell, however, has held firm in his view that only through deeper social knowledge, encompassing knowledge of personality and politics, will humanity be able to survive, let alone achieve "a world commonwealth of human dignity."

Fred I. Greenstein

PREFACE

An understanding of political life can be sought by examining collective processes distributively or intensively. In my *Propaganda Technique in the World War* (New York and London, 1927), I undertook to analyze the factors which modified collective attitudes by examining the symbols to which many millions of people had been exposed, without paying heed to the order in which these symbols entered into the experience of any particular person. In this preliminary treatise on *Psychopathology and Politics*, I am likewise concerned with the factors which impinge upon collective attitudes, but the method of procedure is radically different. It is no longer a question of inspecting the symbols to which innumerable individuals have been exposed; the present starting-point is the lengthy scrutiny of the histories of specific individuals. The procedures and findings of psychopathology are relied upon for the purpose in hand, since they are the most elaborate and stimulating contributions to the study of the person which have yet been made.

Candor enjoins me once more to express my indebtedness to my former teacher and present chief, Charles E. Merriam, of the University of Chicago, who some time ago sensed the importance of psychopathology for political science, and who has been willing to encourage my own forays in the field, without, of course, feeling bound to indorse my results either in principle or in detail. Through him it became possible to have facilities for special work with Professor Mayo, of Harvard University, whose perception of the bearing of psychopathology upon the un-

derstanding of social life is bearing fruit in novel and
important experiments in business. The tenure of a Social
Science Research Council Fellowship (1928–29) made it
possible to continue my studies abroad.

Circumstances have thus been such as to bring me in
contact, sometimes fleeting and sometimes prolonged, with
men who represent divers standpoints in psychopathology.
Many of these have kindly placed their minds and their
facilities at my disposal, and I hereby return thanks for
the generosity and patience with which they treated an in-
quiring, if somewhat innocent, investigator. No one who
knows the lay of the land in modern psychology, deeply
pitted by the trenches and shell-holes of battling schools,
will imagine that all the men whom I am to name see
eye to eye with one another, or that they will look with
equanimity upon the results of my explorations. To name
them is, I hope, not unduly to incriminate them.

Among those from whom assistance has been received
are to be included: Dr. William Healy, Judge Baker Foun-
dation, Boston; Dr. William A. White, superintendent of
St. Elizabeth's Hospital, Washington, D.C.; Dr. Ross
Chapman, superintendent of Sheppard and Enoch Pratt
Hospital, Towson, Maryland; Dr. Earl D. Bond, superin-
tendent of the Pennsylvania State Hospital, Philadelphia;
Dr. Mortimer Raynor, superintendent of Bloomingdale
Hospital, White Plains, New York; Dr. C. MacFie Camp-
bell, superintendent of the Boston Psychopathic Hospital,
Boston; Dr. Harry Stack Sullivan, formerly of Sheppard
and Enoch Pratt Hospital; Dr. N. D. C. Lewis, St. Eliza-
beth's Hospital; Dr. Samuel W. Hamilton, Bloomingdale
Hospital; Dr. Gregory Zilboorg, Bloomingdale Hospital;
Dr. F. L. Wells, Boston Psychopathic Hospital; Dr. Ed-
ouard Hitschmann, Vienna; Dr. Paul Federn, Vienna;

Dr. Alfred Adler, Vienna; Dr. Wilhelm Stekel, Vienna; Dr. S. Ferenczi, Budapest; Dr. Theodor Reik, Berlin; Dr. Franz Alexander, Berlin (now of the University of Chicago). My colleagues, Dr. Stewart B. Sniffen and Professor Leonard D. White, made valuable suggestions during the process of editing the manuscript, several of which I adopted.

Permission to quote freely from my previous publications was received from the editors of the *American Political Science Review, American Journal of Psychiatry, Journal of Abnormal and Social Psychology, International Journal of Ethics,* and from the University of Chicago Press and the Chicago Association for Child Study and Parent Education.

I wish especially to express my gratitude to those who cannot be singled out by name, but whose co-operation in submitting themselves to prolonged scrutiny was of the greatest possible help.

It ought to be pointed out that the cases actually cited are only a fraction of those which I have examined, or which I have in my possession. Only enough cases have been abstracted to serve the purposes of exposition, to supply a background for the theoretical material. The obscurities which result from an unlimited multiplication of "little Willie stories" have been sought to be avoided by curtailing their number and their extent.

The first part of the book proceeds in rather dogmatic fashion, and this no doubt tends to obscure the highly unsatisfactory nature of the materials and methods of contemporary psychopathology. The later chapters are given over to the critical and constructive discussion of these matters, and should fully indicate the highly provisional, though potentially significant, character of the whole.

H. D. L.

PSYCHOPATHOLOGY

AND POLITICS

CHAPTER I

LIFE-HISTORIES AND POLITICAL SCIENCE

Political biography as a field of political science has long been relied upon to furnish a vivid corrective to the overemphasis laid upon the study of institutional "mechanisms," "structures," and "systems." The legal and customary position of the House of Commons, the House of Lords, the monarch and the electorate, as expounded in the commentaries of Gneist and Dicey, suddenly take on new meaning when viewed through the lens of Morley's Gladstone, Strachey's Victoria, or Lee's Edward VII. The German imperial system of Laband is more fleshly and less transcendental when one has studied the lives of Bismarck or William II. An institutional account of the constitutional development of the United States without a life of Marshall and a life of Lincoln would be but the dregs of a rich and ebullient history. Political science without biography is a form of taxidermy.

When the tumultuous life of society is flayed into precedents and tanned into principles, the resulting abstractions suffer a strange fate. They are grouped and regrouped until the resulting mosaic may constitute a logical and aesthetic whole which has long ceased to bear any valid relation to the original reality. Concepts are constantly in danger of losing their reference to definite events. Notions like liberty and authority require a new birth of meaning after they have followed the tempting path of abstraction but a little way. If conceptions are to serve and not to

1

master the mind, their terms of reference must intermittently undergo the most rigorous scrutiny.

The use of "institutional" categories in describing political life is indispensable, but the publicists who employ them have little to say about the "personal" influences which modify the expected behavior of "legislatures," "executives," and "judiciaries." It is no news that "leadership" is an important variable in predicting the course of events, but the standard treatises on politics have next to nothing to offer about the traits of various kinds of agitators and organizers, and nothing to say about the kinds of experiences out of which these differences arise.

This limitation holds for the books about the theory of the state and of politics which are written by Englishmen like Sidgwick and Laski, Americans like Garner and W. W. Willoughby, and Europeans like Jellinek, Schmidt, Kjellén, and Kelsen. No doubt these men possess or have possessed a living sense of political realities. Of Sidgwick it is related that he was wonderfully adept in entertaining his circle for hours with incisive comments and amusing anecdotes about public men. But of this "humanity" of politics there is little to be found in what he wrote. Political biography has been relied upon chiefly to convey a sense of the unpredictable in human affairs, and to adorn an after-dinner tale. At its best, political biography has contributed to an understanding of the factors which differentiate one human personality from another. But it is no secret that the literary biography or autobiography omits or distorts much of the intimate history of the individual, and that many of the facts which modern investigators have found to be important are numbered among the missing.

Where is it possible to secure a supply of life-histories in which the usual conventionalities are ignored, and which are taken by specialists in the sociological, psychological, and somatic influences which play upon the individual? There exist in modern society sizeable collections of such material which have hitherto been accorded slight attention by students of social science. I refer to the case histories of those individuals who have been ill, and especially those who have been cared for in hospitals and sanitariums.[1]

The richest body of psychological and sociological facts is found in the files of the institutions for the care of the mentally disordered, although the material available in general hospitals is of value. The case history of a patient in a good mental hospital is a document to which many have contributed. There is a report of the physical condition of the patient as it is revealed in the routine examination on his admission to the institution. This may be supplemented by transcripts of previous and subsequent examinations. There is also to be found the rating attained by the subject on several general-intelligence and special-aptitude tests. There is a report of the preliminary interview and the diagnosis by the psychiatrist. This is amplified by a summary of the proceedings at staff conferences to which the patient is presented, and which is attended by the whole body of physicians and psychiatric social workers attached to the hospital. The usual routine is for the physician and social worker in charge to present a summary of the case, to introduce the patient for observation, and to engage in general colloquy upon the diagnosis and therapy after the patient has been escorted out of the room. The patient may be brought before several staff

[1] See Harold D. Lasswell, "The Study of the Ill as a Method of Research on Political Personalities," *American Political Science Review*, November, 1929.

conferences for the purpose of discussing whether he is in a condition permitting of release, parole, or transfer. During his stay in the institution the nurses, as well as the physicians who make rounds, add their descriptive comments upon his behavior. The social service department gets in touch with relatives and acquaintances and prepares a biography of the subject. Occasionally the patient will volunteer an autobiography, which is filed with the general record. Correspondence with individuals who have interested themselves in the case will often disclose valuable details. The exhibits frequently include letters written by the patient before, during, and after his illness, together with published works, drawings, paintings, and plastic productions. In some instances the record of a single patient who has been admitted, released, or transferred becomes very voluminous.

It is due to the growing emphasis upon the importance of understanding the personality as a functioning whole that modern medical men are willing and anxious to assemble data about the behavior of the individual in his family, business, and recreational relations. Such facts are often useful to the physician in making his diagnosis and in deciding how to handle the patient. The modern emphasis upon the rôle of reverie in developing one's traits and interests has led to the inclusion of data about night dreams, daydreams, ambitions, grievances, enthusiasms, and loyalties of the subject. Not infrequently the productions of the patient are recorded in his own words by a stenographer who is present during certain interviews with physicians. All these psychological and sociological data increase the significance of the case record for the individual who studies it for the purpose of understanding the total developmental history of the person.

Sometimes the case histories concern people who are without mental disorder, but who have, for one reason or another, been committed for observation. The German government was not the only one in the late war which sometimes resorted to the expedient of avoiding the appearance of internal dissension by referring pacifists to a mental hospital. The records of the kind obtained under these circumstances are often of men and women without pathology, and serve to control the conclusions which rest on the study of pathological cases.

Quite often the specifically pathological features in the record of a sick person are very meager. Thus, one prominent politician, the mayor of a large city, was brought to a mental hospital suffering from an alcoholic psychosis,[2] delirium tremens. He was only "insane" (to use a non-scientific term) when he was passing through this acute alcoholic episode, and was soon released. But the record of what he said and did during the delirium casts a brighter light on the deeper motivations of his political career than many pages of conventional biography. The hallucinations and delusions which he experienced were not entirely stereotyped for the disease. Since he was no longer able to maintain his repressions, his inner fantasy life came out in the clear, and his personality structure stood revealed. Another politician showed nothing abnormal except a propensity for collecting women's shoe heels, which he found sexually stimulating. He came to the medical psychologist to be freed from his fetishist perversion, and in so doing he made possible the preparation of a document which intimately revealed the origin of certain political interests. From the point of view of the political

[2] "Psychosis" means the more serious mental disturbances; "neurosis" means the less serious ones.

scientist the most valuable parts of his history happened
to be quite far removed from the narrowly circumscribed
pathological symptoms.

The value of some records is enhanced by the fact that,
besides the pathological productions of the patient, they
contain much information which is volunteered by the person when he is himself again. Some forms of mental
disorder show recurrent intervals of disturbance and normality, and during the "clear" interludes the patient is
quite competent to furnish autobiographical data. Often
the "remissions" in the individual's condition extend over
several years, although they may be momentary. Another
form of mental disease is characterized by the fact that
the sufferer's difficulties center about a single system of
ideas which, if left untouched by the interviewer, permits
him to be dealt with as an ordinary individual. It should
be evident from the foregoing that, contrary to popular
impression, the histories to be found in institutions for the
care of the sick are by no means exclusively confined to
pathological subjects or to the merely pathological aspects
of the person.

Some of the life-histories which are summarized in this
monograph come from mental hospitals. Others have been
collected from volunteers who were outside mental institutions and who were aware of no serious mental pathology. They have been undertaken on the understanding
that our knowledge of human nature in politics would be
advanced if "normal" individuals were studied with the
same care which is often bestowed on the abnormal.

So the book includes persons who are "sick" and persons who are "well." In the main the material is printed
for the first time. There are no retrospective interpretations of historical personages. The chief unity of the study

lies in the fact that it is restricted to politically interesting people who have been studied while alive by specialists under conditions of unusual intimacy.

The purpose of this venture is not to prove that politicians are "insane." Indeed, the specifically pathological is of secondary importance to the central problem of exhibiting the developmental profile of different types of public characters. Our job is not to catalogue the symptoms at the expense of the main patterns of the personality. We have not finished when we know that a modern Rousseau suffered from paranoia; that a modern Napoleon has partly atrophied genitalia; that modern Alexanders, Caesars, and Blüchers are alcoholic; that a modern Calvin is plagued by eczema, migraine, and kidney stones; that a modern Bismarck is hysterical; that a modern Lincoln shows depressive pathology; that a modern Robespierre displays a eunuchoid habitus; or that a modern Marat suffers from arthritis, diabetes, and eczema. "Psycho-pathography" is legitimate and useful, but pathography is not our aim.[3]

Nor is it the purpose of this book to make a hit-and-miss collection of isolated anecdotes about the relation between early experiences and specific political traits and interests. Not that this sort of thing is not a liberalizing experience. Our conventional schemes of "political motivation" seem curiously aloof from the manifold reality of human life when we discover the private basis of public acts. John B, to choose a random instance, is a busy, aggressive, and successful salesman who spends a great deal of time and money on the care of the blind. He takes time away from

[3] The best summary of this literature is Wilhelm Lange-Eichbaum, *Genie-Irrsinn und Ruhm*. See also the works of Ireland, Lombroso, Möbius, and Gould.

his business to serve on the board of governors of institutions for the blind, and he handles many financial campaigns on their behalf. Measures looking toward the improvement of public or private care for these unfortunates
are certain of his support before legislative committees,
on the platform, and in personal conference. The study
of his early memories finally revealed the incident in which
his ardent interest in the blind was rooted. When he was
between three and four years of age, his little sister pulled
an eye out of his favorite cat, and he was terribly dis-
tressed. His concern for the safety of his pets was the
original drive toward protective work for the blind which
matured into his adult activity. It would be possible to
fill many pages with reports of "critical experiences" of
this kind, and their importance is far greater than is usually supposed.

If diagnostic labels and isolated anecdotes do not satisfy
us, what do we want? The answer can be succinctly stated
thus: We want to discover what developmental experiences are significant for the political traits and interests
of the mature. This means that we want to see what lies
behind agitators, administrators, theorists, and other types
who play on the public stage. Can we conceive the development of the human personality as a functioning whole,
and discern the turning-points in the growth of various
patterns of political life? Can we uncover the typical
subjective histories of typical public characters? Can we
place this subjective history in relation to the physical
and cultural factors which were developmentally significant?

Even this ambitious project does not exhaust the scope
of this study. We want to see whether the intensive investigation of life-histories will in any way deepen our

understanding of the whole social and political order. The life-story of a Hottentot or an American reveals the concrete reality of images and moods as they are experienced seriatim by those whose life is caught up in the web of violently contrasting cultures. The trained student of society discerns a wealth of culture patterns whose full meaning in human experience can only be revealed by securing the subjective history of those who are exposed to them. In some cultures the child is slapped, switched, and beaten; in some cultures the child is rarely the target of corporal punishment. Does this mean that the children in the first culture will harbor revenge and welcome violence in social life? In some cultures, parental control is negligible from the fourth to the fourteenth year, and in other cultures supervision is strict and continuous. What difference does this make in the developing view of the world in successive generations? Those who are within the same culture are exposed to many minor variations in social practice, and we may hope to ascertain the consequences of these differences for the minds of those who undergo them.

This book is in harmony with a trend which has been growing in strength in the social sciences. Social science has been moving toward the intensive study of the individual's account of himself. This is a movement which is poorly conveyed by the phrase, "an interest in human biography," because the term "biography" is full of irrelevant literary and historical connotations. The person's own story is not a chronology of everything he thought and did, nor is it an impressionistic interpretation of what he experienced. The life-history is a natural history, and a natural history is concerned with facts which are *developmentally* significant. The natural history of the earth is not a rehearsal of every event included within the series, but a selective account of major changes within the series. Dated events matter, but they matter not because they have dates but because they mark phases. When biography is treated as natural history, the purpose is to pick and choose the principal epochs of development and to identify their distinctive patterns.

The study of life-histories as natural histories is a very recent phenomenon. The social sciences have barely begun to exploit this approach. It is of very great significance that Comte, after spending a lifetime in the preparation of his great system, finally saw that the capstone was missing, and at the time of his death was frantically trying to improvise it. His projected treatise was to deal with personality development and differentiation (*La morale*). It was never finished. There is something symbolic of the history of the social sciences in this story of Comte's long preoccupation with institutions, his belated recognition of the possibilities of personality study, his hurried effort to make good the omission, and the fragmentary nature of the results achieved. Social science is in the belated-hurried-fragmentary phase of growth.[4]

Comte's fragment was never expanded by French sociologists. The comparative morphology of culture became all-absorbing, and this was concerned with the pantomime of what men did, and sporadically with what men thought. Comte executed his earlier volumes only too well. When the mental processes of primitives came to be studied by Durkheim and the Durkheimians, these "primitive mentalities" were examined for the sake of revealing highly

[4] See De Grange's excellent treatment of this matter in his paper on the methodology of Comte, Analysis 1, *Methods in Social Science: A Case Book.*

abstract "forms" of thought, and not to reveal the individual sequence of human experience under different social conditions. The efforts which have been made to fill the gap have rested upon no massing of empirical data and have been fortified by no critical reflection on the methodological problem of improving the reliability of the data. The most promising sign of the times in France is the synthetic approach to social psychology which is sponsored by Blondel at Strassbourg.

In Germany the social scientists were so occupied with the *Streit um Marx* and the triumphs of the comparative historical school that a comparative morphology of subjective histories, if one may indulge the phrase, did not arise. The prodigious influence of Kant in the direction of multiplying epistemological subtleties stereotyped a penchant for high abstraction in the consideration of psychological phenomena. The great successes of the physical sciences seemed to rest upon the ruthless division and redivision of phenomena until they became amenable to manipulation and control. The combination of Kantian acuteness with scientific atomism was capable of producing the extremes of physiological psychology and the obscurantist revulsion against submitting the sacred mystery of personality to the coarse indignity of exact investigation. Curiously enough, the modern era of personality study was introduced as a protest against the laboratory emphasis, and meant a capitulation to the spirit of scientific irreverance. Personalities could be compared and typologized. The pioneer was Dilthey, the philosophic historian; but neither he nor those who followed him collected and published actual accounts of intimate subjective experiences. Sociological overemphasis on the group was only partially compensated in Simmel's theoretical exposition of individuality, but there was no happy synthesis of category and fact in his work. The field ethnologists neglected to assemble autobiographical accounts, and only the fine sensibilities of Vierkandt made possible the utilization of fragments for the sake of comparing the inner life of primitive man with that of modern man, a task which was performed with rather more subtlety than by the French. The early social psychological impetus of Lazarus and Steindhal produced vast collections of folk-lore materials, but the task of threading folk lore and folk ways onto the developmental history of representative persons remained undone.

The great innovator in the subjective field was Freud. His book on dreams is one of the most unique autobiographies in history, and his publications set the pace for those who wanted to record the actual outpourings of the unrestrained human mind. Here at last was a truly scientific spirit who recorded everything of which the human mind was capable, and looked at it critically in the hope of finding the laws of mental life. He broke through the irrelevant barriers of conventionality and brought dark continents of data into the light of inquiry. He proposed theories which were supposed to be tested by the data, and devised a special procedure for securing data.

The scientific habilitation of the anonymous, intimate life-history document as a source for the study of culture was especially the work of William I. Thomas. He and Florian Znaniecki undertook and completed their remarkable study of *The Polish Peasant in Europe and America*. One volume was devoted to a long autobiography which included the most intimate facts in the life of a Polish immigrant to the United States. The work of Thomas left an abiding stamp on American sociology through the department at the University of Chicago. Franz Boas, dean of American ethnologists, has been keenly interested in the primitive's story of himself, and has collected and urged the collection of many such documents. Paul Radin published the life-story of a Winnebago chief in 1916. The importance of "the boy's own story" was early recognized by William Healy in his study of delinquents, and has been extended in every direction.

So, in stressing the value of the study of the concrete sequence of individual experience for political science, we are expressing a trend of interest which is already well founded in social science. Our quest for full and intimate histories has led to the exploitation of a relatively new source of material, the case-history records of hospitals. It has led to the application of psychopathological methods to the study of normal volunteers as a control on the inferences drawn from the institutional cases. It has led to a detailed study of the prolonged interview technique as a method of personality study (especially psychoanalysis), and to the formulation of improved methods of investigation. It has led to the statement of a functional theory of the state, a theory which springs directly from the intensive scrutiny of actual life-histories, and the realization of what political forms can mean when seen against the rich background of personal experience.

These studies are admittedly incomplete. The documents relied upon suffer from various shortcomings which have been specified in detail at an appropriate place. The number of documents on hand is limited. Caution would counsel deferred publication of even these materials. But the many objections to publication have been outweighed by certain positive advantages. The publication of such a collection of materials will serve to familiarize the professional students of government with the kinds of fact and interpretation which are now current among the specialists in important fields of study. Familiarization is especially necessary in dealing with personality histories because some of the material is unconventional and invariably produces initial emotional difficulties among unsophisticated readers. But science cannot be science and limit itself to the conventional. Some of the facts are not pretty, and they are not the topics of polite conversation. But the medical scientists who dabble with the excretions of the human body for the sake of diagnosing disease and understanding health are not bound by the limitations of banality and gentility in their work. And if political science is to become more of a reality and less of a pseudonym, there must be discipline in dealing objectively with every kind of fact which is conceivably important for the understanding of human traits and interests.

Familiarization, then, is one function of this set of studies. Another purpose is to set up tentative hypotheses about personality growth on the basis of available materials. The mere statement of these hypotheses about the growth of agitators and administrators will sharpen investigation. Perhaps those who have direct access to better histories will be impelled to use them in checking and revising the working conceptions herein set out.

The general scheme of presentation begins with some chapters which sketch the psychopathological standpoint in its historical setting and which review the current criteria of political types. Then comes selected life-history material. The concluding chapters discuss the bearing of personality studies on general political theory and criticize existing methods of study.

CHAPTER II

THE PSYCHOPATHOLOGICAL APPROACH

One of the standing obstacles in the path of personality research is the difficulty of describing the personality as a whole at any given cross-section of its development. In despair at the myriad difficulties of the task, academic psychology has long evaded the issue and concentrated its attention upon the minute exploration of detached aspects of the individual. The manuals of physiological psychology are full of painstaking accounts of how atomized aspects of the individual's environment (the "stimuli") modify the reactions of selected parts of the individual. What these manuals characteristically omit is a workable set of conceptions for the classification of the phenomena which are the objects of investigation in personality research. It is impossible to found a science of geology without inventing terms to distinguish plateaus, plains, mountains, and continental blocs, even though all these phenomena possess the common attributes of "matter." What matters for the geologist is how the differences and not the likenesses come to pass. Much of the academic psychology, in its quest for precision and prestige, has quit studying the problem with which it is ostensibly engaged, and has substituted a minor field of physiology therefor. In so doing, it has lost any criterion for testing the relevance of the results of particular researches for the understanding of personality because it has no master concepts of personality.

The psychopathologist has never been able to evade the

15

necessity of summing up the personality as a whole because he has been compelled to make important decisions about the future of the personality as a whole. The psychiatrist must continually decide whether John B and Mary C will, if released from careful supervision, commit suicide or murder, or whether they will be dependable members of the community. Thus the clinician has found it imperative to search for signs which have high predictive value in relation to the major social adjustments of the individual.

The psychopathologist has had the great advantage of seeing many trends of the personality which are normally subordinated to other trends when they have escaped from control and achieved Gargantuan proportions. The clinical caricature throws into imposing relief the constituent tendencies which make up the functioning person, and draws attention to their presence and their processes. "Normality" involves a complicated integration of many tendencies, a flexible capacity to snap from one mood, preoccupation, and overt activity to another as the changing demands of reality require. The pathological mind, if one may indulge in a lame analogy, is like an automobile with its control lever stuck in one gear: the normal mind can shift. One has a queer feeling as one passes around the wards of a hospital for the custody of the more seriously disordered patients that if one could assemble the scattered parts of the mind that one could create at least a single supermind. There in one corner is a melancholic who is stuck in the mood of despondency; in another corner is a manic who is expansive and elated; elsewhere is a man whose self-esteem has achieved cosmic dimensions; in the back wards is a deteriorated mind in perpetual repose. Every conceivable nuance of preoccupation and mood with which we are normally familiar seems to be dissatisfied with its minor rôle in a healthy integration, and intent upon autocratic mastery of the mind. The clinical caricature draws attention as sharply as possible to the components of the healthy mind. So every theory of pathological manifestations must presently become expanded or assimilated into a comprehensive account of human psychology.

The gross clinical material reveals the intimate interrelationships between soma and psyche. The patient who suffers from obsessive ideas may find relief from obsession by showing hysterical symptoms; and hysterical symptoms may clear up, only to make way for obsessive symptoms. "Pure pictures" are almost pure theories. The patient who is suffering from a definite organic lesion may complicate his troubles by "worry," and "worry" may be one of the factors in bringing about a physical disease picture. There is evidence that psychological factors are among those significantly operating in such diseases as common colds, asthma, catarrh, hay fever, hyperthyroidism, gall-bladder trouble, gastro-intestinal ulcers, irregular menstruation, and sexual impotence.

Fresh vitality has come into modern psychology from the clinic. The psychopathological approach has gradually vindicated itself as more and more of its conceptions find a permanent place in the vocabulary of psychology and social science. Modern psychopathology is itself a recent development, and undoubtedly the most revolutionary figure is Sigmund Freud.

The spectacular and influential nature of Freud's work is sufficient justification for devoting some space to a brief account of his standpoint and his innovation in method. As we shall have occasion to illustrate, his method is of more general application to practical problems of politi-

cal research and political practice than is usually understood.

When Freud was a student in the University of Vienna,
the triumphal progress of microscopic methods of studying cellular structure was sweeping all before it. Congeries
of mental symptoms in the living were frequently found to
be correlated with the discovery of certain definite cere-
brospinal lesions on autopsy. The future seemed to rest
wholly in the hands of those who used the dissecting knife
and the lens. Before Freud graduated from the University,
he became demonstrator to Brücke, the eminent physiolo-
gist; and he labored in the laboratory of Meynart, the distinguished psychiatrist of his day. Freud's first publication was a result of laborious laboratory work.

While materialism reigned, psychological phenomena
were degraded to the status of trivial epiphenomena. But
at this very time a revival of psychogeneticism arose in
French psychiatry under the impetus of Charcot. Charcot
had achieved eminence in pathological anatomy before he
turned in middle life to the study of mental maladies.
By 1883 he had demonstrated the possibility of producing
hysterical symptoms by means of ideas (verbal stimuli).
Time and again he hypnotized individuals and produced
muscular contractures, hypersensitivity, and hyposensitiv-
ity, together with allied symptoms of hysteria.

Breaking away from the laboratories of Vienna, Freud
journeyed to the Salpêtrière Hospital in Paris to work with
Charcot, where he stayed from the autumn of 1886 to the
spring of 1887. Here he was thrown in touch with the
current of ideas which was giving concrete content to the
notion of the "out of conscious" and its dynamic consequences for human behavior. Pierre Janet was busily accumulating the observations which were published to the

world in 1889 under the title, *L'automatisme psychologique*. Early chapters appeared in the *Revue philosophique* as early as 1886. His work was submitted to the Sorbonne for the degree of Doctor of Philosophy. In view of subsequent controversies, it is worth observing that the scope of this research was confined to repetitive and dissociated phenomena. Words and movements of persons who were in somnambulistic, cataleptic, and similar states were described, together with studies of post-hypnotic suggestion, and of total and partial recall. Emphasis was laid upon the "restriction of the field of consciousness" and the "enfeeblement of consciousness."

In Paris Freud acquired a point of view which was bound to bring him into conflict with the materialistic pundits of Vienna. Hypnotism was itself looked upon as an artifice of charlatans. Wagner-Jauregg reflected the ruling tradition when, only a few years ago, he said, "The trouble with hypnotism is that you never know who is pulling the other fellow's leg." Freud was met by derisive laughter when he announced at the Medical Society of Vienna that male hysterics were to be found in Paris. For hysteria, as one of the pedants reminded him, was philologically derived from "hysteron," meaning uterus, and therefore couldn't possibly occur in males. This was an echo of the days when hysteria was supposed to be due to a migratory uterus and women were turned upside down to bring it back in place.

In 1881 and 1882 Breuer had treated a girl suffering from hysteria, and his interest was renewed in the case in conversation with Freud. Breuer remembered that when he treated the patient under hypnosis, she recalled the first episode in which a symptom had appeared, related it with every evidence of excitement, and discovered on waking that the symptom had disappeared. Breuer and Freud began to study hysteria from this point of view and published their results. Charcot had demonstrated that ideas could cause hysteria; Breuer had found that the discovery of pathogenic ideas could cure hysteria.

In 1889 Freud returned to France, this time to the other center of hypnotic research, Nancy, where Liébeault and Bernheim were doing remarkable things. Freud here saw something the full significance of which did not at once dawn upon him.

A subject was hypnotized and given a "post-hypnotic suggestion" to raise an umbrella at a certain signal after coming out of hypnosis. The subject was then awakened from hypnosis, and presently, when the stipulated signal was given, obediently raised the umbrella, although still inside the room. When asked why he raised the umbrella, *he said that he wanted to see whether it was his or not.* Thus did he rationalize (a concept later developed) the gratification of an impulse *which he did not himself at first recognize.* When challenged to explain himself, he merely produced a plausible interpretation of his own conduct.

The immense significance of this train of events is great enough. It at once raises the searching question: To what extent are we in ignorance of our own motives and accustomed to improvise merely plausible explanations of and to ourselves? But an even more notable phenomenon occurred. *If the subject was asked again and again to try to remember why he raised the umbrella, he sooner or later recalled (to his own surprise) that he had been commanded to do it.*

The full import of this observation did not instantly

dawn on Freud. But he continued to have difficulties with the patients whom he sought to hypnotize. They sometimes held out against his suggestions, even though they had accepted them many times before, and seriously impeded the progress of the search for the traumatic episode. He gradually abandoned hypnosis, leaving the patient in a waking state in a relaxed position with instructions to report every incident connected with the early appearance of the symptom under investigation. Vestiges of the hypnotic technique remained as late as 1895, when he would still lay his hand on the patient's forehead as a stimulus to recollection.

This method also encountered crippling difficulties. A patient would sometimes lie for hours without saying a word, totally unable to recover a relevant reminiscence. To meet this obstacle, Freud presently hit upon the simple expedient upon which he thenceforth relied. He instructed the patient to say anything and everything that popped in his head, regardless of its propriety, logic, or triviality.

Freud found that all ramblings of his patient could furnish him with clues to the underlying and unavowed impulses of the sufferer. He became able to guess the nature of the buried episode in which the impulse had received its present type of manifestation. Thus the patient might begin by saying that she had seen a red-headed man in the street and that she always despised red-headed men—except of course her dear brother. Day after day apparently random allusions would build out the picture of her great interest in anything reminiscent of her brother's looks and acts, all of which would be bitterly condemned. But if she were asked directly, she would maintain that her brother was a fine, upstanding man, and a credit to the family.

The analyst, after listening to the eddies of talk, and noting the patterns along which they seemed to whirl, would presently locate a hidden rock beneath the innocent surface of the stream—in this case, an unacknowledged load of hatred against her brother. Bit by bit, stories of real or fancied childhood tyranny would come floating along the stream. Then suddenly, amid tears and violent gestures, might come the story of a long-forgotten incident which involved an intimate aggression on the part of the brother. The patient, manifestly relieved, might speedily recover from her hysterical disabilities and return to the active responsibilities of life.

Freud's theory of what he saw began modestly enough, leaned heavily upon Charcot, Bernheim, and Breuer, and was mostly founded upon observations made upon patients who were handled by hypnosis and not by the new procedure which later was called psychoanalysis. He published a contribution to the theory of the psychoneuroses in which he laid down the proposition that a distinction could be drawn between one group, the anxiety neuroses, which depended on mental conflict, and the actual neuroses, which were not due to mental conflict but to masturbation and coitus interruptus. In the first case, mental energy was converted into bodily symptoms, and in the latter case bodily energy was supposed to be converted into bodily symptoms. In Freud's early articles there is little to forecast the course which he was to follow as his brilliant imagination viewed the behavior of the individual from the new vantage ground which he had discovered.[1]

Whether his particular theories survive or fall, the standpoint which he achieved by ruthlessly applying his

[1] What has been said above is current in the biography of Freud by Fritz Wittals, and in Freud's autobiographical sketches.

method is of the greatest value. His method, which grew
from the necessities of an exasperated physician, led him
*systematically to treat every manifestation of the individ-
ual as part of a related whole.* Freud's mental set had been
furnished by the data of hypnosis, which seemed to show
that patients suffer from reminiscences. When he dropped
hypnosis and tried to force recollections, his mental set
had not altered, for he was still in search of the original,
the traumatic episode. When he asked his patients to say
anything that came into their heads, he was still hunting
the elusive memory of a definite early experience. But
quite without realizing it, his original mental set had wid-
ened, and with momentous consequences for his own subsequent development. If one were given to exaggerations,
one could say that the world of psychological investigation
had suddenly begun to turn on a new axis.

What was the nature of this new mental set? Intently
watching his patients, not for word for word accounts of
what had happened, and looking upon everything else as
"irrelevant," Freud learned to look for meanings and not
for reports. Every dream, every phrase, every hesitation,
every gesture, every intonation, every outburst began to
take on significance as possible allusions to the "traumatic" episode. Allusions to hated objects, reminiscent of
a brother, failure to mention a hated sister until days had
passed, although other members of the family had been
passed in review—every deviation from comprehensiveness—was eagerly scrutinized for the clue it might afford.

The technique of therapy consisted in using clues to
facilitate the patient's search for relief. The problem was
to discover the nature of the patient's conflict and to volunteer interpretations for the sake of helping the patient
to dare to bring into full consciousness the unavowed im-

pulse which had once frightened his socially adjusted self into frantic repression. This involved the interpretation of the symptom as a compromise product of the patient's ideal of conduct; and the out-of-conscious impulse, which, though denied access to the full consciousness of the sufferer, possessed enough strength to procure partial gratification. The symptom was thus a symptom of conflict between the socially adapted portion of the self and the unadapted impulses of the personality, and the symptom was a compromise between partial gratification of the illicit and partial punishment by the conscience. The particular form of the "conflict" depended upon the traumatic experience and the antecedent history of the individual.

Far more important than these therapeutic elaborations is the shift in standpoint which made them possible. Since Freud was on the search for the literal by way of the symbolic, he raised hitherto neglected manifestations of human behavior to the dignity of significant symbols, wrote them out, and introduced them into the literature of human behavior. There could be no sharper illustration of the prepotency of "mental set" for the seeing of "facts" than the difference between the clinical reports of Freud and Janet. Freud, convinced that the eluctable energies of the organism could betray themselves in every image and in every gesture, painstakingly recorded the dreams and day-fantasies of his patients. Janet, who continued to assume that dreams were nonsensical confusions attributable to the diminished tension of the sleeping organism, seldom made any allusion to dreams. His pellucid description of grimaces, gestures, sentiments, and theories of his patients led back to relatively recent moments when the patient failed of adjustment. This failure of the patient to mobilize his energies in smooth adaptation to the exigencies of social reality was then imputed to a defective biopsychical mechanism, to a lowered "psychological tension," due to a miscellany of possible causes, among which was mentioned "the exhaustive effects of emotional excitement." Therapy consisted in restoring the capacity of the individual to mobilize and deploy his energies at the highest "levels" of adjustment. This was to be achieved by a variety of means—by hypnotic suggestion, rest in a simplified environment, and the usual repertory of the psychotherapist.

But the golden flash of psychological insight eluded Janet. At bottom he had little respect for the concrete reality of the mental life of his patients. Although he talked the language of psychogeneticism, it had a poor and not a rich connotation in his mind. I think this is due to his too exclusive reliance upon hypnotism, for the mental set of the hypnotist is derogatory to most of the concrete productions of the patient. The patient, one feels with a shrug, will presently come to the important experience; why take the superimposed material too seriously? Then, too, the patient may be put in order by direct command. Janet relates with some pride how people in the waiting-room of his office would marvel when a woman, bent nearly double, would be admitted into his sanctum, presently to emerge, erect and cured—until the effect wore off.

Freud learned a new respect for the concrete reality of mental life in his concentrated effort to divine the hidden conflict without resorting to hypnosis. His weakness as a hypnotist was in a sense the beginning of wisdom. A patient who is deeply hypnotized is but infrahuman. Barring commands which do violence to the moral code of the individual, the subject will passively execute the commands of the hypnotist. The patient descends from a com-

plicated "nearly normal" person to a waxy caricature of
a human being. The unhypnotized patient of Freud is in
relatively full possession of all the resources of the ordinary waking self, and must be dealt with as a complex human being.

The widest gateway to psychoanalytic development became the study of dreams. And here again we are dealing
with something which came, not from laborious reflection
upon underlying concepts, but from the urgencies of the
clinical situation. Just as we found that Freud had taken
up a new post of observation in practice before he discovered its implications in theory, we find that in such a
detail as the investigation of dreams, his theoretical preoccupations contributed less than his everyday necessities.
Freud's patients continually thrust their dreams upon him;
and he, now in pursuit of clues to what lay behind, presently took them seriously, and found in them many help-
ful indications of unspoken things. He would assist the
free-fantasies of the patient by asking what came into his
mind about any detail of the dream, and he attentively followed the long chains of superficially meaningless associations.

It began to appear that Freud had stumbled upon, and
then brilliantly elaborated the possibilities inherent in, a
new way of using the mind. He trained his patients in a
technique of free-fantasy which they could subsequently
use for themselves as a supplement to the logical technique
which society ostensibly tries to foster. It at once appeared
that he had discovered a method of thinking which was applicable far beyond the confines of the clinic and which
could be added to the repertory of the mind.

The interpretation of dreams was the bridge which
brought Freud from the confines of the clinic to the analysis of the whole psychology of individual development.

The dreams of patients and the dreams of non-pathological persons showed such homogeneity of symbolism that the gap between the "normal" and the "sick" seemed to close. Popular lore already furnished a clue to dreams as wish-fulfilments, whether found in the "well" or "ill," but popular lore also treated them as reminiscences, prophe-cies, and omens, or as confusions, depending on the transitory context of the moment. Freud had a double orientation in dealing with the individual. He regarded him as motivated in the present by impulses which eluded his own consciousness. He regarded these motivations as having achieved their present form in concrete historical events in the life of the individual. The nature of the present could be made clear to the conscious mind if the organizing episode could be recalled. This recall could be greatly facilitated by paying special attention to the "irrational" or non-adjustive aspects of the person's pres-ent conduct. The "irrational" would seem rational enough if the unacknowledged motives were made manifest, and if the historical as well as the contemporary allusions were sought after. Sooner or later the unrecognized mo-tives would disclose themselves in consciousness, if the individual waited attentively; but the process could be greatly helped by using a different style of thinking than the logical.

No one has more dramatically and repeatedly shown the limitations (as well as the advantages) of logical pro-cedures of thought than Freud. No one has made a more important contribution to the technique of supplementing logical thought by other methods of thought than Freud. This is the aspect of Freud's work which has immediate and constant relevance to political as to every other sort of thinking, and to which it is important to devote more extended consideration.

CHAPTER III

A NEW TECHNIQUE OF THINKING[1]

The prevailing theory is that men who make important decisions in politics can be trained to use their minds wisely by disciplinary training in the practices of logical thought. Legal training is supposed to mold the mind to ways of dealing with the world which subordinate whim to principle. Formal instruction in the social sciences is intended to equip the mind for the detached consideration of social consequences, and everyone agrees that this implies a large measure of self-awareness for the sake of reducing the play of prejudice.

The nature of logical thought has been carefully examined by an array of able writers. Their conclusions may be provisionally reported by saying that logic is a guided form of mental operation. It is not something marked off from impulse, but a progressive elaboration and differentiation of impulse. It proceeds by the affirmation of a starting-point, which is in fact a vague indication of the goal to be reached, and develops by the criticism of the material which appears in consciousness according to its relevance to the end in view. If the judge begins by wanting to settle a controversy consistently with precedents, he has indicated in advance the shadowy outline of the desired termination of his efforts. If an administrator wants to reduce complaints against his handling of the postal service, he starts with a different mental set from the judge, but, like the mental set of the latter, his first

[1] Modified from "Self-Analysis and Judicial Thinking," *International Journal of Ethics*, April, 1930.

28

act is to bring into view the state of affairs which he hopes to find when he quits thinking. He is accustomed to guide the operations of his mind by this preliminary character-ization of the terminus sought. No thinker can haul into the center of attention the material which indicates how the terminal situation is to be attained. The thinker must wait attentively for whatever appears. If he wants to deal with such a simple practical matter as getting to the railway station, and his mind continues to fill with images of the one he left behind him, his accustomed means of asserting control is to reiterate the practical end and to hope that he can "keep his mind on" taxicabs or auto-busses. Alternating with periods of reiteration and ex-pectancy and illumination are episodes of "No" and "Yes," which evidence the existence of guided thought.

It would be misleading to stop with this formal de-scription of the characteristics of logical thinking. Logi-cal thinking is not a hocus-pocus to be applied here and there and everywhere. The previewing of events presup-poses familiarity with the sorts of events to which the previewing relates. It usually involves analysis of the con-tingent future in the light of analogies with the past, which is simply a means of refining general familiarity through systematic methods of inspecting reality. General knowl-edge of lending and borrowing must be supplemented, for many purposes, by detailed examination of the quantita-tive dimensions of various routines. The precise nature of the relationship between changes in the rediscount rate and the price of call money requires analysis far beyond impressionistic familiarity.

There need be no illusion that the specification of the terminal situation provides an immovable constant for thought. We can imply, as we have implied, that logical thinking begins by sketching a figure on the canvass and leaves the details to be filled in during the course of the thinking. But the starting-point is often subject to many shifts, and the initial sketch is more or less subject to re-making. The judge who starts in pursuit of consistency-with-precedent characteristically must add conformity-to-principles-of-policy. A plurality of ends is always involved, and usually appears.

Everybody knows that the pluralism of ends goes far beyond "official" ends. A sophisticated and discerning judge may discover an embarrassing conflict in the controlling precedents, and cast about for other social purposes than conformity-to-precedent to guide him. He may scrutinize the principal economic, cultural, and political changes in the society in which he operates, and discern the appearance of a new set of rising dominant values, and decide to diminish the cost of social change by seeking to facilitate their introduction. If this hypothetical judge believes that he should not consciously enact his private prejudices into law, and if the social values are so confused that uncertainty rules, the judge is well advised to flip a coin (in chambers) and govern his decision accordingly. If the judge finds himself favorably disposed toward any alternative to begin with, he will take himself as an object of investigation to determine the extent and origin of his prejudice. His logic thus involves the use of self-scrutiny for the exposure of private values which load the dice for or against a particular point of view. Besides the values which are "public," there are complicating values which are the residue of one's "private" history.

All these points are stressed in greater or less degree in the current writing on the use of the mind. The avowed purpose of our professional schools is to increase the

amount of logical reflection in the world, and the set complaint is that people somehow or another manage to think
very clumsily. In spite of our best efforts to disseminate
logicality, people are always "letting their prejudices run
away with them," even when they have a baggage of good
intentions.

The stock alibi for the failure of the schools to improve
the character of thinking among those who hold positions
of power is that the human mind offers a perverse opacity
to the rays of reason. Somehow or other our training
doesn't take; but this is attributed not to the deficiencies of
logic but to the resistances to it. All this is reminiscent of
the reply of the Christian to the taunt that Christianity has
failed. He says that Christianity isn't to blame, but the
lack of it. The logicians say that the cure of bad logic is
more and better logic. If the human mind refuses to be
educated, that's just too bad.

Our thesis is that our faith in logic is misplaced. Exclusive emphasis upon logic (even where logic is adroitly
used) incapacitates rather than fits the mind to function as
a fit instrument of reality adjustment.

The supposition that emotional aberrations are to be con-
quered by heroic doses of logical thinking is a mistake.
The absence of effective logic is a symptom of a disease
which logic cannot itself cure. We have been misled by
supposing that the mind can rely upon a single technique
of operation when this isolated technique has serious limitations.

A totally different technique of thinking is needed to get
on with the task of ridding the mind of the distorting
results of unseen compulsions. Since our schools have
found no place for the cultivation of this additional technique of thinking, our judges and administrators and

policy-makers are turned loose on the world armed with faith in logic and incapable of making their minds safe for logic. Logical thinking is but one of the special methods of using the mind, and cannot itself achieve an adequate inspection of reality because it is unable to achieve self-knowledge without the aid of other forms of thinking.

The technique of free-fantasy offers many points of contrast with logical thinking. It is unguided rather than guided association. From a given starting-point, no effort is bent toward the exclusion of the trivial, the trite, the embarrassing, the filthy, the nonsensical. The mind is permitted to run hither and yon. It is hospitable to everything which germinates in the mind, and is subject only to the effort to steer clear of the molds of logical thinking. There is no specific definition of an objective, and no intermittent intervention in the flow of material to register its pertinence or impertinence to this rather specific objective.

Free-fantasy is not to be confused with free word associations which begin with simple stimulus words and end when the first few words which pop into the mind are put down. Free-fantasy is not a momentary relaxation of selective criticism, but prolonged emancipation from logical fetters.

Free-fantasy differs from the ordinary daydream, the night dream, and the visions which arise in sleeping or waking by the circumstance that it is embarked upon with the vague, generalized purpose of rendering available new subject matter for logical thought. The frequent interventions which characterize logical procedures are suspended, the better to serve the ultimate purposes of reality adjustment. Daydreaming which is not used for this general purpose does not represent a technique for using the mind.

The ultimate paradox of logical thinking is that it is

self-destroying when it is too sedulously cultivated. It asserts its own prerogatives by clamping down certain restrictive frames of reference upon the activity of the mind, and presently ends in impoverishing the activity which it purports to guide into creative channels. It becomes intolerant of the immediate, unanalyzed, primitive abundance of the mind, and by so doing destroys its own source.

More seriously, too, for the mind which is engaged with social life, logical procedures exclude from the mind the most important data about the self. Directed thinking, whether about the self or something else as an object, is impatient of the seemingly trivial, and this impatience with the seemingly trivial is the rationally acceptable guise in which the impulse to avoid rigorous self-scrutiny gets itself accepted. The mind which is freely fantasying produces distasteful evidence of the facts about the self which the socialized self wants to avoid. This is why free-fantasy is not learned by rote, but achieved through trying experiences, usually under prolonged supervision.

There are wide individual differences in acquiring the technique of free-fantasy. Logical controls are often so gradually released that progress is almost imperceptible for several weeks of daily contact with a psychoanalytic interviewer. Frequently, of course, the logical controls fall away quite rapidly, and the exposure of the underlying preoccupations proceeds apace. Freud developed the technique, and drills his subjects, largely in relation to their dreams, but this is in no sense its exclusive application. The purpose of the psychoanalytic interview is not served if the patient is merely relieved of a few annoying symptoms; its purpose is to equip him with a means of handling his mind which will enable him to go it alone. In developing the free-fantasy procedure, Freud added a powerful

tool to the repertory of those who would use their mind
with some hope of disentangling themselves from the compulsive domination of many vestigial remains of their "private" histories.

It is quite possible to train people to use the free-fantasy
method with considerable success and to outfit them with
a device which they can use in the ordinary problems of
professional and private life.[2] The instances which I shall
presently adduce are from the fantasies which were produced by a judge in the course of a series of interviews
which he undertook after his curiosity about the method
had been aroused by the therapeutic treatment of a member of his family. Any specific allusions are disguised.

One day the judge commented at the beginning of the
interview that a certain attorney irritated him in some un-
explained way. He found himself acutely conscious of his
own prejudice against the man, and in trying to deal fairly with him often leaned over backward and showed him
an embarrassing favoritism in sustaining his objections.
There was always a struggle to hold the balance even.
This seemed to indicate the conspicuous operation of some
unrecognized set of motives in relation to this particular
individual. The judge, who was already partly skilled in
the use of free-fantasy, began to report whatever came
into his mind at the mention of the attorney, without regard to logic or scruple. "Cigar smoke . . . . black cigar
. . . . vile and pungent and stuffy . . . . corridor . . . .
courtroom . . . . ," and so on and on. The word "corridor" reappeared several times in the course of his associations, and the interviewer initiated a new chain by using
the word as a stimulus. After some time, there came up a

[2] The training should, of course, be conducted by a specialist alert to his
responsibilities.

vivid memory of an incident in the corridor of the law school where the judge had studied. A fellow-student, who was a man with a great reputation as a promising mind, dropped cigar ashes by accident on the judge's overcoat. The judge remembered his angry impulse to "sock" the offender, an impulse which he instantly subdued, and that he accepted the apology, which seemed to end the incident. Associations were continued to find why the brilliant rival had so incensed the judge, and the trail led back to certain incidents and reveries in early adolescence, but this material is not relevant here. The connection of his hostility toward his former rival with the attorney before him was due to one of the attorney's mannerisms, which recalled the way the student had flecked ashes off the end of his cigar. When this tie was exposed, the compulsive animosity and the overcompensatory reactions disappeared from the attitude of the judge in relation to the attorney.

Another illustrative detail may be taken almost at random from the record. On one occasion the judge began to enumerate the three principal alternatives which lay before him in deciding a pending case. He remembered two of them but hesitated several seconds before the third came into his mind. This led him to remember that he had often casually noticed that this third possibility seemed to elude him, although on reflection he felt that it deserved as much attention as the other two. He began spontaneously to relax and report everything that crossed his mind, and produced a long string of catch phrases from law and politics like "freedom of contract," "life, liberty, and pursuit of happiness," "freedom of speech and assembly." He presently noted that a picture was forming of one of his old law-school classrooms. He felt that someone was just about to speak to him, and had to resist the temptation to turn around. Then there came across his mind a long series of incidents in which one of his law professors was the principal figure. This teacher was reputed to possess a master-mind and a caustic tongue; and the judge, though he had always wanted to make a great impression on him, had met with no particular success. The professor had a habit of using his most ironic tone of voice when he spoke of "this freedom of contract." Now it happened that the attorney who was arguing for alternative No. 3 before the court pronounced the word "freedom" with unction. This aroused in the judge's mind the ironic tone of the old professor's voice, and this in turn brought back the rather humiliating failure he had been in his efforts to impress the professor. He now exhibited a tendency to repress everything connected with the episode, including the attorney's argument.

The world about us is much richer in meanings than we consciously see. These meanings are continually cutting across our ostensible criteria of judgment, and compulsively distorting the operations of the mind whose quest for an objective view of reality is consciously quite sincere. Good intentions are not enough to widen the sphere of self-mastery. There must be a special technique for the sake of exposing the hidden meanings which operate to bind and cripple the processes of logical thought. With practice one may wield the tool of free-fantasy with such ruthless honesty that relevant material comes very quickly to the focus of attention which we call "waking consciousness."

It would be possible to fill many volumes with illustrations of the hitherto unseen meanings which have been discovered by men and women who have learned to use the free-fantasy technique. They have often been able to find how and why their emotions tended to be aroused favorably or unfavorably toward individuals of their own or the opposite sex who exhibited certain traits, and to understand why they tended to choose certain secretaries, to sponsor certain protégés, and to be impressed by certain witnesses and attorneys. They have been able to inspect the phraseology of law, politics, and culture, and to extricate themselves from many of the logically irrelevant private meanings which they read into it.

Freud developed the technique of free-fantasy well over a quarter of a century ago, but it is still beyond the pale of the schools. Our professional and graduate schools make no effort to readjust their methods to fit the minds of future men of authority for self-knowledge. The sententious admonitions to "know thyself" are no adequate substitute for special discipline in the ways of self-understanding.

We have tried to cure the failures of logical training by homeopathic doses of sermonizing, rather than by the discipline of supplementary techniques of using the mind. The mind is a fit instrument of reality testing when both blades are sharpened—those of logic and free-fantasy. Until this fundamental proposition is adequately comprehended, the professional training of our judges, administrators, and theorists will continue to furnish discipline in self-deception rather than self-analysis.

CHAPTER IV

THE CRITERIA OF POLITICAL TYPES

The free-fantasy method of exploring the mind is of very general application to the problems of life. In particular we are interested in examining the results of its use for the purpose of laying bare the natural history of personality growth and differentiation. All sorts of politicians are met with in society, and our special task is to relate the selection of these adult rôles to certain critical experiences in individual development. But before we can proceed farther, we need to examine the nature of the criteria which are currently used in identifying various political types.

The popular speech of every state and neighborhood swarms with names for varieties of political behavior and types of politicians. The study of political differences may very well begin by sifting the common vocabulary. Some of the popular images are derived from experience with government officials. Within the last hundred years the policeman has appeared over Western Europe, and a history of the popular conception of his rôle could be written around terms like "bobby," "cop," and *"Schupo."* Whatever differences in dress, manner, social position, and common humanity are supposed to exist between a "civil servant," a *"Beamter,"* and a *"fonctionnaire,"* there are common lineaments in the composite stereotype. A thick chapter in human experience could be entitled "The Bureaucrat," wherein would be recorded the innuendo of popular comment on a necessary evil. The "legislator" is identifi-

38

able through all the detailed contrasts between the "congressman," the "M.P.," and the "M.d.R."

The popular tongue is rich in expressions which fill out the official cast of characters in the political drama by peopling the public stage with figures whose traits are essentially irrelevant to their office. There are men of ideas —"anarchist," "socialist," "liberal," "communist,". "conservative." There are men of ideas and of action—"reformer," "revolutionary," "martyr." The history of American, British, French, German, medieval, Graeco-Roman, and every civilization could be written for the sake of showing how the carriers of public power figured in the eyes of the various groups within and without the culture.

This profusion of types in the popular firmament of politics is supplemented by the types which have been isolated by serious students of culture, who have sought to impose order upon the life of the past. Among the political forms which have been described by the historians, the "benevolent despot" of the eighteenth century, the "demagogue" of Athenian democracy, the "prince" of the Italian Renaissance, and the "despot" of the oriental empires spring at once to mind. The masterly sketch of the evolution of the public official with which Max Weber[1] has enriched social science is, it is to be hoped, the forerunner of many elaborate studies. The traits and arts of political leaders have been most systematically handled by Aristotle, Machiavelli, Robert Michels, Christensen, and Charles E. Merriam.[2]

These typologies, whether popular or scientific, possess

[1] "Politik als Beruf," in *Gesammelte Schriften.*

[2] I summarized some of this literature in "Types of Political Personalities," *Proceedings of the American Sociological Society, 1927.* Reprinted in *Personality and the Group* (edited by Burgess).

several features in common. They may converge to what is practically the same picture. When W. B. Munro described the "reformer," he filled out the popular image which arose in the American mind at a certain phase of American political evolution.[3] Practically every scientific conception is a refinement and generalization of some term in general circulation, though with local connotations.

The scientific and the popular typologies may include the same kinds of fact as their starting-points. The fact of supposed political conviction gave rise to the "liberal," but it is a far cry from the rather shadowy lines of the popular image to the finely wrought lineaments of Ruggiero.[4] The means employed in encompassing political objectives christen the "lobbyist," "propagandist," and "agitator." The idea that private motives are not merged in public motives is carried in "renegade," "sorehead," and "tyrant." The idea that private motives have been firmly fused into public purposes is one connotation of the "martyr." The fact of informal ascendancy is celebrated in the "boss." In the "bureaucrat" it is implied that the office has molded the man, and that the office tends to attract those especially likely to develop such qualities. The Western European idea of a judge almost necessarily refers to a functionary who carries certain paraphernalia and proceeds with ceremony. The leanness of the "fanatical agitator" figured in the popular mind long before Kretschmer gave it his scientific blessing.[5]

Both popular and scientific conceptions range from the particular to the general. The British "election agent" is closely bound to a recent, special social setting. The "lead-

[3] *Personality in Politics.*
[4] *The History of European Liberalism.*
[5] *Physique and Character,* chap. xiii.

er" keeps a stable nucleus of meaning for the description of a social rôle among widely separated peoples in widely separated periods.

Popular and scientific conceptions are at one in that they may present developmental and not merely descriptive implications. The notion of a lean and bitter agitator is not entirely a static, cross-sectional description of a fortuitous juxtaposition of traits, but a hypothesis that bodily irritations operate dynamically to foster the selection of forms of activity which enable the individual to give rather free vent to his animosities.

Both popular and scientific types may be taken as objects of study to determine the factors in their formation. The popular idea of a "reformer" in America bears a certain photographic resemblance to actual personalities who figured as public advocates of restrictive laws. It is possible to study the process by which the stereotype of the lean and spinsterly kill-joy arose, and to see why it persisted. Every body politic has its gallery of political mummers, and political history needs to be rewritten to explain the unique and the typical qualities of these popularly conceived rôles. Stuart A. Rice has developed a technique for the identification of contemporary stereotypes of this kind.[6] Rice took photographs of a senator, a bolshevik, and a bootlegger, and after obliterating the names asked various test groups to tell what designation best fitted each picture. By examining the erroneous identifications, it became possible to detect the mental pattern popularly associated with the class name.

An interesting contribution to social science would be the detailed examination of the factors affecting the rise and fall of those political typologies which have been seriously

[6] *Quantitative Methods in Politics*, chap. v.

proposed by scholars. The exaggerated picture of the omnipotent leader drawn by Carlyle no doubt had something to do with Carlyle's sexual impotence and his compensatory idealization of the potent; but the popularity which this exaggeration enjoyed among certain classes of English society was due to the dislocation of older economic institutions and the rise of threatening collective ideologies. The new business enterpriser felt the intoxicating vanity of the self-made man, and the decayed landlords felt the necessity of individualistic protests against the age of cities and machines.

Suppose we examine in more detail the intellectual structure of scientific political types. This requires special attention to the two terms involved, the "political" and the "types." Two ways of defining the "political" are current in social science. I will speak of them as the "institutional" and the "functional" methods of definition. Within any community there are many patterns of activity whose form and whose magnitude may be singled out for study. There is the production and distribution of material goods and services; the main patterns by which these operations proceed can be called the economic institutions of the community. There is the settlement of disputes, and the defense and extension of interests which are believed to be collective; these are the political or governmental institutions of the community. In the same way religious, charitable, and a host of other institutions may be discerned.

These institutionally derived categories fall short of clarity and comprehensiveness. Some social processes occur within the framework of every institutional process. Thus the settlement of disputes is a prominent characteristic of government as we know it; but it is not, and never has been, and cannot by the nature of things be, a monopoly of government when government is defined as an institutional division of social labor. No institution ever quite monopolizes the function which it most distinctively exercises. But this need not lead to confusion. When the settlement of disputes is a prominent function of one group in society, and there is no other group which participates in the same function in the same degree, there is no hesitation in deciding to call the first group the "governors" and to call the patterns according to which they are selected and operate the "political or governmental" institutions of the community. If there is a rival adjuster of differences, the distinction is by no means clear, as when the "church," "business," and the "state" are rivals. Perhaps the governors can be identified by finding who it is who handles the coercion employed in defending or extending communal enterprises, though this criterion may from time to time fail to differentiate. But, on the whole, these doubts are marginal doubts. Ordinarily it is possible to find a division of labor and a set of sentiments which can be called the "government of the state." The marginal instances call attention to the fact to which allusion has been made, the fact that no "institutional" process quite monopolizes the function which it most distinctively exercises. It is therefore advisable to describe communal processes by two sets of terms, one of which refers to "institutions" and the other to "functions" which are found within the various institutional frameworks. Much of the literature of social science consists in terminological quibbles about the "proper" words to use in this institutional or functional sense, often without appreciating the essential nature of the matter at issue. It is, of course, of the highest importance to understand the difference, and of minor importance to agree upon the words with which to describe the distinction.

From what has been said, it is clear that a word like "political" may be given an "institutional" or a "functional" meaning in a particular context, and that—and this is the most important consequence—any contribution to the understanding of the "institutional" process is a contribution to the understanding of the wider "functional" process, and the reverse. In this resides the unity of the social sciences. The apparent disunity arises from the differences in starting-point of particular inquiries. One begins with a series of phenomena which are selected from a single institutional process, and another begins with a series of phenomena which are selected from several institutional processes according to some functional conception.

This unity of destination and disunity of starting-point is abundantly manifested in the scientific study of human behavior. The specialist on some phase of the political process, institutionally conceived, who is asked to classify the types of political behavior, devises his categories on the basis of the institutional processes which he knew best. It would be possible, were it worth the effort, to pass in review the typologies which have been propounded from time to time by specialists in executive organization, public administration, judicial administration, legislation, political parties, propaganda and conspirative organizations, political revolution, nationalism, imperialism, interstate methods of adjustment (war, diplomacy, conference, adjudication, mediation, arbitration), and all the other topics in political science.

At first glance, the functional method of defining political types would seem to lead to even greater congeries of categories than the institutional method. From the functional standpoint politics is found wherever, to use the older terminology, "wills" are in conflict. This implies that intensely political manifestations in society are not confined to government officials and parties, but to banking houses, manufacturing enterprises, distributing services, ecclesiastical organizations, fraternal associations, and professional societies. It is probable that the most aggressive, power-lusting individuals in modern society find their way into business, and stay out of the legislature, the courts, the civil service, and the diplomatic service. If this be true, the student of political personalities will find the most interesting objects of study in J. P. Morgan and Company, in the United States Steel Corporation, and among the clerical or educational or medical politicians.

It follows from what has been said that the study of politicians who are chosen from a single institutional process makes a contribution to the general study of politicians in every institutional process, and that the conscious abstraction of categories until they are comprehensive opens a wider range of exact comparison. This may eventuate in an actual simplification of some fundamental conceptions. Of course, institutional processes differ in the scope which they give to certain human drives. Today the church offers less opportunity for the use of physical violence than it did in the sixteenth century, and very much less opportunity than the police force, the private detective agency, or the political gang.

The advantages of comprehensiveness and possible simplification have been sacrificed by the political scientists of the schools because they have conceived their task in too narrow a spirit. They have been slow in studying the manifestations of human nature in politics because they have been saturated with sectarian pride in legal and philosophical distinctions; or they have checked their theories with their coats, and plunged into technical work. A body of theory which interacts fruitfully with philosophy, law, and technology is still very poorly developed. The formal sociological systems have been sacked for "premises" but neglected for hypotheses. (Witness the exploitation of the concept of "solidarity" in recent juridical theory.) The task of the hour is the development of a realistic analysis of the political in relation to the social process, and this depends upon the invention of abstract conceptions and upon the prosecution of empirical research. It is precisely this missing body of theory and practice which Graham Wallas undertook to supply in England and which Charles E. Merriam has been foremost in encouraging in the United States. It is the deficiency which led Catlin to propose to substitute what I would call the "functional" for the "institutional" definition of the field of political science.[7] This necessarily implies a new respect for the possibilities of using the ingenious suggestions to be found in the sociological systematists, a new curiosity about diverse ways of approaching events, and a new sympathy for parallels to institutional phenomena.

Various obscurities can be removed if we generalize our terms from the narrowly institutional to the broadly functional plane. Terms like "statesman" and "despot" were minted of the metal of political experience in communities where the high road to power was governmental. It is true that in Athens it was difficult to draw very sharp lines between governmental and other forms of communal activity, on account of the intimate interlacing of all institutional processes. Nevertheless, terms like "statesman" and "despot" came to refer to forms of political activity in a narrowly institutional sense, and such is their connotation today.

[7] *The Science and Method of Politics.*

But this connotation requires generalization and revision. The road to power in our civilization is by no means
an exclusively governmental highway, for technical imple-
ments have scattered authority and created an industrial
feudality. The directors of large corporations have to
make decisions which are far more important for the daily
happiness of mankind than most of the decisions of governments. Since government is so largely the agent of
corporations, the government is hardly master in its own
house.

The concept of the statesman has long carried the implication that anyone who exercises social power outside the
government is in hot pursuit of an exclusively private advantage. Is this any longer tenable? Is there not such a
thing as the "institutionalization of business" which arises
when a given enterprise plans to operate indefinitely and
is thus forced to calculate its interests over long periods of
time? One of the major elements in this calculation is the
necessity of taking precautions against a withdrawal of
favor on the part of the community at large. This is the
core of the political way of thinking, and assimilates the
policy of aggregations of private power to that of the state
which is guided by statesmen. It is timely, therefore, to
disentangle the concept of statesmanship from its historical
association with a single institution.

Some of the many senses in which the "politician" is
used may be disposed of by drawing a clean distinction between the "business man" and the "politician." The business man may be defined as one who pursues a private advantage with little regard for conceptions of public right.
The politician, in the here-selected "best" sense of the
word, uses persuasion on behalf of his conception of public
right. The politician pursues a genuine integration of in-

terests in the community; the business man is satisfied with a compromise among competing private interests. The importance to political theory of the distinction between integration and compromise has quite properly been stressed by Mary P. Follett.[8] An integration of interests is the solution of a conflict in such a way that neither "party" recognizes that so much has been won and so much has been lost in the outcome. It represents a reinterpretation of the situation in a sense which renders the old line of battle, the older definition of interest, irrelevant. It is illustrated when a wage controversy is disposed of by the decision to try to divide the advantages of economies in production which may be brought about through new co-operative procedures. The essence of the contrast between integration and compromise is that between a synthesis and a trade. The politician is a discoverer of inclusive advantages, and the business man is a higgler for special advantages. Whether, as Adam Smith said, an invisible hand shapes a social synthesis from the general pursuit of private profit, we do not have to decide upon here. The contrast is between the conscious objectives of the individuals concerned. It should be observed that politicians are not limited to government and that business men are not limited to private ventures. The "boss" is one form of the business man in government; the director of a large private concern may be a politician in the sense used here.[9]

Having drawn a necessary distinction between the insti-

[8] *The New State.*

[9] It is not profitable to pursue these distinctions farther. I should prefer to distinguish the statesman from the politician by treating the latter as a function of a democratically organized community and as one who is limited to persuasion in the advancement of his conceptions of public right. The statesman may use force, and is not necessarily a function of democratically organized society.

tutional and the functional meaning of the "political," we are in a position to discuss the "type" concept. A "type" is a relation, and we may classify types according to the relations chosen. Political types may be set up on a three-fold basis: by specifying a nuclear relation, a co-relation, and a developmental relation.

What is meant by the choice of a nuclear relation may be illustrated by the concept of the *Machtmensch* as elaborated by Eduard Spranger in his *Lebensformen*. Spranger, the distinguished educational psychologist of the University of Berlin, has developed a morphology of personality on an original basis. Dilthey, it will be recalled, ushered in the modern era of typological inquiry in his famous address before the Berlin Academy of Science.[10] Dilthey selected forms of distinguished cultural activity and posited trait-constellations to fit. By the process of abstracting from many concrete fields of achievement, he finally built up his description of the sensual, heroic, and contemplative types. Most eminent political figures naturally fall in the second category. Spranger's approach has much in common with that of Dilthey. He proceeds on the hypothesis that all possible valuational dispositions are shared by all men. By inspecting human culture, Spranger comes to the conclusion that six distinctive cultural fields have materialized six valuational dispositions in man. Thus the cultural activities having to do with wealth production correspond to the economic value tendency. Science corresponds to the theoretical, art to the aesthetic, religion to the religious, the state to the power tendency, and society to the love tendency. Spranger goes on to deduce the at-

[10] His viewpoint is best expressed in "Die Typen der Weltanschauung," in *Weltanschauung-Philosophie und Religion in Darstellungen* (edited by M. Frischeisen-Kohler).

tributes of each personality in which one value tendency predominates, and traces out the implications for each field of activity of the predominance of this tendency. Thus the political man is the one whose principal value is the pursuit of power. The essence of power is understood to be the capacity, and usually the will, to impose one's own values as permanent or transitory motives upon others. The political man in science tends to substitute rhetoric for truth and to use ideas as forces (in the sense of Fouillée). In economics the political man tends to reach his ends by diplomacy and negotiation, by intimidation or violence, or by other political means. In art the political motive leads to efforts to impress by flamboyant decorative display. In social life the political motive, with its forcible urge toward self-aggrandizement, must usually disguise itself in fostering the interests of some collectivity. The god of the political man in religion is a god of might who requires mighty men to serve him.

In developing his image of the *homo politicus*, Spranger is fully aware that his "pure" type seldom exists. The bold, frank aggrandizement of self is rarely tolerated in society, for "the greatest power manifests itself as collective power," and the man who cherishes power must achieve some measure of socialization or he is outlawed. Although in principle no warm-hearted lover of his fellow-men, he must keep his contempt to himself or feign expansive sentiments of group loyalty. Indeed, self-deception is perhaps the rule, for the political personality with a strong artistic component possesses a florid imagination which dramatizes his personal history and subordinates all reality to ambitious plans. It seems to me that Spranger does not sufficiently stress this aspect of the political man, this large capacity for playing the impostor upon himself and others.

The gist of Spranger's generalization of the political man is schematically expressible in terms of desire-method-success. The political man desires to control the motives of others; his method may vary from violence to wheedling; his success in securing recognition in some community must be tangible. These are the nuclear relations which are essential to the type definition.

Naturally there are a number of necessary annotations to be made on this formula. Sometimes the man with a thirst for power is unable to indulge and quench his thirst, for his physical and social equipment may be too meager. And how are we to appraise results? *Wer regiert denn?* Power over others is partially exercised by every living being; but in any hierarchy of the powerful, some are on the lowest tier, if current social criteria be applied. The bedridden, complaining wreck may be of no significance except as a burden upon the care of a single nurse. Accepting the current values of society, such an individual would be on the very bottom of the heap. And yet, as Alfred Adler has so often insisted as to make the point peculiarly his own, the hysteric may use his symptoms to win a high degree of submission from his immediate environment, and this may be all that he cares about. And some of those who give up the visible struggle for social influence may retire to distil their bile into poisoned darts against the pursuit of external pomp, and secure reputation and eminence by embodying the results in sparkling rhetoric.

The man who runs his village may become more acutely aware that he does not run the county; and when he runs the county, that he does not run the province; and so on up the ladder. His appurtenances of power may be deferred to by those about him, yet his own soul may smart with the shackles of a larger slavery. Thus, Spranger is right in saying that, when one succeeds in penetrating the psychology of the search for power, it becomes comprehensible that he whose nature is bound up in the pursuit of authority is most keenly sensible to the limits of his own freedom, and consequently suffers so keenly from nothing else in life than his own subordination. Sensing this, the Stoics long ago contended that the essence of liberty is the self-sufficiency which makes no demands on others. Ascendancy involves dependence, a reciprocal relationship which has been exhaustively described by Simmel.[11] But there are some who combine easy success with indifference. These are no doubt recruited from among those who have natural suggestive power to certain groups—they possess the *charisma* of Max Weber.[12]

Allowing for these annotations, the nucleus of Spranger's thinking may be repeated. The *homo politicus* is characterized by the following relationship between desire, method, and success: desire to control the motives of others; methods varying from violence to wheedling; and success in securing communal recognition.

Spranger's subtle comments in elaborating this simple, central conception are among the most valuable in the literature of society. Starting from bold simplifications, he succeeds in formulating pictures which give richer meaning to the details of political life in all the institutional processes of culture. Of course the literature of political science is full of types which are described as Spranger has described the political man. Michels and Merriam have listed the qualities which they find in political leaders as a class. Conway has propounded his fa-

[11] *Soziologie*, chap. iii.
[12] *Grundriss der Sozialökonomik*, III, 1.

miliar trichotomy: crowd-compellers, crowd-exponents, and crowd-representatives. The possibility of defining types according to the reactionary, conservative, liberal, or radical nature of the opinions championed has often been discussed.[13]

The scheme which will be employed in presenting case materials stresses the capacity of political personalities to play rôles which are either specialized or composite. Hobbes was a theorist and an agitating pamphleteer; he is scarcely thinkable as an agitating orator and organizer like Garrison. The "pure-type" agitator is represented by the Old Testament prophets. Bodin combined a memorable contribution to political theory with the arduous duties of a successful administrator. Masaryk won his spurs in philosophy, sociology, cultural history, agitation, and organization. Numberless are those who have shown excellent organizing ability but who have been innocent of theoretical interests or of agitating power. Some political assassins and tyrants have enjoyed the use of violence as a *ding an sich.* The central point in deciding where to place a political figure is to discover the form of activity which means the most to him, and to modify the classification according to his success in combining this with other rôles. Marx wanted to impress himself upon mankind, certainly; and he craved the skill of a Lassalle, who could step on the platform and dominate the turbulent emotions of the crowd. But more: Marx wanted unreserved admiration for the products of his mind. He toiled through years of isolation and poverty to make his assertions impregnable.

[13] See Robert Michels, *Political Parties;* C. E. Merriam, *American Party System,* and *Introduction* to H. F. Gosnell's *Boss Platt and His New York Machine;* Martin Conway, *Instincts of the Herd in Peace and War;* Lowell, *Public Opinion in War and Peace;* Rohmer, *Die Vier Parteien;* A. Christensen, *Politics and Crowd Morality;* W. B. Munro, *Personality in Politics.*

It was more important to attain theoretical completeness than to modify his technique of social intercourse. Lassalle was the composite leader who could woo an audience, organize activities all over Germany, write excellent books, and win a place for himself in many circles of life. Marx was the limited specialist who had to exact submission to the assertions of his mind, come what may.

Table I brings out the distinction between specialized and composite types.

TABLE I

POLITICAL RÔLES

	Administrator	Agitator	Theorist
Specialized types:			
Hoover	*	....	....
Old Testament prophets	....	*	....
Marx	....	....	*
Composite types:			
Cobden	*	*	....
Bodin	*	....	*
Lenin	*	*	*

Other combinations may be indicated. By adding a fourth column for those who resort to violence, the schematic possibilities are enlarged. Most theorists have been agitators in some measure, and it is often a matter of taste whether emphasis is to be placed on one or the other feature of their activity. Characteristically, the theorists have sought to appeal to the sentiments of their contemporaries by pamphleteering or by the direction of their speculative interests to immediate ends. Hobbes and Rousseau were shut off from oratory and organization, but no small part of their writing was intended to add fuel to the flames around them. Such men as Tom Paine are able to strike

THE CRITERIA OF POLITICAL TYPES

off excellent formulations of political theory in the heat
of the fray.

So far we have been discussing types which are distinguished according to some nuclear relation among a few
variables. The characteristic mode of elaborating such a
type is to imagine a host of situations in which the type
may be found, and to describe the resulting picture. This
is the elaboration of the preliminary sketch on the basis of
sophisticated experience with social life. For these im-
pressionist methods it is possible to substitute a more
formal procedure. Having chosen a central primary relation, is it possible to find, by reference to specific instances,
the relative frequency with which other traits are associated with the nuclear ones. The starting-point may be
either institutional or functional, of course: those who are
"judges," "legislators," or "bosses" may be investigated,
or those who are "statesmen," "conciliators," or "administrators." We have already had occasion to stress the
point that institutional definitions and functional definitions do not precisely coincide, although either is a valid
point of departure for research.

The result of the formal procedure outlined is to define
"co-relational" (correlational) types. A recent monograph
by Fritz Giese may be used to illustrate the possibilities.[14]
This is a statistical treatment of the data available in the
German *Who's Who* of 1914. After Giese had eliminated
those who were included on account of their hereditary
position only, he had over ten thousand names left. He
then distinguished thirty-three varieties of activity, which
were grouped into the five major categories of art, social
science, physical science, technology, and practical life.

[14] *Die öffentliche Persönlichkeit.* Beihefte zur *Zeitschrift für angewandte
Psychologie*, Vol. XLIV.

He also classified his subjects into those who were honored because of high-grade but essentially routine professional accomplishment, those who enriched their field of activity by some creative contribution, and those whose creativeness was unrestricted to their occupational field. The three types were the skilful, the productive, and the freely creative. Since the individual is not confined to one field of activity, the following scheme of connections was built up to show the relation between the person and the form of activity: (a) income source (the person regards a particular field as a "bread and butter" occupation); (b) successive activity field (the individual has deserted one field for another); (c) field of simultaneous double-production; (d) recreational activity. The relation of a person to a field of activity may show a splitting of his personality or a compensatory function. When a politician consciously decides to play golf or to collect pictures to relieve his mind from exclusive political preoccupations, he is realizing a compensatory value in this chosen field. When he finds himself impelled to try to live a double life of scientific investigation and political propaganda, he is exhibiting major, and contrasting, tendencies in his personality (splitting). Sometimes the tie between fields of activity which the same individual exploits is factual similarity, as when a politician becomes a literary man to the extent of writing the political history of a period. Sometimes the connection is a functional relationship, in that the same biopsychic dispositions are to be assumed to operate. Thus, business promotion and politics are intimately allied; sculpture and politics are not.

Giese's detailed analysis showed that those engaged in politics reveal the most heterogeneous affiliations and backgrounds. He raised the question whether it was proper to think of a distinctive functional gift which would characterize all those in political positions. When compared with art, especially architecture, and engineering, the heterogeneity of the political population is very evident. Indeed, the manifold connections of politically active persons with other fields suggest that political life depends upon very widely dispersed capacities of human nature, as does teaching, history writing, and journalism. But there is one important exception which is clearly brought out by the figures. This was a group of politicians who rose from humble circumstances and devoted themselves assiduously to organization and agitation. They offer a sharp contrast to those for whom political life was a sport, hobby, or honorary distinction. For the organizing and agitating group we may postulate a functional disposition of some kind.

The results show how the institutional approach to a problem may eventuate in the isolation of one group which very probably coincides closely with a functional group in other institutional activities. Some of the agitating and organizing people weren't yet in politics at the time the 1914 census was made, and some of them were so busy with private organizations that they never made the formal transition to politics in the institutional sense.

Another conclusion which bears on the same point is Giese's discovery that those who were freely creative in politics had much more in common with those who were freely creative in other fields than they had with those who were merely productive in their own. Giese's method of classifying his freely creative group is too ambiguous to justify one in considering his conclusion of more than suggestive value, but it is possible that he has isolated a functionally homogeneous group which cuts across all institutional lines.

Some of the studies of political personalities have carried the quantitative method far enough to substitute scales for rank orders at various points. Various reaction tests have been used in the hope of discovering constant differences among those who play different political rôles. Henry T. Moore undertook to decide whether there is such a thing as a temperamental predisposition toward conservatism or radicalism. He defined radicalism as "an attitude favorable to sweeping changes in social institutions, especially changes along lines opposed to class interest," and classified the opinion expressions of students according to the degree of radicalism or conservatism indicated. He then applied a series of reaction tests to the students and reached the following conclusion:

Our evidence so far as it goes points to some innate basis of difference. This basis does not seem to be the level of general intelligence or of emotional stability, nor in any general superiority or inferiority in learning or attention, but in such specific factors as greater speed of reaction, ease of breaking habits, readiness to make snap judgments, and independence in the face of majority influence. The last of these differences is the one most clearly indicated. . . . . If one man is by nature more keyed up for speed and flexibility, and the other is more designed for regularity of function, we can hardly expect that government of the hyperkinetic by the phlegmatic and for the phlegmatic can fail to develop periods of stress and strain.[15]

Floyd Allport classified students into typical and atypical members of the community, discovering whether they took up prevalent or minority positions on various political questions. He then applied a battery of tests to the

[15] "Innate Factors in Radicalism and Conservatism," *Journal of Abnormal and Social Psychology*, XX (1925–26), 234–4.

students and found that certain traits of the atypical (whether the opinions were "radical" or "conservative") proved to be homogeneous. Thus, not only do the "extremes" meet, but also those who hold minority positions along a hypothetical continuum of opinion distribution.[16]

W. H. Cowley, at the instigation of Charles E. Merriam and L. L. Thurstone, undertook to compare leaders in chosen situations. He used twenty-eight tests of such traits as aggressiveness, self-confidence, intelligence, emotional stability, and speed of reaction. While his tests were differentiating within the same group between leaders and followers, he reports that they did not distinguish between leaders as a class and followers as a class. He thus felt justified in denying that leadership is a universal trait of particular persons, and criticized efforts to itemize "traits of leadership."[17] Further applications of the blanket-test technique are under way.[18]

Gilbert J. Rich opened out a new field of investigation when he studied certain complex physiological and biochemical variables among leaders and followers. He measured the hydrogen-ion concentration of the saliva, the acidity of the urine, alkali reserve of the blood, and creatinine excretion of the urine. The least excitable subjects showed the most acid saliva and the most acid urine. The

[16] Allport really used a rank-order method of handling opinion expressions which he unjustifiably treated as marking definite positions along a base line. Thurstone has greatly improved the technique of opinion measurement. See Thurstone and Chave, *The Measurement of Attitude* (Chicago, 1929). For Allport's original paper (with D. A. Hartman), see "Measurement and Motivation of Atypical Opinion in a Certain Group," *American Political Science Review*, XIX (1925), 735-60.

[17] "Three Distinctions in the Study of Leaders," *Journal of Abnormal and Social Psychology*, Vol. XXIII (July–September, 1928).

[18] By Keith Sward, Social Science Research Council Fellow, and others. I discuss the problem of evaluating test results later on.

rating of the subjects was open to criticism, and was obviously much less refined than the biochemical techniques employed.[19]

The types which we have just been considering show more than a cross-sectional picture of the adult personality. They have made the transition from itemizing the instantaneous pictures to the selection of features of the immediate picture which show how the type has come to be. They are thus more than co-relational types; they have made some progress toward developmental types. When Giese found the group of political personalities of humble origin and persistent organizing and agitating activity, he postulated a common dynamic of development, a homogeneous functional disposition toward this sort of thing. Moore wanted to extricate the formative influence of temperamental reactive sets, and the other investigators have likewise sought to ascertain developmental factors in the production of the adult picture of traits and interests.

Almost every nuclear and co-relational type carries developmental implications. The terms which are used to characterize motives have dynamic, genetic, formative coronas of meaning which, vaguely though they may be sketched, are emphatically present. When Michels says that a "Catonian strength of conviction" is one mark of the political leader, it is implied that if one pushed his inquiry into the adolescence, childhood, and even infancy of the individual that this ruling characteristic would be visible. Of course, Michels does not himself develop these implications; it is doubtful if he has tried to find the early analogues of the trait which he called "Catonian strength of conviction" on the adult level. But the dynamic penum-

---

[19] "A Biochemical Approach to the Study of Personality," *Journal of Abnormal and Social Psychology*, Vol. XXIII (July-September, 1928).

bra of the term can lead empirical investigators to scrutinize the behavior of children from a new point of view.
Many of the terms which are used to describe adult traits
are no doubt unpredictable from the less differentiated
traits of infancy, childhood, and youth. But the growth
of full-blown developmental types requires the sifting and
refinement of terms until they are adequate to the description of sequences of growth. Developmental types will
describe a set of terminal, adult reactions, and relate them
to those critical experiences in the antecedent life of the
individual which dispose him to set up such a mode of
dealing with the world. Developmental types will not
only include the subjective account of the history of the
personality but will embrace the objective factors which
were co-operating to produce the patterns described.

The notion of a developmental type may be illustrated
by examining the place which is assigned to the political
man in the chief modern characterological systems. Hans
Apfelbach has used five dimensions for the description
of characters. Each one is described as a gamut between
two polar opposites, and a sixth pair of polar opposites
is introduced into the system. The scheme is indicated in
Table II.

This gives a formal range of sixty-four types of character formation without allowing for subtle variations in
quantity. The first combination which Apfelbach specifies
is, symbolically, ABCDEF. This is a very masculine,
sadistic, hyperemotional, moral, intellectually keen, and
upright character. Among men this is the type of the
organizers, politicians, the great preachers, generals, dic-
tators, and the like. Among women, this is the type of the
organizer of every description, especially the political or
patriotic enthusiast, like Joan of Arc. It should be ob-

served that the terms "masculine" and "feminine" are not used in a mutually exclusive sense. Carrying on the tradition of Weininger and Fliess, these terms are employed to designate traits which may be present in different proportions in the same person.[20]

The political man appears in Jung's system at various intersections of his underlying scheme. The essential

TABLE II

Dimension	Polar Elements	
Sexuality	Masculine	A
	Feminine	a
Psychomotility	Psychosadistic	B
	Psychomasochistic	b
Emotionality	Hyperemotional	C
	Hypo-emotional	c
Morality	Moral	D
	Immoral	d
Intellectuality (specialized)	Superior	E
	Inferior	e
Accessory elements	Altruistic	F
	Egotistic	f

cleavage in Jung's classification is between those whose psychic energy (libido) flows outward toward objects (extraversion) and those whose libido flows inward (introversion). The former enter into full affective relations with the world around; the latter are mainly focused on their private interpretations of experience. In addition to these fundamental dynamic relationships, Jung subclassifies with reference to our fundamental psychological functions: thinking, feeling, sensation, intuition. These functions may operate against one another consciously or unconsciously. So, when thinking predominates in con-

[20] Hans Apfelbach, Der Aufbau des Charakters. Cf. Otto Weininger, Geschlecht und Charakter; Fliess, Ablauf des Lebens.

sciousness, feeling is repressed; and the reverse. Intuition is understood to be a kind of instinctive comprehension, a function peculiarly dependent upon the unconscious. According to the predominance of one or another of these basic functions, Jung constructs four special types of extraversion and introversion.

Certain conspicuous political types belong to Jung's category of extraverted thinkers. These individuals try to bring their whole life-activity into relation with intellectual conclusions, which in the last resort are always oriented by objective data, whether objective facts or generally valid ideas. By his formula are good and evil measured: all is wrong that contradicts it, and all is right that corresponds to it; all is accidental that is neutral toward it. Just as the extraverted thinking type subordinates himself to his formula, he seeks to subordinate all others to it, as a manifestation of a universal inspiration. His moral code forbids him to tolerate exceptions, and he would bend all to suit the scheme. "One really should" or "one must" figure largely in his program. If the formula is wide enough, Jung remarks that the extraverted thinker may figure as a reformer, a ventilator of public wrongs, and a propagandist. But the more rigid his formula, the more likely he is to grow into a grumbler, a crafty reasoner, and a self-righteous critic.

Many politicians answer to the general description which Jung gives of the extraverted, intuitive type. The intuitive is unattracted by the established values; he is drawn to the possible rather than to the actual. He seizes hold of new objects and ways of doing things with eager intensity, only to abandon them cold-bloodedly, when their implications become obvious. The irresistible magnet of the rising sun fires his imagination and guides his activity. For the risen sun and the setting sun there is no enthusiasm, no special hostility, only indifference. Here is the facile promoter, who senses the dawning future and speeds from project to project, bored with routine and detail after projects have been accepted and the blueprints finished.[21]

The types of Apfelbach and Jung are based upon a small number of reactive mechanisms which are supposed to influence in different degree the growth of the personality. These "mechanism" types may contain many useful leads, but the methodological problem in isolating these hypothetical mechanisms is unsettled. A "stable" reaction in adulthood may be far from stable when viewed at successive growth periods. These "mechanism" types seem to encourage endless classificatory ventures at the expense of detailed reporting of life-histories. For reasons which have been set forth, subjective histories are of the greatest importance to social science; and any excessive interest in "mechanism" which minimizes the importance of elaborate individual records is to be deplored. Jung and Apfelbach say very little about the principal epochs of individual development, and distract attention from the career as a whole, as this career is structuralized in successive phases.

Before outlining our developmental conception of the *homo politicus,* we return to the work of Freud, for his method has enabled him to keep close to the subjective sequence and to use classificatory terms in relation to the successive phases of impulse organization in the developing personality.

[21] C. G. Jung, *Psychological Types,* chap. x.

CHAPTER V

THEORIES OF PERSONALITY DEVELOPMENT

It will be remembered that Freud's search for signs of the traumatic situation led him to uncover the contemporaneous functioning of all sorts of unconscious motivations in both the diseased and the healthy personality. The quest led him farther. Freud felt impelled to set up a schematic representation of the typical genetic development of the human personality. This grew out of the comparative study of very thoroughly analyzed cases and was rooted in empirical observation. Freud has always kept close to his data; and no matter how far his imagination soared, actual clinical experience was the starting-place and the landing-field for the flight.

The energy of a developed personality can be treated as dispersed in three directions: in the affirmative expression of socialized impulses, in unsocialized impulses, and in the maintenance of resistance charges against unsocialized impulses. The original forms of energy expression which are available to the infant are in many ways incompatible with the demands of human intercourse. The infant must surrender many primitive forms of gratification, if he is to be loved, and to avoid discomfort and pain. He must build up a self which represents the demands of society. The surrounding adults coerce and wheedle him into taking their commands for his own laws. The conscience is the introjected environment which imposes limitations upon the antisocial impulses. As the infant and child grows, he avoids conflicts with the environment by removing the locus of the conflict within himself, and plays nurse, mother, and father to himself. He learns to control his own excretions and to chasten his own murderous rages. He achieves individuality of emphasis by accepting the socialization of his major impulses.

But this incorporation of the requirements of the social order into the personality does not proceed smoothly, nor does it abolish the primitive psychological structures which have been developed and apparently discarded at each step of the way toward adulthood. Much of the energy of the personality is spent in blocking the entry of the unadjusted impulses of the self into consciousness and into overt expression. Careful scrutiny of individual behavior over a twenty-four-hour period strikingly shows the extent to which the personality is controlled by very elementary psychological structures. Moments of fatigue, moments of deprivation, moments of irresponsible reverie, all betray the presence of tendencies which are unassimilated to the world of adult reality.

Freud began to build up his conception of personality development by the gradual universalization of phenomena which he encountered in actual clinical work, and which he first described in relatively modest and restricted terms. He began his original psychological contributions by stressing the rôle of sexuality in the etiology of certain neuroses. He found that all sorts of pathological conditions and developmental abnormalities were apparently due to some shortcoming in sexual integration. This emphasis upon sexual adjustment as a necessary prerequisite of healthy adulthood met with so much opposition that Freud's energies were taken up with defending and elaborating his position. Now the sexual function is essentially a species function and stresses the biological uniformities of man at the expense of individuality. A topic like "personality development" requires a comprehensive theory of individuality, and this Freud did not develop until the split with Adler, who insisted upon the rôle of a drive toward individualization and who denied that the much neglected "ego instincts" of Freud were enough to support a comprehensive theory.

The story of Freud's neurosis-sexuality-personality theories begins with his earliest independent psychological contributions. Many clinicians before Freud had been abundantly impressed by the frequency with which sexual troubles seemed to beget "nervous" troubles. In his hypnotic work, Freud was especially struck by the frequency with which specifically sexual episodes were involved in the pathogenic experiences. Freud now proceeded to generalize about the sexual element in neurosis, and announced that neurosis was a function of deviated sexual life.

Freud armed in defense of his generalization with two new weapons. The first was his experience in letting his patients talk it out and in treating most of their productions as symbolic of something else. He acquired facility in interpreting what other people took literally as being a disguised representation of something else. So, when Freud was confronted with cases which were not manifestly sexual, he felt able to treat the non-sexual elements as symbolic representations of sexuality and to justify himself by claiming that his more intensive research procedure supplied him with the sustaining facts. Needless to say, those who had not themselves experienced the shift in standpoint which Freud had achieved were alienated by his seeming arbitrariness.

Freud's second reliance was on an inclusive theory of

sexuality. Undaunted by the ridicule heaped upon his sexual theory of the neurosis, he carried the war into enemy territory by extending the whole concept of sexuality backward from puberty through the life of the growing child to infancy.

At first glance this might appear to be a cheap, dialectical trick to confound his critics by telling them that "sex" meant all the things they had called by other names. Freud's *Three Contributions to Sexual Theory* was saved from being a rhetorical quibble by the virtuosity of his imagination and by the apparent definiteness of the connections which he traced between the various features of childhood development and the patterns of healthy and perverse adult sexuality. Careful analysis of biologically efficacious intercourse shows that it is a complex integration of many acts. It involves a partner of the opposite sex. Its essential feature is an increasing tension until the point of explosive release, followed by perfect relaxation. The male must be sadistic enough to run the risk of hurting the female by injecting the penis in the vagina. The participants must be willing to indulge in all sorts of preliminary play for the sake of heightening the critical tension, involving tongue, lips, nipples, and all the erogenous zones of the body.

Comparing the details of this completed pattern of the unambiguously sexual act with the earlier activities of the infant and child, Freud drew a host of analogies. Children indulge in play in sexual postures, exhibit their sexual parts to one another, and take pleasure in sexual peeping; but Freud carried his analysis of the sexuality of children much farther. Child specialists had often remarked that the nursing male child frequently exhibits the phenomenon of an erect penis and a desire to suckle for some time after hunger contractions cease. The general pattern of the sequence hunger-nursing-peaceful relaxation follows the characteristic curve of the sexual act. Freud suggested that inspection of the nursing pattern reveals that the pleasure derived by the child goes far beyond immediate biological necessities. This excess gratification Freud treats as a primitive outcropping of the sexual instinct, which need not be supposed to appear suddenly with the maturation of the glandular apparatus, but may be thought of as growing like the usual biological process by integrating partial components into one complex synthesis.

Sexual differentiation arises gradually, for at first distinctions of sex are not recognized by the child. The human animal is bisexual, a concept which Freud took over with some reservations from Wilhelm Fliess. Distinctions are achieved within the world of family experience. The child is attracted sexually toward the parent of the opposite sex but is too weak to compete for the loved object. Thus the father, who is too mighty to be killed and put out of the way, is copied by the son, who seeks to absorb his power into his own personality. The repression of the father-hostility, mother-love sentiments produces the Oedipus complex. The child achieves a socialized self by playing the rôle of the father in relation to his own impulses. The "latency period" arises from four to six, according to Freud, when the early sexual struggle against the father is given up. The fear of the father (the "castration complex") leads to the passing of the Oedipus phase of growth.

Now Freud specified a variety of difficulties which arise whenever there is failure to achieve successful integration of the partial components of the sexual instinct. He connected homosexuality, psychological frigidity and impotence, exhibitionism, sadism, masochism, voyeurism, and a variety of other abnormalities with definite failures in integration. Sometimes the individual becomes obsessed by ideas which have a disguised sexual meaning, and sometimes he indulges in physical symptoms which possess a similar unconscious significance. The first is an obsessional neurosis, and the second is hysteria.

The stress which Freud laid upon the sexuality of the child, and upon socialization by intimidation, broke with revolutionary violence in a culture which swaddled its infants in sentimentality. The child of the poets was like this:

> Not in entire forgetfulness,
> And not in utter nakedness,
> But trailing clouds of glory we do come
> From God, who is our home:
> Heaven lies about us in our infancy!
>
> —WILLIAM WORDSWORTH

The child of the Freudians was like this:

The child, at one time or another in its life, is, in a sense, auto-erotic, narcissistic, exhibitionistic, inclined to play the rôle of "Jack the Peeper," incestuous, patricidal, or matricidal, homosexual, fetichistic, masochistic and sadistic [G. V. Hamilton, *An Introduction to Objective Psychopathology*, p. 301].

As early as 1898 Freud had begun to elaborate the idea that sexuality begins at birth. But as late as 1900, when the *Interpretation of Dreams* appeared, he wrote in a footnote that "childhood knows nothing, as yet, of sexual desire." With the elaboration of his sexual theory, Freud became less preoccupied in defending himself against his psychiatric colleagues than in perfecting defenses against his friends. Freud began to build up a circle in 1903. Of the original group, Alfred Adler and Wilhelm Stekel were the two who were destined to achieve the most subsequent attention. By 1906 Ferenczi of Budapest and the Zürich contingent—the eminent Bleuler and his assistants—became cordial and interested. In 1908 a conference was held at Salzburg, and in 1909 G. Stanley Hall invited Freud to lecture at Clark University. In 1910 an international society was organized at Nuremberg, and the institutionalization of the psychoanalytic trend was well launched.

The first cleavage came about when Freud and Adler finally broke in 1911. In and out of season Adler stressed the "masculine protest," the drive of the human being to master every situation in which he finds himself. The individual specializes in overcoming his short stature, his enuresis, his ugliness, and his other defects; his principal drive is to differentiate himself rather than to perform his species function.

Adler represented several other currents of dissent from Freud. Freud had felt compelled to stress the antisocial drives of human nature, and Adler held a less Hobbesian view. The "social-feeling" component of human nature was accorded a place in the Adlerian system; and when the "socially useful" norms of individual adjustment were violated by the individual, "inferiority feelings" ensued. Therapy consisted in bringing this interpretation home to the maladapted person, leading him to relinquish his socially useless means of mastery and to allow his "social feelings" to express themselves more freely. Adler's therapy showed that he represented a pedagogical-ethical reaction against Freud's denial of the training function of the scientific analyst. Freud said repeatedly that the business of the analyst is to expose the patient to himself, and to leave it to the patient to work out his particular modes of adaptation to reality. Adler wants to give the patient a general scheme of thinking and to let him have some practice in indulging the "social feelings" of his nature.

Adler likewise represented a protest against the complexities of Freud's style of thought. The distinction can be drawn best, perhaps, by saying that Freud proceeded from symptoms to meanings, and from meanings to other meanings, and from other meanings to conditions. The analysis consists in uncovering lifelong chains of meaning attached to particular objects. Janet never achieved this process, and Adler short-circuited it. Adler begins with the symptom and proceeds as directly as possible to the condition. His books abound in succinct characterizations of cases, and "symbolic" material is at a minimum. Employing his orienting principle, he directs attention to a sympathetic reconstruction of the social relationships of the patient and selects those problems which the individual has tried to master by antisocial or personally crippling devices. The "common-sense" simplicity of Adler's observations commends his doctrines in circles which are repelled by the alien terminology and the elaborate interpretative machinery of Freud.

Under the perpetual hammering of Adler, Freud undertook to expand upon his sketchy theory of the ego. At first Freud was inclined to say that Adler had nothing to add because he had himself spoken of the ego instincts as well as the sexual instincts. Such a solution was hardly satisfying, and the self did not find a suitable resting-place in Freud's theoretical system until the rôle of narcissism (love of the self) was taken up and set forth at length. This "saved" the sexual theory, and it made the analysis of ego processes a problem of major interest to psychoanalysis. Stress was laid upon the fact that when the individual's libido flows outward toward objects, and when obstacles or deprivations are imposed upon this outward reaching, the libido turns back upon the self. This excessive libidinization of the self rendered subsequent adjustment to reality very difficult, and many personality deformations and formations are traceable to this developmental warp.

The break between Freud and Jung in 1913 had less immediate importance for personality theory than the previous schism. Like Adler, Jung undertook to subordinate the rôle of sexuality; but Jung accomplished his purpose, less by postulating concurrent ego-instincts than by invoking an inclusive energy concept which would embrace sexuality, ego-drives, and many other accessory manifestations. Jung, paralleling Adler again, came to the rescue of human nature, postulating a moral trend in the unconscious. And Jung, like Adler, frankly advises and trains his patients. Jung's two distinctive lines of innovation were concerned with dream interpretations and ethnological applications. Jung expanded dream interpretations for the sake of laying bare the "racial unconscious." Using saga material and dream material, Jung undertook to deflate the claims of sexuality and to demonstrate the limited applicability of the Oedipus idea.

Freud was assailed at a vital spot and rallied to defend himself in *Totem and Taboo*. He scored a point over Jung, who had relied on saga material, by drawing heavily on the ethnological summaries of Frazer in the *Golden Bough* to justify the universality of the Oedipus complex. This was Freud's first contribution to systematic social theory, and will come up for consideration in that connection. From the standpoint of personality theory, perhaps the most valuable passages are those which describe the infant's overvaluation of thought—the "omnipotence of thought," as it was phrased by a patient.

Some years later Jung, now on his own for some time, devised his classification of personality types and vastly increased popular and technical interest in the subject. This in turn has stimulated the group around Freud to develop a formal psychoanalytic characterology. In this task they were assisted by some early communications of Freud, wherein he took note of some of the character types met with in his practice. This literature will be referred to in connection with the case histories which are to be discussed immediately.

The other schisms between Freud and his pupils (involving Stekel and Rank) have been less significant for personality theory thus far, although Rank's sociological interests may germinate now that he is away from the immediate presence of the master.

Freud, who had obstinately clung to the phraseology of sex, rejecting every proposal for an overmastering set of terms which would carry less restricted connotations, executed a brilliant maneuver in 1926 and proposed to regard human activity as manifestations of two principles, the life and the death instincts. Life consists in accumulation and the release of tension; and, generalizing this phenomenon, we have the life and death drives.[1]

Suppose we put aside further exposition of the analytical personality theories, and in the light of these conceptions set up a general formula which describes the developmental history of the political man. The most general formula would employ three terms. The first component, p, stands for the private motives of the individual as they

[1] *Beyond the Pleasure Principle.*

are nurtured and organized in relation to the family constellation and the early self. We shall have occasion to see that primitive psychological structures continue to function within the personality long after the epochs of infancy and childhood have been chronologically left behind. The prominence of hate in politics suggests that we may find that the most important private motive is a repressed and powerful hatred of authority, a hatred which has come to partial expression and repression in relation to the father, at least in patrilineal society, where the male combines the function of biological progenitor and sociological father.

The second term, d, in such a formula describes the displacement of private motives from family objects to public objects. The repressed father-hatred may be turned against kings or capitalists, which are social objects playing a rôle before and within the community. Harmonious relations with the father of the family may actually depend upon the successful deflection of hatred from private to public objects.

The third symbol, r, signifies the rationalization of the displacement in terms of public interests. The merciless exploitation of the toolless proletariat by the capitalists may be the rational justification of the attitude taken up by the individual toward capitalism.

The most general formula which expresses the developmental facts about the fully developed political man reads thus:

$$p \ \} \ d \ \} \ r = P \, ,$$

where p equals private motives; d equals displacement onto a public object; r equals rationalization in terms of public interest; P equals the political man; and } equals transformed into.

The p is shared by the political man with every human being. Differentiation rises first in the displacement of affects on to public objects, and in the molding of the life in such a way as to give an opportunity for the expression of these affects. The non-political man may feel himself aggrieved against a brother and against every fellow-worker with whom he comes in contact. His mind may be taken up with personal fantasies of love or hate for specific people, and his ideological world (his attitudes toward the state, the church, the destiny of man) may be very poorly elaborated. He is a fly in the meshes of his immediate environment, and his struggles are fought in terms of the world of face-to-face reality. When such a man displaces his affects upon a person who happens to be a public object, this does not make him a political man. Impulsively killing a king who happens to insult one's sister does not make a politician of the regicide; there must be a secondary elaboration of the displacement in terms of general interest. It is the rationalization which finally transmutes the operation from the plane of private to the plane of public acts. Indeed, the private motives may be entirely lost from the consciousness of the political man, and he may succeed in achieving a high degree of objective validation for his point of view. In the "ideal" case this has gone so far that the private motives which led to the original commitment are of feeble current importance.

Upon what does the displacement and the rationalization depend? No doubt the general answer is that the selection of certain public objects depends upon the "historical" accident of the patterns offered by the personal environment of the individual at critical phases of growth. It is safe to predict that more politicians rise from families with political traditions than without them. But this very broad conclusion requires no technique of intensive investigation of individual instances to support it. If the psychopathological approach to the individual is worth the trouble, it must disclose a variety of relatively novel circumstances which dispose individuals to adopt, reject, or modify the patterns of act and phrase which are offered in the environment. Provisionally, we may assume that the puberty phase of biological growth, which coincides with increasing social demands, may be the period in which the attitudes toward the invisible environment most rapidly crystallize.

The details may be more hopefully dealt with if somewhat homogeneous groups of politicians are investigated for the purpose of bringing out significant differences in their developmental history. The agitators are the first to whom special attention will be paid.

CHAPTER VI

POLITICAL AGITATORS

The essential mark of the agitator is the high value which he places on the emotional response of the public. Whether he attacks or defends social institutions is a secondary matter. The agitator has come by his name honestly, for he is enough agitated about public policy to communicate his excitement to those about him. He idealizes the magnitude of the desirable social changes which are capable of being produced by a specific line of social action. From the standpoint of the administrative mind, we may say that an agitator is one who exaggerates the difference between one rather desirable social policy and another, much as the lover, according to Shaw, is one who grossly exaggerates the difference between one woman and another. Whether agitators behave like physicians or surgeons, as Munro would have it, they are united in expecting much good to come from single acts of innovation. The agitator easily infers that he who disagrees with him is in communion with the devil, and that opponents show bad faith or timidity. Agitators are notoriously contentious and undisciplined; many reforming ships are manned by mutineers. The agitator is willing to subordinate personal considerations to the superior claims of principle. Children may suffer while father and mother battle for the "cause." But the righteous will not cleave to their families when the field is ripe for the harvest. Ever on the alert for pernicious intrusions of private interest into public affairs, the agitator sees "unworthy" motives where others see the just claims of friendship. Believing in direct, emotional responses from the public, the agitator trusts in mass appeals and general principles. Many of his kind live to shout and write. Their consciences trouble them unless they have periodic orgies of moral fervor. Relying upon the magic of rhetoric, they conjure away obstacles with the ritualistic repetition of principles. They become frustrated and confused in the tangled mass of technical detail upon which successful administration depends. Agitators of the "pure" type, when landed in responsible posts, long to desert the official swivel for the roving freedom of the platform and the press. They glorify men of outspoken zeal, men who harry the dragons and stir the public conscience by exhortation, reiteration, and vituperation.

The first life-history to be excerpted here is that of Mr. A. This is no "institutional" case. Mr. A is aware of no mental pathology, and has never consulted a neurologist, psychiatrist, or "nerve doctor." He is one of those who at first reluctantly, then whole-heartedly, allowed himself to be studied with the same thoroughness, intimacy, and detachment with which an obviously unstable person would be scrutinized. Mr. A at once saw the advantage for the progress of science of an accumulation of life-histories taken from men who regard themselves as perfectly normal, since so much of our case material is from the ill.

A's claim to a place among the agitators is not open to question. He was compelled to resign his position when the United States went into the World War on account of the tenacity with which he argued the pacifist position. He had previously run for Congress on the socialist ticket. Suspected of unorthodoxy in the theological school, he steadily became more radical in his views, and was expelled from one denomination. Previously he had been the secretary and principal spokesman for a civic reform organization which had vigorously attacked corruption in municipal affairs. He gradually became convinced that "white collar reforms" were futile as long as the capitalistic system prevailed in this country, and presently threw his energy into the propaganda of labor organization and socialism.

A leading characteristic as moralist, socialist, and pacifist has been his truculence in public on behalf of his cause. Mr. A speaks rapidly, with great fervor and earnestness, and his discourse is studded with abusive epithets, sarcastic jibes, and cutting insinuations. He confesses that he has taken an unmistakable pleasure in "rubbing the fur the wrong way." He enjoyed nothing better than accepting invitations to lecture on social and economic subjects before conservative audiences, and scandalizing them by declaring that "organized business and organized crime are hard to distinguish from one another," "corruption and capitalism are one and inseparable," and "capitalism depends on markets, markets ultimately depend on force, and force means war." Thus war was the logical result of the capitalistic system.

Mr. A prides himself on his ability to cut holes in the logical fabric spun by conspicuous men. He has engaged prominent preachers of the gospel in correspondence, arguing that something in their writings leads logically to the conclusion that any war, not excepting the last one, is wrong, and that they should confess this openly, declaring their sorrow for having been infected with un-Christian war-hysteria.

He believes that right reason is the hope of mankind,

and the name of science is exalted in his mind. He was glad to lay his own life-story on the altar of science, and in the name of science to endure the embarrassment of recalling private facts which most of us try to forget.

Mr. A's later convictions have been held with enough intensity to redefine many of his earlier opinions. Thus his pacifism brought him into sharp opposition to the government, which resented his expression of the truth as he understood it. Mr. A warmly champions the cause of the individual against official interference in matters of taste and conscience, and has modified his early enthusiasm for prohibition.

Although censorious, accusatory, didactic, and defiant in public address, he is cordial and winning in those face-to-face situations where he is unaware of hostility. His eyes twinkle with good humor, and he is gentle, responsive, and anxious to impress. His speech and gestures are quick, and his manner is alert and often tense.

A's physique inclines toward the asthenic end of a hypothetical pyknic-asthenic scale, such as Wertheimer and Hesketh have constructed from Kretschmer's observations on physical types.[1] He is noticeably lean, but strikes the impressionistic observer as being toward neither the tall nor the short end of the scale. The legs are somewhat longer than the length of the body warrants, and the bony structures of shoulder, hip, knee, and ankle are prominent. The thin face is rather delicately molded, and is given added dignity and distinction by a neat Van Dyke beard. The chest is flat, and the upper ribs fall inward. His erect carriage seems to be a compensation against a predilection toward a scholarly stoop. In middle and later

[1] "The Significance of Physical Constitution in Mental Disease," *Medicine*, V (1926), 375–451.

middle life he has been bothered by gastro-intestinal disorders.

The second son of an impecunious village parson, he grew up in straitened circumstances with a brother somewhat his senior. The mother died when A's youngest sister was born, and the children were cared for by the father and a succession of elderly housekeepers who left faint memories behind them. A and his brother went to an old-fashioned ungraded school, entering at the same time in spite of their disparity in years, so the younger one would not be left alone in the house.

From a very early age A had a certain sense of hostility toward his brother, and a feeling of his own superiority. For a reason that is not clear, the school children teased his brother as the preacher's son, but left him alone. A was more agile than his brother, and climbed trees and wriggled into tight places with ease. He prided himself in doing things which his brother hesitated to try, and seems to have awed him somewhat, for he remembers having heard his brother tell another schoolboy to let A alone, "because when he gets mad, he can lick me."

The older boy was held responsible by the father for pranks which were really joint enterprises. On one representative occasion, the father left the house to make a call, ordering the boys to stay indoors. They decided to go out, and their father, who discovered footprints in the snow outside the door, gave the older boy a sound whipping, but let A off scot-free. The younger son was unquestionably the favorite, and his father would frequently chide the older boy for being a dullard, and point with pride to the ease with which A could get his lessons.

Indeed, A got on famously at school. One of his teachers, who chanced to be a college man, told his father that

A was brilliant and promising. A also remembers a glow
of elation when a relative wrote to say that arrangements
must be made for him to have a college education, since
he had shown that he could be a worthy successor to his
uncle. This uncle was a famous professor, who had written well-known philosophical books, and remained a great
hero in the eyes of the family.

The father slept in the same bed with his two sons
until they were well along in the teens. For as long as he
can remember, A found the touch of his father very pleas-
ant, though the touch of his brother was repugnant. A's
strong hostility against his brother, based on their rivalry
for the affections of the father, received a certain justification in the critical episode which occurred as his older
brother, who matured early, approached puberty and began to have emissions. The preacher was horrified, for
he took this as a sign of masturbation, and masturbation
was sinful and dangerous.[2] When he thought that A was
sound asleep, he would gravely lecture the older boy on
the evil consequences of self-abuse. Sometimes the son
would wake up in the morning and discover that an emission had taken place during the night. In a hushed and

[2] The popular superstition about the dangers of masturbation seems to
have become widespread in Western Europe in the eighteenth century.
Havelock Ellis dates it from the appearance of a sensational book by an
anonymous English doctor which was called *Onania: or the Heinous Sin
of Self-Pollution and All Its Frightful Consequences in Both Sexes, Considered, with Spiritual and Physical Advice, etc.* This is said to have
passed through eighty editions and to have been translated into German.
Tissot, a physician of Lausanne, contributed his *Traité* on the same subject
in Latin in 1760. This appeared in French four years later, and subsequently in nearly all European languages. His watchword was that masturbation was a crime, "an act of suicide." Voltaire popularized his viewpoint
in the *Dictionnaire philosophique*, and the tradition became firmly set. See
Havelock Ellis, *Studies in the Psychology of Sex*, I, 248–49. The cultural
relativity of this attitude toward masturbation is brought out in ethnological
reports.

contrite whisper he would say to his father, "I've gone and done it again!" at which the parent would exclaim reproachfully, "Oh!" The boy was presently taken to a physician who seems to have modified the excitement of the father and in some measure to have reassured the son that his manhood was not irreparably lost. Dark rumors about self-abuse were whispered through the village from time to time. The neighborhood idiot was supposed to have brought idiocy upon himself by self-abuse, and a bachelor in the village who went insane was supposed to have suffered from the same vice.

A listened to the rumors and to the nocturnal dialogues between his father and elder brother, and gathered that ominous things were connected with handling one's self. He felt ashamed of his brother, who brought so much suffering on his father, and silently determined never to be a disappointment to his father. The tag end of a biblical passage about bringing the gray hairs of his father to the grave in shame ran through his mind, and he resolved never to repeat his brother's weaknesses.

A's older brother surprised everybody about this time by suddenly changing from a phlegmatic lad into a fervent religious enthusiast. He became converted under dramatic circumstances and joined the church, thus propitiating the unknown powers which might visit horrible punishment upon him for his private iniquities. In this he was running true to the adolescent pattern. Adolescence is notoriously the time when the temptations of the "flesh" multiply and when many youths, oppressed by their "animal" impulses, seek to escape from the burden of guilt by adopting the ceremonial patterns provided in the religious observances of society. Adolescence is so often a period of high ideals, which are typically reaction formations to "low desires," that adolescence is the happy hunting ground for proselyters of every breed.

When A's own emissions began, he was terribly upset by worry and self-accusation. About fifteen he got an emission after a boy had fooled with his genitalia, thinking he was asleep. He was taut with sinful pleasure while the seduction was taking place, which added to his guilty feelings. This was the time when he, too, exhibited a fervent interest in the church. He quickly "overcame" masturbation, but until late in life there was always a "fight" to overcome his "wayward" impulses and his erotic imaginings. In his dreams he often saw roosters and hens performing sexual acts in the barnyard of his old home, and the reappearance of the old scenes is indicative of his early sexual curiosity. Many more of his dreams used common sexual language. Sometimes he was making his way across a valley of snakes, or he was naked and walking toward a goal he could never quite make out. The nude female figure was usually repressed, though it occasionally came through.

He was taken off the farm, on which his father eked out a supplement to his meager salary, by an aunt, who insisted that the boy must have better school facilities. This aunt had always taken a great interest in this promising motherless nephew, and tried to fill his life with the affection which would have been his had his mother lived. As a small boy he had often come on short visits to his aunt. He had slept in the same bed with her, and his lively curiosity about the female figure was partly satisfied by glimpses of his aunt at the morning bath. The aunt had a family with all of whose members he was on good terms, and he was supremely happy to live in town with them. Out on the farm he had been undernourished, but here he was filled out and flourished. He took an active part in the church and in the social activities of the neighborhood.

The early intellectual promise which A had displayed was no mere flash in the pan. He was one of the brilliant students in high school, and passed his college-entrance examinations with such distinction that he entered college with a mild intellectual halo. He resolved to make good scholastically, and this he did, finishing the four years at a first-rate institution at the top of his class.

As time passed, he began to dissent from many of the dogmas of his immediate social environment. During high-school days he had been assigned to act the devil's advocate and defend the free-trade side in a tariff debate. The more he read and thought about it, the more convinced he was that the free-trade position was sound. His relatives without exception were high-tariff Republicans, and his arguments were countered with sentimental rather than rational appeals. A's conversion to free trade led him to come out for the Democratic candidate for the presidency. He remembers that the first time he announced this heresy one of his aunts violently pushed her chair away from the table, exclaiming in vexed, incredulous, and reproachful tones, "And to think that my own sister's son could say such a thing!" His college course in biology converted him to evolution, and he argued this out at great length with one of his uncles, who was a traditionally minded preacher. A began to develop a feeling that intellectual brilliance meant dissenting from the convictions of middle-class people like his own relatives.

So far his nonconformity was strictly confined to a few theories. He was a member of the prayer-meeting group in college, and his fraternity consisted mainly of embryo doctors of theology who scrupulously upheld a rigorous code of personal abstinence from alcohol, tobacco, strong language, and women. One of the young men who had the temerity to enter the house with a lighted cigarette had it gently but firmly removed from his lips. It was in college that A took part in his first law-enforcement drive. The state prohibition law was poorly observed, as A had good reason to know, since he had a collection route which took him to "drug stores" and other equivocal establishments about town. "Tea" was openly ordered at the bar and drunk on the premises. A conceived the idea of leaving posters in these places to advertise the law-enforcement meetings, thus creating something of a stir.

Just before graduating from college A had a talk with a favorite professor. The professor asked him what he proposed to do, and was much interested when A said that he wanted to become a minister. The professor said that during his own active years in the pulpit, before he began to teach, he had learned at least one thing. Every man who was intellectually honest and independent would sooner or later discover that he questioned his own dogmas, and a period of bitter anguish would ensue. If a man were intellectually honest, he would never flinch from the truth, even for the sake of wife and family. But when the period of doubt arose he advised A not to abandon his work too abruptly. He had himself lived through six months of torture during which he had been on the verge of dropping everything and going into business. But finally he had arrived at a faith which he could defend, and stuck to it. "I would rather be drawn and quartered than preach anything I do not believe," he declared emphatically. This conversation made a deep impression upon A, leading him to anticipate doubts as a mark of intellectual keenness and honesty.

Thus far in his life he had never questioned the tenets of the strict and simple theology of his immediate surroundings. Indeed, he had never met anybody who questioned it. Only a single episode had slightly jarred his complacency and left a tiny scar behind. At one time his Sunday-school teacher had been a young professor of theology who was much more liberal than his contemporaries. A boy in the class had dared to ask something about the authority of the Bible, and the teacher, without the least trace of embarrassment, had replied that authority should not rest on blind faith but upon clear reason. "If the Bible told you to kill your father and your mother, you would not do it. You would not be bound to do it. The justification of the Bible is that its teachings prove to be sound in the experience of all reasonable men."

In the divinity school the first course which A attended was on the authority of the Bible. It was taught by a smug and full person of some eminence. A was accustomed to distinguish himself by bold opinions, and he undertook to challenge several of the propositions which were supposed to be accepted and repeated by rote. His main point was that authority rested on reason, not on faith. For his pains he got the reputation of being a smart and troublesome upstart of doubtful orthodoxy. His former Sunday-school teacher was a member of the faculty, and A wrote a thesis on the authority of the Bible, in which he elaborated the line of argument which had so much impressed him. Only the constant intercession of this professor kept A from being disciplined, or even expelled, at various times.

The young man was disposed to take rigid theology none too seriously on account of his increasing disrespect for his father. A and his brother both felt duty bound

to return home every summer to help with the farm work.
Their father was happy enough to have them rejoin him,
but matters never ran smoothly. The father was quick
to reassert his parental authority and to criticize freely.
Most of the unpleasantness was as usual at the expense of
the older son, but some of it was deflected against A. Both
sons were uncomfortably aware of the uncouthness of
their father in comparison with city preachers. He laughed
too boisterously at his own stale witticisms. His ever present dignity was a little ludicrous when he wore an alpaca
coat into the fields on the hottest midsummer day.

The social life at the divinity school was wholly satisfying. The students were warmly welcomed by the maid-
ens of the local churches, and several became engaged.
A proposed to two girls during his career there, and was
turned down as often. He very quickly recovered his good
spirits after a night or so of melancholy. The first girl
was a relative whom he had known for many years, and
the second was a close friend of the family. The double
defeat was something of a bruise to his dignity and fed his
determination to make a dent on the world.

A's first congregation was in one of the poorer quarters
of a little city. A had no doubt of his towering intellectual
superiority over his parishioners, and he found it exasperating when an uneducated housewife presumed to gossip
about the dubious orthodoxy of his beliefs. At the end of
three years he resigned in disgust at the peppering of
criticism directed against his ideas. Looking back at the
incident, he feels that he was too hasty.

It was at this first charge that A began to make good
copy for the press, and to win a reputation as a sensational-
ist. He organized a Law and Order League to harry criminals and the police. His pulpit rang with stinging philip-

pics against law-breakers and cowardly public officials. All this gave him a zestful sense of making a stir in the world of real affairs, so that he turned down an offer to join the faculty of a famous university where his old Sunday-school teacher was now located.

A's new pastorate was among working people in a large city. He at once began to hound the officials for non-enforcement of the law. He led raiding parties to visit the biggest gambling hells and put it up to the police to shut them. Renewed criticisms began to appear of his opinions, and the governing body of his denomination asked him to recant or resign. He refused to budge, and he was soon expelled. He was immediately called to lecture before an ethical society, where his comments on current religious and social problems won a wide hearing. Although attracting much attention, the society was exceedingly poor and A spent a little legacy which he had received upon it, indifferent to his own future.

During these exciting troubles he became a socialist and joined the socialist party. He had sympathized with the hard lot of the poor since he could remember, and had cast his vote for Bryan as a symbol of protest against the indifference of the privileged classes to the privileges of anyone but themselves. His favorite college professor had lost his job during the anarchist hysteria, when he came out against the "judicial murder" of the Haymarket suspects. A was profoundly moved by the spectacle of a man who backed his precepts of independence with sacrifice for their sake. The argument which finally won him for socialism was that political democracy is impossible until economic democracy is realized, and that socialism is simply democracy in industry. The principles of democratic brotherhood, once put to practice in the world of work, would soon govern public relationships of every kind.

His new convictions opened to A a new field of agitation and publicity. Ignoring or overcoming the coolness of certain "horny-handed" elements, he rushed into the little band of socialists, and was presently the congressional candidate. In this campaign he conducted a whirlwind tour of the district and enjoyed himself immensely.

A finally married a capable, motherly school-teacher whom he had known for several years, but whom he had been prevented from marrying until the death of her parents, who heartily disapproved of him. During his bachelor years in the ministry he had certain knowledge that various women were far from averse to becoming the preacher's wife or mistress. One married woman became the foremost worker in the church and passionately assured him, "I am at your service day or night." Another woman, whom he barely recognized, came to the pastor's study, declaring that they must be married at once and "end this awful agony for both of us." He had not been aware that any agony had begun, and was in no mood to begin it. He recognized that a wife would be a protection, but most of the women who threw themselves in his way were so homely that abstinence remained a pleasure as well as a principle.

For many years there had lurked in his mind the fear that he might not be potent, and he was humiliated to find that he was at first unable to consummate the sexual act. Since he first attempted sexual intercourse when nearly fifty, and had practically never masturbated, his troubles were not atypical, and they fortunately proved to be transitory. He regretted having failed to consult a physician before marriage, and was not at ease until the first of his children came.

Shortly after marrying, A came to the end of his financial resources, and found it necessary to relinquish his lecturing for other work until a suitable congregation should requisition his services. When a call finally came, the war broke out in Europe, and A denounced it with his customary ardor. He had read a book which popularized Prince Kropotkin's thesis that mutual aid and not struggle is the key to the evolutionary process. War was irrational because it contravened the principle of mutual aid, and it was un-Christian because it set the hand of man against his brethren. As the hour of America's participation drew nearer, A saw that his outspoken position would cause trouble. But he was accustomed to take a radical view and stick to it, and the idea of compromising his independence for the sake of family obligations was intolerable. His characteristic optimism also misled him into overestimating the amount of pacifism which his congregation would put up with, and soon he was forced to resign.

A was left financially high and dry, and rather hoped that his wife would be willing to starve with him, if need be, as a gesture of sanity in a war-mad world. He was left financially dependent upon his family, and upon such support as was forthcoming from wealthy radical sympathizers. Since his own professional opportunities were curtailed, and he never applied for other types of work, he was left dependent upon others. He was somewhat embarrassed by this, but was never depressed by it, or by the social ostracism which was entailed by his unpopular stand. As he once expressed it, "melancholy is alien to a fighting nature."

Looking back over A's career, certain private motives appear which were well organized in his early family life, and continued to operate with considerable strength during his adult years.

A had a strongly repressed hatred for his brother. He

was consciously aware of his own coldness toward the brother, but succeeded in barring from consciousness any recognition of the emotional charge on this attitude. The older boy was his rival for the affection of his father, and A's quickness and boldness were cultivated in an effort to outstrip his brother. He showed many of the traits of the overactive younger child, as Adler has frequently described them. A felt rather ashamed of his brother, who went through school and college with no special distinction, and whose modest subsequent career was prosaically respectable. A struggled to keep hostile thoughts about his brother out of his mind, and sought to keep his attention away from the brother by corresponding or visiting with him infrequently.

Although A never frankly faced his own animosity toward this brother, he was plagued by a sense of guilt for his unfraternal attitude. This conflict was partially resolved by a reactive formation and by displacement. The reactive formation was the reverse of the anti-brother drive, but it was only supportable by displacing his affection upon remote social objects. He generalized his own prohibition against brother-hatred to all society, and identified himself with the workers and with humanity at large, serving a poverty-stricken congregation, spending his own money on the work of the church, adopting the socialist dream of a brotherly state, and demanding the abolition of fratricidal war.

His love for the downtrodden and for humanity (this reactive displacement of his own brother-hostility) was buttressed by the usual rationalizations. The democratic ideal in politics, the ideal of effective equality in political power, had his support, and he adopted socialism when it was presented to him as industrial democracy (brotherhood), the indispensable antecedent of genuine political democracy (brotherhood). His early prohibition appeals were cast in the form of an appeal to the brotherhood sentiments. He argued that every man was his brother's keeper, and therefore bound to refrain from an example which might lead his weaker brother to dash his foot against a stone. War meant the destruction of mutual (brotherly) aid among those who were brethren in Christ. A's brother-hatred, so manifest in his younger days, and so potent in arousing guilt feelings, created this disposition to choose generalized brother-substitutes to love, and to elaborate brotherly ideologies to defend his position. Then by keeping his distance from the physical brother, he could maintain a comfortable adjustment.

Another significant private motive, whose organization dates from early family days, but whose influence was prominent in adult behavior, was A's struggle to maintain his sexual repressions. He erected his very elaborate personal prohibitions into generalized prohibitions for all society, and just as he laid down the law against brother-hatred, he condemned deviations from the rigid puritanical code by which he lived. Individuals who possess superego structures of such rigor often try to protect themselves from the strain of sexual excitement by keeping away from "temptation," or by removing "temptation" from their environment. Thus Mr. A avoided exposing himself to "lewd speech" and "immoral suggestion." Consciences of such severity can often be traced back in deeply analyzed cases to unusually strong repressions at the time when infantile masturbatory activities are being curbed. And it often happens that the rôle of the intimidator is taken not only by the male but by the female imago. In another highly moralistic person, who was thoroughly psychoan-

alyzed, this came out distinctly. Thus for several days the
subject dreamed of standing before a butcher shop where
he had been sent by his mother, and where he saw his
father sharpening long knives. Or he saw his mother,
dressed as Brünnhilde, carrying a sword, while he cowered
on a marble stairway. After many dreams of this kind,
the original situations finally burst into view. They involved what were interpreted as direct threats to cut off a
hand if the child didn't cease handling himself.

That A was never able to abolish his sexuality is sufficiently evident in his night dreams and daydreams. In
spite of his efforts to "fight" these manifestations of his
"antisocial impulses," they continued to appear. Among
the direct and important consequences which they produced was a sense of sin, not only a sense of sexual sin,
but a growing conviction of hypocrisy. His "battle"
against "evil" impulses was only partially successful, and
this produced a profound feeling of insecurity.

This self-punishing strain of insecurity might be allevi-
ated, he found, by publicly reaffirming the creed of repression, and by distracting attention to other matters. A's
rapid movements, dogmatic assertions, and diversified activities were means of escape from this gnawing sense of
incapacity to cope with his own desires and to master himself. Uncertain of his power to control himself, he was
very busy about controlling others, and engaged in endless
committee sessions, personal conferences, and public meetings for the purpose. He always managed to submerge
himself in a buzzing life of ceaseless activity; he could
never stand privacy and solitude, since it drove him to a
sense of futility; and he couldn't undertake prolonged and
laborious study, since his feeling of insecurity demanded
daily evidence of his importance in the world.

A's sexual drives continued to manifest themselves, and to challenge his resistances. He was continually alarmed by the lurking fear that he might be impotent. Although he proposed marriage to two girls when he was a theology student, it is significant that he chose girls from his immediate entourage, and effected an almost instantaneous recovery from his disappointments. This warrants the inference that he was considerably relieved to postpone the test of his potency, and this inference is strengthened by the long years during which he cheerfully acquiesced in the postponement of his marriage to the woman who finally became his wife. He lived with people who valued sexual potency, particularly in its conventional and biological demonstration in marriage and children, and his unmarried state was the object of good-natured comment. His pastoral duties required him to "make calls" on the sisters of the church, and in spite of the cheer which he was sometimes able to bring to the bedridden, there was the faint whisper of a doubt that this was really a man's job. And though preaching was a socially respectable occupation, there was something of the ridiculous in the fact that one who had experienced very little of life should pass for a privileged censor of all mankind.

He had long practice in the art of the impostor. From the plight of his older brother, A learned that he would lose the affection of his father if he was discovered to have indulged in certain practices like masturbation. He resolved never to do anything to cause his father to withdraw his affection, and when he was not entirely successful in living up to this ideal, he pretended to virtues which he did not possess. Never once was he found out, and his life was the life of a "model" boy and man. This reputation he owed in part to his abstinences, but likewise to his concealments. He learned to cultivate the mask of rectitude, and succeeded in carrying off the rôle so successfully that he was never found out during adolescence or adulthood.

Cut off by his impotence fears from loving others fully and completely, A loved himself the more. He had unbounded confidence in the brilliance of his mind, and this intellectual arrogance was nourished by the easy ascendance which he won over the poorly educated people among whom he worked. He was careful to keep in environments where his mind would not be put to the test of keen competition. A didn't compete with the clergymen who had the largest posts in his denomination, he struck out for himself in no hazardous business or professional enterprise, he took up and finished no piece of investigation; instead he cut a big figure among the workers, among whom he was the best-educated and the best-known leader. His chances of being elected to Congress when he was nominated were never good, and he had everything to gain and nothing to lose by making a campaign. After the days of his scholarly ascendance in high school and college, A fell out of competition in academic pursuits.

He valued his capacity to produce words. Ferenczi remarked in conversation with me that the revolutionary agitators who had come to his attention had been noticeably deficient in the intensity of their emotional attachment to objects. They were notably indifferent to the accumulation of property, and they were lacking in possessive jealousy in their sexual life. This deficiency in warmth of affective experience was sensed by the revolutionaries themselves, who felt that they were in some way estranged from others. Their orgiastic indulgence in language is to be interpreted as an effort to heighten the affective intensity of their own lives. Either because the emotional life is physiologically

defective or because the libido is too narcissistically fix-
ated, this general description holds true of some obsessive
and many psychotic persons. It was no doubt a factor
in the history of A.

Before following out the full implications of this struggle of A's to repress his sexuality, we will take up another
topic of major and not unrelated importance. I refer to A's
ambivalence toward his father. A was not conscious of the
full force of his hatred and his love for his father, but his
personality history is full of evidence of the formative
influence of these bipolar attitudes. In the course of his
competition with his older brother, A accepted abstinence
from genital indulgence as the price of holding paternal
preference. Now psychoanalytic findings are unanimous in
showing that genital indulgence is not given up without a
continuous struggle, and that recurring waves of sexuality
break against the barrier of the introjected prohibition, and
reanimate hostile impulses against the sanctioning authority. It is of the utmost importance for A's development that
he fought to bar from consciousness any hostile thought
directed against his father, and that he succeeded in re-
pressing his father-hatred very deeply. He was able to
identify himself with the father, and to copy many of the
paternal standards and attributes. The strength of these
identifications is indicated by the tenacity with which A
held to certain paternal patterns. Although his much-
touted uncle had been a famous writer and professor, A
remained a preacher, even when tempted by a flattering
offer to leave his first humble parish for the faculty of a
great university. He cherished the paternal prejudice
against money-making and money-makers. His boyhood
home was where some wealthy people spent their summers,
and A's father would speak contemptuously of "the fash-

ionables" who loitered ostentatiously past the house. This was an additional determiner of A's subsequent devotion to the welfare of the poor, which manifested itself in financial sacrifice and socialist agitation. A was very susceptible to old men, and idealized not only his early teachers, but a venerable pacifist who approved of his wartime conduct.

The negative side of A's attitude toward authority came out in the choice of the abstract (remote) objects upon which to vent his hatred. The hostility which was denied conscious recognition and direct indulgence against the actual father was displaced against substitute symbols, such as the dogma which required the acceptance of the Scriptures by faith, of the capitalistic system, and of the militarists.

When A was introduced to a stranger, he was genial, talkative, and anxious to impress. When he was aware of opposition in his environment, he overreacted at once, hurling a vast repertory of jibes and flouts and sneers at the offender. This gives a clue to an important element in his makeup which will come out very distinctly in subsequent cases, namely, a strong latent homosexual trend. When the individual is not able to achieve full heterosexual adjustment, the sexual libido tends to work itself out in more primitive ways, and one of the phases of emotional development is the homosexual epoch. Earlier, however, than the adolescent homosexual period is the phase connected with the suppression of auto-erotic activities. The child characteristically uses its nutritional object (nurse-mother) for the sake of stimulating his own erogenous zones as much as possible. This "incestuous" drive is curbed, and the child is denied the pleasure of promiscuously fingering others, and of manually stimulating his own genitalia.

Though the nurse or mother, who is the target of the desires of the child, also administers the prohibitions, the
sanction which lurks most prominently in the background
is the strength of the father. Reduced to its ultimate expression, this sanction is the threat of depriving the child
of his much-valued organs unless he observes the "hands
off" prohibition. The "normal" development is for the
hostile protest at authoritarian interference to subside, and
for the child to copy the idealized father. The repression
of hostilities and the identification with the father do not
take place instantly. Identification is not achieved without a phase in which the child plays a femininely passive
rôle toward the father, and this is the passively homosexual reaction which may for one reason or another be
unusually strong. A's fantasies of his father's beautiful skin
are common screen fantasies for more primitive drives.

A's tendency to overreact to the stranger who is merely
polite, and to interpret the stranger's interest as a "personal" one, is characteristic of the one in whom this passive
"winning" rôle is of some importance. He tries to create
an overpersonal relationship in those somewhat formal
situations where ordinary conversational requirements are
such as to force conventional compliments.

The overreactive hostility toward those who merely differ from him is partially motivated by the desire to punish
those who have rejected the affection which he all too quickly volunteers. This wound to his narcissism demands that
wounds shall be inflicted on the offending objects. Now it
is commonly observed that repressed drives are likely to
secure partial gratification in the very activities which are
in part a protection against them. Sneers and jibes would
at first seem to free him from those who arouse and reject
him, but this is not the whole result. A exceeded the bounds

of convention and became recklessly provocative. His wild assaults and defiances tended to provoke the social environment into attacking him, and thus to gratify two powerful unconscious drives. He wanted to be forced into a passive, feminine, victimized rôle, and to inflict upon himself the punishment which he deserved for excessive hatred of others. Thus A felt quite happy, escaping moods of depression, as long as he was indulging his hostility against conspicuous conventional authorities in society, and as long as he was suffering from society's retaliatory measures. His romantic idea of starving to death as a gesture of sanity in a war-mad world is indicative of his pleasure in the "martyr rôle."

He could not endure "inharmonious" people, and built up a "soft" and overindulgent group around him. He had a small group of admirers who turned to him for advice and who looked up to his superior wisdom and moral courage. Nothing pained him more than the slightest jar in personal relations. This disparity between his demands for gentleness in the primary group, and his genius for creating a disturbance in a secondary group, suggests the tension produced within his personality by the struggle with the feminine component. He was careful to keep away from close-working subordination to a powerful personality. He stayed in environments where his authority was unchallenged. In the church he was both a financial pillar and the pastor, and among the socialists he was sustained by the halo of moral and cultural prestige.

It is noteworthy that though A was venomous when publicly opposed, he was capable of a wooing and persuasive strain which he could effectively use in his proselyting work. His humor was of the mock-modesty variety, and relieved the moral earnestness of his discourses. A showed much tenacity and skill in following people whom he once loved and respected, and in attempting to convert them to a community of views with him. He displayed a strong impulse to enter into and to cultivate personal interchanges by correspondence.

That A found the task of asserting himself in the world rather arduous is suggested by the desire for dependence upon women. He entered into a whole series of "platonic" friendships ("platonic" in the popular and not in the correct use of the word) with women, and he accepted economic support from his wife for several years. He was very "sensitive," and required a great deal of coddling in the home.

There are indications of the way in which his very early experiences influenced his trait formation. The infant takes pleasure in activities centering about the mouth, and this at first involves pleasurable sucking and later on, as the teeth begin to push through, this involves pleasurable biting. In our culture this leads to a withdrawal of the nipple, precipitating one of the major crises of growth. Weaning is the first substantial loss which is inflicted upon the individual after birth, and the way in which it is met establishes reaction patterns which may serve as important prototypes for subsequent behavior. About the time that the weaning deprivation occurs, the child is exposed to another set of conditions which demand sacrifice. He is supposed to control the elimination of his feces by giving up a part of his body at regular intervals. The growing child is also supposed to sacrifice another source of irresponsible pleasure by blocking his impulses to handle his genitalia. When the taboo on handling the genital organs for erotic purposes is set up with particular stringency by the methods adopted to curb early masturbation, some of the energy of the personality regresses to reanimate previous auto-erotic dispositions. This involves strengthening of the anal and oral components of the personality.

On the basis of the oral and anal origin of various traits, Karl Abraham has worked out a psychoanalytic theory of character formation.[3] The material which is available on A is too scanty to reveal the psychological mechanisms of infancy and early childhood. If a cross-section of his later character traits be tentatively interpreted in the light of Abraham's scheme, it may be said to show a predominance of traits from the oral phase of development. A striking characteristic of A has always been his optimism. He has never become despondent and passed through serious "blue spells," whether he lost his job, reached the end of his financial resources, lost a bride, or suffered social ostracism from all but a small though admiring circle. Disappointments and some illness have brought him comparatively little worry. Abraham traces this trait to the earliest level of character organization, saying that it indicates a child who, thanks to the abundance of nursing care, is accustomed to find the world responding copiously and quickly to his demands. A always felt an inner assurance that he would be cared for, and that all would come out for the best in the end "to those who serve the Lord, and are called according to his purpose." He accepted a position of economic dependence upon his wife, and upon the charity of radical ladies, without conflict. His nurse was still there to provide for him. A never showed any interest in

---

[3] *Psychoanalytische Studien zur Charakterbildung* (International Psychoanalytische Bibliothek, 1925), Nr. XVI. Freud's first contribution to the subject was published in 1908. His brief article, "Charakter and Analerotik," is reprinted in the fifth volume of the *Gesammelte Schriften*. Others who have written in the same field are Sadger, Ferenczi, Jones, and E. Glover.

104   PSYCHOPATHOLOGY AND POLITICS

accumulating money, and generously shared all that he possessed. His small legacy was eaten up by the society over which he presided, and he was always on the poverty line.

He not only gave bountifully of such money as he possessed, but copiously of his ideas. Automatically he took the lead in conversation, genially pouring forth streams of ideas. The savagery of his attack on those who disagreed with him, though an oral trait in part, stems, according to Abraham, not from the sucking phase of early development, but from the next succeeding or oral-sadistic phase.

Those individuals who have difficulty in accepting their heterosexuality are cut off from normal sex life, and seek to emphasize the acts preparatory to, and not consummatory of, copulation. An interest in sexual peeping was in some measure gratified by A's experiences in listening to the personal difficulties of those who came to him for counsel. The high value which he placed on appearing before the public, while perhaps adequately accounted for on the basis of his father-identification, probably had the additional advantage of gratifying his exhibitionistic drive. Since drink is in legend and life a frequent precursor of copulation, the reformer exaggerates its importance, and tries to stop it. Alcohol was early associated with sexual excesses in the mind of A, and his hostility to it was something more than a simple reflection of his milieu.[4]

A's intensity of manner betrayed the magnitude of the neurotic conflicts within his own personality. This intensity is not alone due to the insecurity arising from the failure to exterminate his own conscious awareness of sex, nor to

[4] Joel Rinaldo paraphrases Freud in his *Psychoanalysis of the "Reformer"* and without supporting cases argues that the reformer is always a meddling hysteric. This is not to be taken for granted, for he may more often prove to be an obsessive type, when he shows mental pathology. For the best picture of the two clinical types, see Janet, *Les névroses.*

his sense of sin for erotic impulses, nor to his fears of impotence, nor to the reaction organized when he was competing with his brother for the attention of the father. His sexual inhibitions removed from him one of the most dependable means of disposing of the tensions which arise from the miscellaneous frustrations met with in the course of daily life.[5]

We have traced A's demand for widespread emotional response to his difficulties of personal adjustment, especially in the field of early sexual development. We have followed through the displacement of the drives, which were originally organized with reference to the family circle, on to remote social objects, resulting in the espousal of ideals of social change. We have seen that A's particular technique for arousing emotional response was denunciatory oratory, and that such a technique expressed important underlying drives of his personality. Since A happened to be a socialist, it is natural to compare him with the socialist thinkers studied by Werner Sombart in *Der proletarische Sozialismus*. There is no doubt that A is numbered among the "artificial" rather than the "natural" men, since his relation to reality is less direct than with the "natural" type. But it cannot be said that social criticism was as deeply motivated in his life as among the men mentioned by Sombart. He expressed himself not only in radical agitation but in conservative, moralistic agitation. His career was not wrecked at any particular point in his history, and he possessed no mania for destruction, although showing much resentment against his family, and indulging in an active fantasy life. He was fundamentally an agitator, and secondarily a social radical.

[5] See Ferenczi, *Versuch einer Genitaltheorie* (Internationale Psycho-analytische Bibliothek, 1924), Band XV, esp. Sec. V. Also Wilhelm Reich, *Die Funktion des Orgasmus*.

CHAPTER VII

POLITICAL AGITATORS—*Continued*

B is an agitator who uses his pen instead of his tongue. He has achieved eminence in newspaper work, beginning as a news editor and editorial writer. At twenty, when he held his first newspaper job, B led a fight against the red-light district of the city, exposing the pimps, panderers, and prostitutes in sensational style. He has always responded quickly to the appeal of the underdog and revealed injustices wherever he found them, and he won great popularity among minority racial and national groups whose claims he championed before the American public. It is noteworthy that B has never been converted to "isms" and responds to the call of specific abuses. No one who knows B has ever questioned his sincerity, for the news value of his campaigns is often much less than the personal risks incurred.

B has a high reputation for absolute truthfulness and reliability, often carrying his scruples to what his fellow-newspapermen think are unwarranted extremes. On one occasion, he threw up an excellent job on a very well-known newspaper on a point of honor. The paper had divulged the source of a story which he had received in confidence, and which he communicated to the editor in confidence. Later he was made the editor of an important newspaper. For five months he produced brilliant results, when a misunderstanding arose with the proprietor over another point of honor. In a despondent moment he resigned, but the proprietor refused to let him leave, offering a substantial raise. He let himself be persuaded to go back, but refused to accept the raise. Before long, new points of honor arose, and he broke away for good. His passion for justice made him a favorite with his staff; and his quiet good sense and studiousness made him a name among older men and intellectuals.

Some of his reforming campaigns were very thinly veiled displacements of his own private motives. At the age of fourteen he was seduced by a colored woman, and he reacted to this experience with fright and disgust. He left a school which he attended after a series of boyish escapades which culminated in an argument over missing laundry. The laundryman was a negro. It was on his first newspaper job that he led the fight to clean up a red-light district, featuring the fact that both colored and white prostitutes were available.

B was one of the numerous family of a Civil War veteran on the Confederate side. His father carried himself like a soldier and expected his children to act like soldiers under all circumstances. He was spare, thin, and active, and his temper was short. He was boss in the house, ordering his wife about a great deal, and demanding implicit obedience from the children.

The mother of B was eleven years younger than her husband. She had ten children in quick succession, and she spoiled them, and was much beloved. She did all the cooking, washing, and ironing for the household, and slaved to allow the children to obtain an education. Everybody but her husband thought she worked too hard. She was herself eager for learning, but had no opportunity to continue her studies after marriage. Although poor, she was proud, and never asked alms or assistance of any kind. Though "obstinate as a mule," she was timid and shrinking in ordinary relations. Her routine was only broken by occasional headaches.

The father was a very suspicious man, and B bore the brunt of it. B was the sixth child and from an early age had trouble with his next older brother, who was three years his senior. On one memorable occasion the elder brother attacked him with a knife. B was able to take the knife away from him without being hurt. The affair was reported to the father by an aunt who was living in the house, and who always sided with the older boy. She said that B had been the aggressor, and in spite of his indignant assertions of innocence, B was soundly whipped. Such episodes aroused in him a deep protest against injustice, and an abiding hostility against his father. Years afterward the truth came out, and the father apologized, but animosities had grown too formidable to be ceremoniously brushed aside. B cherished a long list of grievances against his father. Once his father asked him to print some letters; he presently found that this was for the purpose of comparing them with an inscription on the lavatory wall.

Genital activities had their usual connotation of sinfulness. His father went so far with his prudery that B, who was once discovered naked in his own room, where he was slowly dressing, was severely reprimanded. Shortly after being seduced by the negro woman, his sense of guilt, combined with his ever present resentment against his father's unjust treatment, led him to run away from home. After staying away from home and working his way through school for about a year and a half, he returned home and went to work in the neighborhood, attracted chiefly by the prospect of being back with his mother.

It is noteworthy that in his career B was constantly finding pretexts to escape from a situation in which he was

popular and successful. Salary increases, promotions, and
social recognition came to him, but he managed to extricate himself from every such situation, often on a "point
of honor." An excellent journalist, he always had a new
door open. Thus he passed from one editorial desk to another, and even to a private news-service venture which
turned out well in spite of the heavy handicaps on such
an undertaking.

How can such behavior be accounted for? Let us suppose that friendly treatment on the part of superiors tends
to activate a strong homosexual drive which has been repressed, but which continues to threaten to find expression.
This unconscious drive urges him to intimacy with persons
in the environment, whereupon his conscience, reacting
blindly against the outlaw impulse, seeks to provoke a
flight from the environment, and thus to escape from the
exciting objects of desire. The outcome is a compromise
formation in which the illicit hope of being attacked and
violated by the environment is gratified by imagining that
the environment has compromised his "honor." The conscience is gratified by the retreat from temptation. No
sooner is B in a new environment than the tension begins to
accumulate all over again. By throwing himself with zeal
into a new and strange position, where the environment is
impersonal, success comes, and with success and habituation
to the milieu, there come familiarity and friendship. This
produces the familiar strain by reactivating the unconscious homosexuality, and the defending conscience finds
another retreat imperative.

What specific justification is there for the hypothesis
just proposed? B finally came into a situation from which
he could scarcely escape by the usual tactics. He scored
one of the great successes of his career by being invited to

accompany a government commission which investigated conditions abroad, and covered the assignment in brilliant style. He was shown all manner of courtesy. Working under high pressure, he plunged into another assignment, and once more had the journalistic world at his feet. But the strain of success was too much. This time he sought release, not by flight to a new job, which was difficult, but by developing a delusional system. In short, B went into a psychotic phase, and substituted for the world of reality a fantasy world of such sinister dimensions that he was justified in trying to escape from it. Unable to concentrate on his work, he moved restlessly from one town to another, and launched forth on long automobile tours with his wife.

The actual content of his delusional productions gives a clue to his mental conflict. He had ideas of reference, imagining that people on the street were looking at him mysteriously. He claimed that he was a party to the Teapot Dome scandal and that there was a dictaphone in the house. On the way to be examined at a sanitarium he claimed that he was being trailed by policemen. Upon admission he claimed that the orderlies were policemen, that he was being electrocuted, that his bed was wired to record all his movements, and that filthy songs were sung to him (with homosexual content). Discharged from the sanitarium, he was taken to a family reunion. He claimed to be treated as a negro, and declined to eat with family or sleep in the house. B claimed that a forest fire was caused by him and that books in the library were re-written on his account. On a motor trip he claimed that insulting remarks were made to him at every gas station. He turned against his wife (he had been sexually inactive in marriage), and finally called her a snake who ought to be killed, and proceeded to try it.

During the course of his psychosis it emerged that he recalls a sexual seduction by his older brother, and that he had been bothered by this fancy all his life. There was material to show that his father was likewise implicated in his homosexual fantasies, and that he had "eroticized" the injustices of his father and the physical attacks of his brother.[1]

The history of B belongs to a borderline group between agitators and administrators. His administrative ability is manifest in the managing editorships which he held, and in the special service which he organized and for a time conducted. His rôle as an agitator (in writing) began when he was twenty, and continued for more than another score of years. When this record is taken in juxtaposition to that of A, it shows how differences in displacement affect the growth of the personality. B was never able to displace his hatred and affections to remote, impersonal objects with the degree of success which characterized A. The campaigns of B against injustice were more concrete, more limited, and more personal than the agitations of A. It will be remembered that B's first crusade was against black-and-tan houses of prostitution, and this was in the nature of a revenge and a penance for his early experience with the colored woman. B was raised in a relatively inarticulate environment. His father made no public appearances, no member of the family achieved more than a rudimentary education, and no conversation was possible beyond the visible environment. Since B went to work at sixteen, he saw the world more from a concrete point of view while A was peering at the universe through the theoretical lenses of the schools. His history shows

---

[1] See Freud's discussion of paranoia in his "Psychoanalytische Bemerkungen über einen autobiographisch beschriebenen Fall von Paranoia," *Gesammelte Schriften*, Band VIII.

prolonged preoccupation with his own specific grievances against the original objects—against the father, brother, and aunt. This was a factor which disposed him to greater susceptibility to persons in the immediate environment than A. Although driven to become a rather seclusive child who read books more often than he played, no one took a special interest in his intellectual prospects. His maternal grandfather was said to have been a brilliant teacher, but not much was made of this model when B was a boy.[2]

Unlike A, B lacked the trick of dramatizing himself before a crowd. Inspection of his early history in the home shows that he lacked the practice in imposture which may be a prerequisite of this ability. B was never able to carry off a pose to impress his family with his own virtue and promise. Indeed, he had very early evidence of his own shortcomings, and his father not only accused him of sins he did commit, but padded the record with many that he had not contemplated. B was never able to get away with much.

The foregoing excerpts from the history of B illustrate how closely the behavior of the victim of a functional disorder may connect with the fundamental drives of the personality. Functional mental disorders are efforts at adjustment that fail, and the materials employed are those which the personality has available on the basis of its developmental history.

In the paranoid case just discussed, "grandiosity"—delusions of grandeur—was not as prominent as it often is.

[2] This grandfather committed suicide at an unreported age, and his youngest son is said to be "very nervous." B's oldest sister had a nervous breakdown in high school. The third sister is "neurotic." B is described as having been a frail infant, and a shy child. Bed-wetting continued until he was twelve or fourteen, and he occasionally had attacks of indigestion. Physical examination failed to disclose any significant physical factor in his difficulties.

Grandiose delusions seem to be linked with very strong impotence fears. This connection may be shown in gross clinical caricature in the case of C. This man belongs to the well-known group of verbose cranks who often surround themselves with admiring circles of disciples, and do nobody much harm. C went so far as to run for president of the United States on a minority ticket.

C came into medical hands quite by accident. He belongs to a very common type which preserves the personality sufficiently intact from deterioration to pass for well, though eccentric. C got into a dispute with a colored expressman over the charge for moving his goods to a new apartment, and the expressman called the police, who presently turned C over to a hospital. C imagined that the negro was plotting to ruin him by stealing his most valuable books and manuscripts. He announced that he was going to be the next president of the United States of America, since the reign of the present incumbent was to be short, and damned short at that. On the next inauguration day he will take charge by divine power, and after that his red-headed wife will be given full authority. He said that during the last presidential campaign he had a conference with the governor of New York concerning the leadership of American parties. At that time the governor told him that he was a wonderful man and a logical party leader. He declared that though as a rule he does not believe in prophets, one absolutely reliable prophet had testified that he would be president. This man had a vision in which a wedge was drawn between the Democrat and Republican parties, and an unknown man arose who was to rule the world. This man would have six letters in his name. He is "Six and Six," and this exactly fits C. C's real name is "Arabulah the Divine Guest." Using this name, he wrote a nine-thousand-word treatise on politics and world-peace which he said was thought to be supernaturally brilliant.

He was sure that he got into the hospital through a damnable trick of his enemies. "It is prophesied that I am to be the next president. To defeat this, they put me here. I'm just a martyr, but I'll come out on top in the end." He would be president in fulfilment of prophecy.

C more than hinted at the scientific secrets at his command. He had recently consulted Dr. A of the government about his process for the manufacture of diamonds. More pressure was all that was needed. He declared that he is a wonderful amateur chemist, and that he has a process for manufacturing coal that he learned confidentially from a shoemaker.

When a young man he was appointed a clerk in one of the government departments, but was thrown out of a job when the Democrats were elected in the late eighties. He then became what he called a promoter of inventions and an inventor.

A clue to the source of his delusional system is furnished by his sexual history and fantasies. At the age of fifty-nine he married a widow with two children. He describes his wife as of surpassing beauty, and as for himself, he declared that he possessed three testicles, and that he is a perfect specimen of a man, a most beautiful Apollo from the neck down, and asked to pose as a model. He refused, however, to be photographed, or to disclose anything further about his sexual history.

Impotence fear as the root of the luxurious tree of grandiose delusions is sometimes directly demonstrated by the obvious nature of the invention on which the individual is engaged. The mysterious perpetual motion machine turns out to be a crude version of the sexual organs.[3]

Shortly after C left the hospital, he was busy on the stump, haranguing large audiences as a presidential candidate on a protest ticket.

C would not be taken seriously by many people of much culture and discernment, but there are paranoid types who are plausible enough in their accusations to win the support of discriminating men. Many of them are "litigious paranoids," and, as implied by the term, they are characterized by the legal and agitational means which they exploit for the redress of grievances. They succeed in rationalizing their motives so adroitly that they are very dangerous troublemakers. Even when psychiatrists diagnose them as psychotic, they are able to put up a front so successfully that they are often released from custody by judge or jury. Were the data available it would be interesting to calculate how much this active and by no means uncommon element in society costs in terms of litigation fees and damaged reputations.

One of the smoothest customers of this description is D. After leaving high school because of his ambition to earn money, he presently became a traveling salesman for an electrical company. He was very successful and soon accumulated enough to start himself in business, aided somewhat by the money of the woman whom he married. From the beginning he was involved in numerous lawsuits with big corporations. He was finally sent to the penitentiary for having assumed the name of another company which was already operating. Since the address of the new com-

[3] Examples are given in Kempf's *Psychopathology*, and in other textbooks on the subject.

pany, as well as the name, was so similar to that of the older concern, he received mail and checks intended for the corporation. His own story is that he was persecuted by a certain big corporation, which tried consistently to ruin his business, even poisoning the mind of his wife against him (who soon divorced D). Whenever a suit was being tried against him, he claims always to have found a representative of the big corporation in town. These ideas of persecution extended through the trial, which he asserts was unfairly conducted, and to the penitentiary, where he claimed that officials were in league with the corporation to keep him imprisoned. His conduct was such that he was finally transferred from the prison to a mental hospital, where his attitude was that of contemptuous superiority. He collected evidence against the hospital, listening to all who complained of any sort of cruelty and incompetence, and constantly occupied himself with schemes to release prisoners and expose his persecutors.

D has an impressive, deliberate manner. There are no marks of the maniac about him to fit into the popular idea of a "crazy man." In conversation with strangers he puts his own case, and the case of others, with seeming moderation, emphasizing the obvious difficulties in the way of collecting conclusive evidence, and showing scrupulousness about affidavits and other documentary material. IIe has succeeded in establishing connections with prominent people in many walks of life, and is devoting himself to the cause of the underdog, with special reference to those unfortunates who are thrown into insane asylums and kept there by enemies who league themselves with doctors and superintendents.

He is associated with groups of people who band together in little agitational organizations with such unexceptionable names as Vigilantes of the Constitution, Foundation for Legal and Human Rights, American Equity Association. Their indictment of modern jurisprudence is pithily formulated in the slogan, "One Law for the Rich —Another Law for the Poor." The object of one of these associations is:

To secure to all persons the rights, privileges, and immunities which are theirs under the Constitution and laws of the United States, and to which they are justly entitled as members of the human family. . . . . Those aided are: worthy cases unable to hire legal counsel; victims of corrupt practices; friendless and unfortunates restrained in Institutions, who require assistance; ex-service men who have not been able to have legitimate claims considered, etc., etc.

One of the cases which is often referred to in the papers published by this group is that of William J. O'Brien. The headline of one article reads as follows: "Poor Private Wm. J. O'Brien, Sane Veteran of the Apache Indian Campaign, Railroaded to the Madhouse. Denied Justice—Denied His Day in Court—No Trial—No Lunacy Proceedings—Illegally Held 34 Years. . . . ." In the body of the article this statement occurs: "Mr. O'Brien indulged in some disorderly conduct in the office of the War Department. He was immediately arrested, charged with assault which he did not commit, and brought into the Supreme Court." I examined the record of the O'Brien case and found that "some disorderly conduct" consisted in visiting the War Department, shooting two clerks, and trying to shoot some more before his gun jammed.

The inference should not, of course, be hastily drawn that all the claims made by agitators, even of the psychotic stamp, are pure fabrications. That is to be determined in the individual instance. Thus the slogan about "One Law

for the Rich—Another Law for the Poor" has very repu-
table support in the findings of such surveys of criminal
justice as the one at Cleveland, in which Dean Pound of
Harvard had a responsible share. But in the case of the
litigious paranoids the underlying private motivation is so
imperious that wholesale distortions of truth are inevitable.
Sometimes reckless accusations bring cruel results, as
when another psychotic, E, claimed that a certain Captain
K was shot in the back while circling over a flying field.
This fabrication got to the family of the soldier, who had
been informed that the Captain had been killed in an aero-
plane accident, and caused much unnecessary suffering.

The history of F affords some contrasts to what has gone
before. F took up agitation in middle life. It will be remembered that A directed much of his agitational zeal
against culture objects which were sanctioned by his family
and the "substantial" elements in the nation. F was the
reverse of a nonconformist. He was no pacifist, but a
soldier-patriot. The enemies of his country were his enemies, and he denounced them up and down the land. The
authority of revealed religion was not a debatable question; the enemies of Christianity were his enemies and he
went on the platform to expose them.

Several of his patriotic and religious lectures became
famous among the smaller communities of the land. He
told the story of a renegade who impersonated Christ for
the purpose of collecting funds to start an insurrection
against the American government in one of our dependen-
cies. He gave a thrilling account of how he sought out and
apprehended this monster. A Y.M.C.A. worker, in a testi-
monial letter, declared, "Every man sat spellbound as the
speaker bared the facts in the most sacrilegious undertak-

ing of modern times to thwart the plans of the American government."

F was a moving spirit in the opposition to the Covenant of the League of Nations because the name of God was not mentioned in it. His argument on the point is said to have impressed President Harding. One of F's public pronouncements on the subject read as follows:

There might be no trespass in an "Association of Nations for Conference" coming together if they did nothing but *confer*, and did no acting or legislating whatever, *if* they beforehand and by common consent did the following before the whole world:

1st, Acknowledge Almighty God before the world, with a promise to serve *Him!*

2nd, Acknowledge allegiance to God's Peace Plan—the Kingdom of the Prince of Peace—for world peace, which the Bible provides for!

3rd, Ignore all man-made plans for peace, such as World Federations, Hague Tribunals, World Leagues, World Courts and all forms of *Human* world-governments, which the Bible provides against!

4th, Refrain absolutely from everything that has the slightest tinge of world-alliance, world-control, or world-domination influence or world concert of civil action, the human instrumentalities that Holy Writ severely prohibits.

5th, Especially for the United States. Refrain absolutely from everything that contravenes our U. S. Constitution and the Declaration of Independence! (And every nation should alike protect their Constitution!)

When thru centuries of trial the world failed to keep *the Covenant* written at Sinai by the Hand of Almighty God Himself and *He* promised that *He* would give the world "A New Covenant" for peace, which *He* did, then how can the world, except anything whatsoever from *The League of Nation's Covenant* written at Paris by the mortal hands of just mere men like Wilson, Lloyd George, Clemenceau & Co.?

After serving in the army as a young man, F joined the secret service, and spent several years in pursuit of the enemies of law and order. His record was excellent, and when the World War came he was put in charge of secret military police. He became overzealous in the perform-ance of his duties, spending an altogether disproportionate amount of time investigating two Mennonite ministers who were alleged to have letters in their possession written in German criticizing the Liberty Loan. He claimed to have found ground glass in the bread served to men in camp. When the laboratory did not confirm his findings, he said that he mixed ground glass with flour and submitted a sample to the laboratory, which reported no ground glass, thus confirming his suspicions that the laboratory staff was composed of aliens—a German, an Austrian, and a Turk. He began to make direct accusations that some of the camp officers were in league with the enemy. One of them he accused of using a German private in his office for translation work, and intrusting him with a key to the iron safe where the United States secret codes were kept. Pres-ently F was referred to a psychiatrist for examination, to whom he complained that he was the victim of a persecu-tion by a little clique of officers. He managed to publish an interview in the press asserting that ground glass in the food had made fifty men ill at a certain training camp, and this led to much unnecessary anxiety among the folks at home.

F's anxiety to "do his bit" in the suspicion-ladened at-mosphere which surrounded America's entry into the war led his suspicious nature to overdo the matter. When some of his efforts were blocked by fellow officers, he began to develop persecutory ideas. But he was soon able to dis-pense with them by reinforcing his identification with the interests of the nation and God, and displacing his sus-picions upon more generalized foes. When his secret-service work was blocked, he was able to make a transition to agitation, where he balanced the lost gratification of cherishing secret knowledge with the pleasure of exhibiting it in public. The record does not contain enough early childhood material to justify one in venturing to select the determiner of his capacity to make such an adjustment. The history simply furnishes a striking example of how a flight into agitation may perform the function of keeping the personality in some sort of passable relation to reality, when it has met a serious setback. It gives another instance to the sum of those which show the difficulties which may be created in society by those whose personality is influenced by strong paranoidal trends.

The histories so far abstracted have had to do with male agitators of various kinds. Miss G, when thirty-five years of age, came to the physician complaining that she was constantly bothered by blushing, stage fright, uncertainty, palpitations of the heart, and weeping spells. She is known to be forceful, ambitious, and aggressive. Her contentiousness is notorious. She is active in the support of all kinds of measures, particularly for the emancipation of women from the domination of men. She rose to her present distinction from a very humble position as a handworker, and she champions the radical cause.

An early reminiscence was recovered during analysis which had been completely buried before. Sometime between the ages of five and three she had been asked by a nurse to touch her nurse's genitals, and threatened with dire things if she told. When she was in bed with her mother, she had to fight against a powerful compulsion to touch her mother's genitalia. This early assumption of the male rôle was strengthened by her father-identification. In the analysis she reported that she and her father possessed many common traits, such as stubbornness. As sometimes happens with children showing traits of the opposite sex, their brothers or sisters reveal cross-traits. Thus her younger brother cooked and sewed. Her father took her side in family altercations with the mother (the father was an artist). The mother was religious, and on the death of her mother the patient was religious for six months from a sense of possible guilt for having precipitated her death. Everybody said that she ought to have been a boy since she showed so much physical dash and hardihood. Between six and ten she often stole money from her parents, and was caught reading other people's letters.

As a child she suffered seriously from vague worries. At the age of seventeen she was unable to read her own compositions before the class. She talked rather badly in groups and before strangers, but was very effective in face-to-face conversations. In public she spoke best when attacked. She had a constant fear of being subordinated to a man, and was constantly on the alert to assert herself. She had a horror of marriage, which she thought of as gross subordination to the crude physical desires of men. One budding love affair broke up when the man went insane and died.

For a long time she longed to have a child, but only one child. She wished that there were some other means of impregnation than by using a man, but finally decided to bend to the inevitable. Several years before analysis she looked around to select a man to be the father of her child. It was a year after she became acquainted with the man before she could bring herself to coitus, and she felt befouled. After the birth of the child she became utterly indifferent to the man, and broke off their relationship. She was, of course, sexually frigid.

What is the meaning of this demand for a child, and for
but a single child? It was essentially a subconscious demand for the penis to finish her assumption of the male
rôle. The psychoanalytical study of the growth of the female personality stresses the importance which this motive assumes.[4] Gregory Zilboorg has analyzed certain post-
pregnancy psychoses from this point of view, and in so
doing has thoroughly surveyed the theoretical field.[5]

Castration dreams appeared in the guise of losing muffs
and keys. Homosexual dreams took the usual shape of a
nude homosexual figure. Horrified by dreams of sexual
intercourse with her father, she began the analytical process. Her narcissism expressed itself in both simple and
disguised form. She dreamed of being the mayor and of
humiliating men in all manner of ways. She dreamed of
influencing the whole world (telepathic dreams). Incidentally, she credits dreams with some prophetic significance. Once she dreamed of a clay field over which she
was passing which changed to plowed land, signifying
work, and, sure enough, she found a job the next day.
Another time she was crossing a brook and saw an ugly
body in the stream, and developed laryngitis the next day.

The narcissistic component was strong. She felt the
universal rule of the analytical situation to say everything
that crosses the mind to be a personal command from the
doctor. She bitterly resented this subordination to a man,
and finally broke off the analysis. She showed a record of
having been quite rebellious against those in authority
over her—shop foremen and party leaders.

Miss G had an enormous masculine complex. She chose

[4] See Helene Deutsch, *Psychoanalyse der weiblichen Sexualfunction.*

[5] See "The Dynamics of Schizophrenic Reactions Related to Pregnancy
and Childbirth," *American Journal of Psychiatry,* VIII (1929), 733–66.

masculine goals, and ruled out the female rôle as far as she could. Her narcissism brought her from obscurity to distinction, though at the cost of several neurotic difficulties in which her repressed drives found crippling expression. She swings between vanity and inferiority feelings. She blushes when praised, she blushes in public because of the dependence of her sex on men, and she is timid in the presence of academic people. She always feels ill at ease with strangers, and lives in isolation from society.

In theory and in practice Miss G is for free love, and for the complete equality of the sexes. She sought out politics as a career as a means of expressing the male rôle of dominance, a drive which was powerfully organized in her early childhood experiences.[6]

What has been said about the agitator may be brought together at this point in a provisional summary. Our general theory of the political man stressed three terms, the private motives, their displacement on to public objects, and their rationalization in terms of public interests. The agitator values mass-responses. Broadly speaking, this requires an extension of the theory to make it possible to divide politicians among themselves according to the means which they value in expressing the drives of their personalities. Now what is there about the agitator's developmental history which predisposes him to work out his affects toward social objects by seeking to arouse the public directly? Why, to state it another way, is he the slave of the sentiments of the community at large? Why is he not able to work quietly without regard to the shifts of mood which distinguish the fickle masses? Why is he not able to cultivate interests in the manipulation of objective materi-

---

[6] The physician in charge of this case comments that there may be a homosexual *anlage* on the physical level, but that this is not certain.

als, in the achievement of aesthetic patterns, or in the technical development of abstractions? Why is he not principally concerned with the emotional responses of a single person, or a few persons in his intimate circle? Why is he not willing to wait for belated recognition by the many or by the specialized and competent few?

Agitators as a class are strongly narcissistic types. Narcissism is encouraged by obstacles in the early love relationships, or by overindulgence and admiration in the family circle. Libido which is blocked in moving outward toward objects settles back upon the self. Sexual objects like the self are preferred, and a strong homosexual component is thus characteristic. Among the agitators this yearning for emotional response of the homosexual kind is displaced upon generalized objects, and high value is placed on arousing emotional responses from the community at large. The tremendous urge for expression in written or spoken language is a roundabout method of gratifying these underlying emotional drives. Agitators show many traits which are characteristic of primitive narcissism in the exaggerated value which they put on the efficacy of formulas and gestures in producing results in the world of objective reality. The family history shows much repression of the direct manifestation of hatred. There is often a record of a "model boy" during the early years, or of a shy and sensitive child who swallowed his resentments. Repressed sadism is partly vented upon objects remote from the immediately given environment, and favors the cultivation of general social interests. The youth has usually learned to control by suppression and by repression the full amplitude of his affects, and this is a discipline in deceit. The narcissistic reactions prevent the developing individual from entering into full and warm emotional relationships during his puberty period, and sexual adjustments show varying degrees of frigidity or impotence, and other forms of maladjustment.[7] Speaking in terms of early growth phases, the agitators as a group show marked predominance of oral traits.

Distinctions within the agitating class itself may be drawn along several lines. The oratorical agitator, in contradistinction to the publicist, seems to show a long history of successful impostorship in dealing with his environment. Mr. A, it will be recalled, was able to pass for a model, and became skilled in the arts of putting up a virtuous front. Agitators differ appreciably in the specificity or the generality of the social objects upon which they succeed in displacing their affects. Those who have been consciously attached to their parents, and who have been successful impostors, are disposed to choose remote and general objects. Those who have been conscious of suppressing serious grievances against the early intimate circle, and who have been unable to carry off the impostor's rôle, are inclined to pick more immediate and personal substitutes. The rational structure tends toward theoretical completeness in the former case. Displacement choices depend on the models available when the early identifications are made. When the homosexual attitude is particularly important, the assaultive, provocative relation to the environment is likely to display itself; when the impotence fear is active, grandiose reaction patterns appear more prominently.

[7] Harry Stack Sullivan has stressed the critical importance for personality growth of the adolescent phase in which the individual is impelled to enter into intimate emotional relations with one or two other persons of his own age. Those who partially fail in this show various warps in their subsequent development.

CHAPTER VIII
POLITICAL ADMINISTRATORS

Some administrators are full of ideas and others are seldom attracted by novelty. Some do their best work under a rather indulgent chief; others fall to pieces unless there is strong pressure from above. There are administrators who derive their influence over subordinates from the authority of their positions rather than from the authority of their personalities. There are some who may be depended upon for the conscientious performance of detailed tasks, while others neglect details and think in terms of general policy.

Viewed developmentally, it appears that one group of administrators is remarkably akin to the agitators, differing only in the fact that they are bound to particular individuals more closely, and thus displace their affects upon less generalized objects. This gives a certain independence to the administrator from the compulsion to "get a rise out of" large numbers of the population. It ties him more securely, however, to the members of his own environment, whose relations he seeks to co-ordinate. The administrator is a co-ordinator of effort in continuing activity.

The group which is allied to the agitators includes those who show imagination and promoting drive. The history of H belongs in this class, and has the incidental interest of showing how H behaved in war time.

While it is accurate to say that H is diplomatic and seemingly open and frank in dealing with his superiors, it should be added that in situations which involve the fate of his own projects, he is noticeably overtense, and likely to evaluate himself much higher than others. He becomes slightly accusatory if his demands are rejected. The elderly executive with whom H did his best work sometimes complained that a conference with H was as fatiguing as a whole day's work. The older man felt that H might be entirely broken up if his projects were rudely rejected, and he also believed the young man to be too valuable to damage. H recognizes that he has often found himself shirking when his superiors let him alone, and wonders why this attitude, which is contrary to his own interests, should take hold of him. H displays a tendency to behave arrogantly toward subordinates, and when he was in the army it was obvious that he could maintain discipline only through the formal authority vested in him.

H is an only child. His father was a big, overpowering person, who was a strict disciplinarian. The parents were very prudish in sexual matters, and one of his embarrassing memories is the confusion and vexation of his mother when he asked her about babies. Left to his own resources, and stimulated by a variety of incidents to explore sexual problems on his own initiative, the boy became involved in a set of episodes and reveries which he tried to keep from the family, and thus met every family situation with some anxiety lest his sins should find him out. H grew into a hyperactive and seemingly light-hearted youngster, who obeyed his parents implicitly and met strangers with ingratiating charm. H was constantly occupied with the task of adopting a manner toward authority which would conceal his secret preoccupations.

About the age of four, H surprised his parents in a sexual embrace, and vividly recalled his own mixture of burning curiosity and embarrassment. Some of his early dream fragments indicate that he repressed a powerful hostility toward his father, who he thought was hurting his mother, and likewise repressed hatred of his mother, who he felt was disloyal to him.

His experiences continued through a long chain of incidents. There was mutual exposure of sexual parts between him and a playmate of his own age. A deeply repressed episode was a seduction in which he played the principal part. He was meanwhile completely successful in playing the rôle of model boy.

When H was ten years of age, however, there transpired an incident which for a time branded him in the neighborhood as a nasty little renegade, and which had many subsequent repercussions. He touched the exposed sexual parts of a neighbor girl, who was somewhat his junior. The sister and brother of the girl were interested spectators. The children told the cooks, and the news finally got around to the mother of the girl. She took it calmly enough, but thought she ought to tell the boy's mother. H's mother passed the story to his father, which was the worst thing that could happen, from H's point of view. His father administered a sharp dressing-down, and forbade him to play outside the yard for a fortnight. H's father was very angry, and lectured him about his sins every night for a while. Presently the father went over to see the neighbor, and seems to have taken the line that the girl was as much to blame as his son if not more so. This tactless behavior completely alienated the neighbor.

Now this neighbor happened to edit an important newspaper, and ever afterward this newspaper lost no opportunity to assail the efficiency of the department in the city government headed by H's father. These attacks continued over many years, and H's father occasionally threw it up to him that he had been responsible for the original quarrel.

As it was, the boy was ostracized in the neighborhood for a year or more, and was not invited to go to parties, although he could play with the children. But H was self-conscious, and sought companionship farther away. The brother of the girl thought that he ought to turn against H, and there were some fights.

At fourteen H began to go to high school. He kept away from the swimming pool during the first year or two because he was much embarrassed by the lack of hair around his genitals. This supposed retardation, about which he worried a great deal, lasted but a short time, when a new set of worries came up. He now believed that his penis was abnormally large, and that his testicles were too low-hanging and perhaps deformed. In college he was nicknamed "Cocky," on account of his jauntiness, but he secretly suspected that this was an allusion to his penis.

A chum taught him how to masturbate, and he continued to do so for about six months, when his emissions became so frequent that his mother told his father. For once, H's father handled the situation with good sense, and after a kindly interview in which the father explained that it was not a good idea to indulge excessively, H quit. But even this matter was not terminated, for the disturbing reverie remained that perhaps his excessive masturbation had permanently impaired his manhood.

H had a lively curiosity about his mother's body of which he was intensely ashamed. He recalls loitering in his mother's room while she made ready to change her clothes, hoping that she would forget to send him out. He found himself speculating about the shape of her body, and was several times on the verge of spying through the keyhole. But his impulse was inhibited when he remembered the story told by his father in which a "peeper" was spoken of with the greatest contempt. H dreamed of sexual intercourse with his mother on several occasions, nearly always during periods of unusual strain. These dreams were deeply buried and came out into the clear with great difficulty.

His sexual curiosity extended to animals, and he stimulated the sexual parts of his dog. This further associated sex with the bestial and unclean, and convinced him of his own guilt for so much as wondering about it.

H's first sexual intercourse cost him much worry. It occurred during his second year in high school. He had been sent with the family automobile to drive home a guest, and noticed a girl of about his own age who was gay and flirtatious. On the way home he picked up the girl with two boys whom he knew slightly. All of them had sexual intercourse with the girl. He was terribly worried that he might reach home too late. His strict father had laid down the rule that if he got home at any hour of the night, he was to wake up the family and give an account of himself. In his haste he neglected to inspect the car and his father found some hairpins in the tonneau. H denied that he knew anything about them. The incident, however, was not closed. He saw an item in the newspaper about several men who were arrested for rape, and wondered whether he had committed a horrible crime himself with his companions. Before long the girl became pregnant and was brought before the juvenile court. She named another gang of boys, and this gang accused H and his two companions of being to blame. He was horrified at the prospect of going into court and dragging his family to disgrace. H was afraid that his partners in wrongdoing would confess, but he denied everything to his father, and his father's political influence kept him from being haled into court. But for at least a year the black cloud of possible exposure hung on the horizon of his mind.

All during his high-school days he had occasional sex intercourse, but every episode was marred by some disagreeable features. While there were such experiences with girls of low social standing, he had many friendships with girls of good social position whom he idealized as above sexuality. He attended a private school which was patronized almost exclusively by children from very wealthy families, and H, who was handsome, well dressed, quick, and agreeable, found his friends among them. He was often in their homes and admired the signs of wealth and culture. He became sensitive of the cultural limitations of his own parents, and was afraid to entertain his school friends at home, but fortunately from his point of view his father was willing to furnish enough money to make it possible to hold up his end of the social bargain at exclusive clubs and restaurants.

In college H continued to draw a sharp line between those who could be petted, but who were too rich and refined to be approached for intercourse, and those who could be petted, and who were poor enough to be asked for intercourse. He continued to associate with a smart and wealthy set, and finally concentrated his attention on the daughter of a rich business man whom he wanted to marry. His left-handed affairs continued at irregular intervals, and he felt remorseful when he had the perversions performed on him.

Enough has been reported to convey an impression of H's inner state. His unsatisfied sexual curiosity had been whetted by his prudish parents. His father defended his own ascendancy in the home by ordering the boy about a great deal, and H responded to authority by a system of reactions which became characteristic of him. He was tactful, deferential, and acquiescent, qualified by inner resentment and rare gestures of defiance. The father was not a friend but a barrier to be circumvented, and the father's hegemony was protected by the sense of guilty inferiority which he had created in his son. Family differences, such as arose when the father objected to house-keeping details, or when the boy wanted more freedom to use the car, always showed the same balance of forces —mother and son versus the father. The mother did not defend herself by robust contradiction but by weak complaints. There were only two instances in which the boy flared up enough to resist his father openly.

If H had been more successful in winning applause outside the family, it is quite possible that his position would have been made much easier inside it. His social charm brought him into the most influential circles, and this gratified his parents, but his father was a man of action who felt that while wealthy friends were an asset, his son ought to show more positive achievements. Though he never nagged H, the father's sternness, suspiciousness and absence of praise made a deep impression on the boy, and gave him a sense of insecurity and inadequacy. Although H scored no great successes, he went along without academic catastrophe until college. He was suspended at the end of his Freshman year for poor work, but came back after six months, during which he pretended to his father that he was still in school. The suspension was partly due to the advice given to the dean by his fraternity brothers, who had found him very hard to manage, and wanted to "bring him to his senses." H was having a fling, since he was away from home for the first time, and away from the intimidating father. Presently he steadied down enough to get along.

Reminiscences of his guilty sexual experiments, deeply charged with guilt-feeling, were continually bobbing up to interfere with his progress. Once he was assigned to debate in high-school public-speaking class. His opponent proved to be the brother of the girl with whom he had the notorious incident several years before. The brother was a prominent school leader who had no doubt forgotten the affair, but it continued to weigh on H. He always had felt uncomfortable in the other boy's presence, and on this occasion, being poorly prepared, the situation became so unbearable that he fainted.

He began to study agriculture at college, but soon found that he had made a mistake. His family owned a ranch which he often visited during vacations, and very much enjoyed. Farming was an avocation of his father, and H had the idea that ranching was a genteel occupation without much work, and with much ordering of other people about. He vaguely thought of himself as a country gentleman of cultivated leisure. The war saved H from agriculture. He took up aviation, without losing "credits," partly because the snobbish mother of his favorite girl was bowled over by the uniform, and partly because he thought it would be better to go into the war, if he had to go, as an officer than as a private. His father's influence secured a deferred classification for him in the draft, and H, though feeling quite small about it, said to himself that it was better for people to die who were without his own advantages and achievements.

His career as an officer in the camp brought out the traits to which reference has previously been made. His engaging deference toward his superiors won them all, but he had trouble with the men. His own insecurity led to an arrogant pose on his part that offended every man in the company. He also discovered that the moment discipline was relaxed he became very careless in performing his own duties.

The same constellation of traits reappeared in his administrative career, modified by the fact that he learned to assume a less provocative attitude toward his subordinates. He made a very good record, and proposed a number of changes that were adopted for the improvement of the service.

Looking back over H's history, the striking thing is his prolonged worry about his adjustment to specific persons. H was never able to make the hurdle into abstract interests. Even his administrative ideas were closely tied to the immediate context of the service. H's life was very much dominated by his relationship to definite people, and this meant a prolonged carry-over of early attitudes to these individuals. Unlike B, who could rightly feel that his father and brother and aunt were treating him unjustly, H was all too aware that he "deserved" more than he got. His success as an impostor was rudely interrupted in some early episodes.

Another "marginal" history shows what happens to some men with agitating aspirations who are not able to disentangle themselves from a place inside an organization and to give themselves up wholly to agitational work. Mr. I is a type occasionally met with inside administrative staffs who makes a serious problem for himself and others. He radiates plans that he neglects to execute, and he is supercilious and defiant toward superiors. He lacks the drive, however, to move over into agitational work entirely by identifying himself with a sufficiently dramatic cause. Sometimes this is due, as in I's own case, to powerful early identifications with particular projects, and with administrative work as such. When such a person can be pried loose from certain of these early fixations, he often proves capable of fulfilling the expectations which he is able to arouse.

The father of I was a man whose extraordinary talents won him great distinction, but who never quite managed to come through as brilliantly as people had a right to expect from one so richly endowed. I's father could talk five or six languages and read many more. He was educated in England, France, and Italy, and after serving as a professor of modern languages, his interest in educational problems led him to become the head of a famous preparatory school, and later of a public school. He spent most of his time reading, and during the last decade of his life drank heavily, but without impairing the quality of his work. Someone who knew him pronounced the man "a self-centered intellectual who died without a friend." The mother of I was an adopted daughter of a member of the British aristocracy, and was brought up in distinguished social and intellectual circles. The mother was exceptionally active in all sorts of humanitarian enterprises but lavished much time and love on the boy, who was "dreadfully spoiled," and accepted everybody's judgment that he was a budding genius.

True to anticipations, the boy shot through school like a meteor, ranking first in his subjects, and taking every available honor with ease. In college he branched out into social and political life on a large scale, and joined about twenty organizations, managing to have himself put on every important committee.

Like his father, the son took up public-school work. Becoming interested in psychology, he did some graduate work, and quickly published a book that received very favorable comment among those best qualified to judge it. The idea of educational reform fired his imagination, and he lectured far and wide, engaging in agitations to secure legislation which would authorize a number of experimental schools.

The part of his history which is especially interesting to the student of administration is this: He was continually at outs with his superiors and colleagues. His first teaching position began with a feud, and lasted but a little while. He was invited to resign his next post. He was asked to resign the next position. He was asked to resign the next position. These entries appear monotonously through his record.

Everybody conceded the brilliance and fertility of his mind, and did homage to the originality of his plans. He began work but failed to carry it far, seeming to think that work planned was work done. His methods were always aggressive. Seized of an administrative idea, he went to his superiors. When they criticized the scheme, or rejected his suggestion, he often took the bit in his teeth and tried to run the ship in his own way.

More than once financial irregularities have been discovered in connection with his work. He has given out checks when no funds were available, and run unduly large expense accounts. Whenever he has been in financial jams, he has turned to other people for aid as a matter of course, seeming to feel that he has a claim on the world for support.

He has always been childishly dependent on his wife for praise. He resented his wife's motherhood, but has been overindulgent with the two children, who, his wife says, have no respect for him. He likes to be the center of attention, and is a clever showman, and a great deal of a bluffer. He is usually not high tempered but affectionate. He is inclined to be accusatory toward his wife—"a vixen" —but his wife appears to be a keen person, who was enough impressed by his precocious brilliance to marry and to pamper him, but who in later years has delivered herself of pointed comments on his character.

It seems that he has gone through several periods of alternating exhilaration and despondency. The exhilarations came when he had a position and when life became a little monotonous or a little hard. At least one of these swings was sufficiently pronounced to lead to a period of retirement in a sanitarium. During this time he was asked what kind of work he liked best, and replied, "Reforming the world—my first choice; second, exploiting the world."

The strength of his narcissism is self-evident, and the feminine marks in his character are numerous. He expects to be nurtured and supported by the world as a matter of right. He demands constant "mothering" from his wife, and coddles the children. His father-hatred, which was thoroughly repressed in the family, comes out in his difficulty with father-surrogates, and in his determination to change the educational system at points where the father took it for granted or overtly defended it. The selection of the pedagogical rôle is itself indicative of the strength of his father-identification. What seems to have happened in his development is a fixation of interests in a relatively narrow sphere in which the affects are so powerful and at the same time so contradictory that difficulties are assured. He finds it impossible to shake off his managerial aspirations sufficiently to devote all his time to the propagation of ideas. Although his affects are displaced upon abstract problems, they are not displaced upon objects sufficiently removed from his father, and the displacement does not succeed in making it possible for him to achieve an impersonal attitude toward his superiors and colleagues in educational administration. The exaggerated praise heaped upon him as a boy had much to do with the narcissism. His incapacity to follow through is no doubt related to his early conflicts over genital activity. The chief point of significant contrast with A is that the narcissistic component interfered more seriously with H's development, since it led him to insist upon playing an administrative rôle. A's environment was less prostrate before him, and he was able to avoid assuming administrative obligations where he would be cramped and subordinated.

The history of J, which has been reported by Alexander,[1] shows what lies behind a powerful administrator's thirst for responsibility, and reveals how changes in the working relations inside an organization may disorganize the individual.

J was a driving executive whose superiors deferred to his judgment and accepted his plans. His abounding energy sought an outlet through the assumption of heavier and heavier responsibilities inside the organization. Finally, a change in the chief executive brought J under the immediate control of a man who handled him with cool assurance, holding him firmly but considerately to his own formal sphere of action. Confronted for the first time in his life by a more powerful personality who knew how to regulate him, J took the wife of another man for his mistress, and in spite of the remonstrances of those

[1] "Der neurotische Charakter," *Internationale Zeitschrift für Psychoanalyse*, XIV (1928), 26–44.

who knew him, he held tenaciously to both the mistress and the wife.

An analysis showed that J was characterized from early childhood by a notable split in his personality. Side by side with his aggressive, masculine drive there existed a strongly repressed, though powerful, feminine tendency. His personality is to be rendered intelligible only as a compromise formation between those two incompatible motives. The repression of the passive component produced a regressive fixation upon the wife, who was compelled to play a markedly maternal rôle, and to humor his every whim. He resented it if his every wish was not defined and fulfilled before he had to go to the trouble of putting it into words. J has delicate aesthetic sensibilities, and is a cultivated amateur in the arts.

In sharpest imaginable contrast to his behavior at home was his insatiable thirst for authority and responsibility in his professional life. One of his dreams acutely symbolized him as a giant automobile of untold horse-power, whose body was a light French coach of the rococo period.

As Alexander comments, J's life-problem was to indulge his passive demands without doing violence to his masculine ideal. But this was not accomplished without strain. He could earn periods of indulgence in aesthetics by exaggerated aggressiveness in his work, but as his feminine tendencies were gratified, his masculine ideal was endangered, and he would be driven back to high-pressure management. The psychological significance of his work was symbolized in the following dream: He was penetrating a thick sheet of cardboard with a needle, and continually asking for new sheets to bore through. He succeeded in going through several thicknesses. The cardboard represented his occupational problems, and the needle his penis.

His professional activity was largely a sublimation of his aggressive, active sexuality.

The equilibrium between his aggressiveness in work and his passivity in marital life was upset by the new chief executive, who skilfully hemmed in his activity. Alexander remarks that it is impossible for a man who has struggled all his life against very strong unconscious homosexuality to serve under a strong man. The dominating personality arouses the latent attitude, and the subordinate must resort to special means of maintaining his repression. In the case of B, which we have previously considered, the means of restoring some sort of equilibrium was escape (by resigning), but when that became very difficult, he fled into a world of fantasy (a psychosis). J met the crisis by breaking through the sublimation of his heterosexuality, and taking a mistress as an outlet for his thwarted drives. Further than that, he vindicated his masculinity in a very dramatic way. He not only took a mistress, but he took the wife of another.

From now on, he was dependent on both women to preserve the equilibrium of his personality. Previously the equilibrium had been maintained between wife and work; now it depended on wife, mistress, and work, for the aggressive, masculine component required the mistress to make up for the limitations imposed upon his working sphere.

Alexander reports that in the course of a long analysis this remarkable split in the personality was traced back to early childhood. "At the age of four he was already the same person." At the age of four he continued to drink milk out of a bottle, stubbornly resisting every effort to break him of the practice. But—and it was with an emphatic "but" that J produced the reminiscence—at the same time the boy was especially adventurous and independent, riding all by himself out on the highway. Here was the same antithesis that later expressed itself in his peculiar relation to wife and work. The child won the right to indulge his infantile, oral tendencies in one particular by exaggerated boldness in other respects. This solution was the prototype for his later life.

The rôle of the bottle was later taken by his wife, whom he often treated like an inanimate object whose only function was to minister to his needs, while his work, and later his mistress, were the successors to the bicycle, by means of which he was able to prove his independence and his masculinity to himself and the world.

The castration fear, which was aroused by the means adopted to break up his infantile masturbation, favored the oral fixation, and came into conflict with his strong masculine genital drive, laying the basis for this notable character split.

The records so far discussed have had to do with inventive or driving administrators. A type often met with in the public service is the conscientious, overscrupulous official, whose touchiness, fondness for detail, delight in routine, and passion for accuracy at once preserve the integrity of the service and alienate the affections of anybody who has to do business with the government. K was such a man. For some years he was in the forestry service, where part of his duties was to mark the trees that might be cut by private lumbermen. The lumbermen naturally argued that the straight, sound trees should be cut and the damaged ones left for seed. K took a variety of other factors into account, and spent days measuring and estimating position, growth rates, and shade area, exasperating the lumbermen with his everlasting and often superfluous scrupulousness. He keenly felt his responsibilities as a public servant, and disliked the very appearance of succumbing to private pressure. At one time K resigned the service in disgust because of "uncivil" treatment by a superior, but his "touchiness" was much more deeply rooted in his nature than he had any idea.

The record of K is not only the story of a pedantic official but of an ardent patriot. One of the highest forms of patriotism is supposed to be volunteering for posts of conspicuous danger in war. K pulled all the wires within reach to get a place on the front line, and only the point-blank refusal of his superiors to allow him to squander his technical ability prevented him from achieving his desire. From a close examination of his intimate history we learn how one variety of superpatriot comes to be.

K was the youngest of four children. His next brother was eight years his senior, his sister was five years older than this brother, and his oldest brother was eighteen years ahead of him.

He never remembered a time when his mother and father, who were divorced when he was eight, were on good terms with each other. They seldom spoke, except to quarrel. This family background was reflected in the mental life of the growing child. K was notoriously nervous and timid. From a very early day he began to be preoccupied with why he was different from everybody else in the world. His sense of isolation and strangeness led him to believe that perhaps he was the only real person ı the world and that everybody else was an illusion. He would sometimes come up wonderingly to touch his mother, and then himself, to see if she, too, were real. He speculated on how he could get away from the human shadows around him, and became convinced that he could fly. Sev-

eral times he laboriously climbed up on the seat of a
kitchen chair, spread his arms like a bird, and leaped into
space. Every time he crashed to the floor, his frightened
mother rescued him, but he always felt surprised and
rather aggrieved that he should fall, and secretly believed
that he could fly after all. This type of reaction characteristically appears where emotional conflicts in the home
create an acute problem of emotional orientation for the
child.

As a small boy he was sent by his mother to follow
his father when he left the house, and to report where
he went. K developed a strong sense of guilt for this, and
after the divorce was afraid that his father would return
and take revenge on him in some unknown and horrible
way. His father did occasionally reappear, and once invited the boy to spend the night with him, but K was too
frightened to accept.

The family often lived in the country, and the self-con-
sciousness of K in the presence of strangers was heightened
by frequent removals into new and often isolated places.
One of the towns near which he lived when about nine
was on a frontier. Gun-play was frequent, and K remembers having seen the corpses of men who had been shot
down in street brawls. There were ominous-looking fel-
lows around town, and the boy gave them a wide berth.

The death of his mother when he was twelve robbed K
of his main emotional support in a dangerous world. She
died after two years of suffering from an infected limb.
She would also spit into bits of papers and burn them in
the stove. K wondered why she did this, and later developed a reverie the importance of which will soon appear.

The older members of the family were left with K on
their hands, and they decided to club together and put all

thought of marrying out of their heads until he was able to stand alone. The boy did not then realize the sacrifices they made for him, but he later discovered that his older brother put off marrying the girl of his choice until she broke off the engagement and married someone else. It was not until about the time that he graduated from high school and the home was broken up that he became aware of what he owed them, and ever after he was plagued by the thought of his unworthiness, and his incapacity to repay his brothers and sister for their care. Up to that time he had experienced no particular sense of gratitude, and although his older brother once or twice referred to his dependent position, his private feelings were mainly of resentment against the restrictions imposed upon him.

And these restrictions were not inconsiderable. The family ran a greenhouse, and the drudgery involved in such an occupation was incessant. There were slips to transplant, beds to weed, and loads to pull and carry. There were long hours of boredom over routine occupations. K was expected to dash home from school at the earliest possible moment, and to lend a hand with the endless chores about the place.

Occasionally he succeeded in evading his duties. He stopped to play on the way home from deliveries, and he stayed at school on some pretext or other to join the drill squad. But he was always haunted by fear and guilt. His older brother was a strict disciplinarian, and beat him several times. His sister occasionally let him have some spending money, but as a rule he was tightly cramped financially. When his gang organized into a drill squad, and chose their uniforms, he was humiliated when the necessary dollars were not forthcoming from home.

K was worried by what appeared to be a lack of physical stamina and endurance. This idea (which had no basis in fact) in part grew out of his efforts to do what his brothers did. They occasionally broad-jumped or pulled weights, and of course K made a poor showing beside them. But for the unconscious hostility against them, such unequal results would not have disturbed him. His morbid worries about his strength led him to submit to a great deal of bullying by town toughs.

His adolescent years were marred by perpetual anxieties about his social adequacy. He had been the victim of an explosion which left his face marked with powder stains, and this repugnant tattooing, which disappeared very gradually, embarrassed him for years.

K's older brothers and sister sometimes took him with them to parties because there was nobody to leave him with, and an annoying sense of being in the way added to his growing sense of social inadequacy. During high-school days he fell in love with the daughter of the most influential man in the locality, but as her social standards became more exacting, his lack of money, leisure, and prestige made it impossible for him to travel with her set. One of the most humiliating episodes in his life was the one which broke up their relations. K had arranged to meet her at a dancing class. Another girl called up to see if he would take her, but he said he wasn't going. His oldest brother had listened in on the telephone extension, and was astonished to see K appear all dressed up and on the way out. He launched forth on a tirade, declaring that K gallivanted around throwing money away and shirking his job, though he was absolutely dependent on others for his daily bread. K was cut to the quick, and went back to his room churning with too many emotions to call up and offer explanations to the girl.

K had taken it for granted ever since he was a small boy that he would go to college. He traced back his determination to an incident when he was driving across the plains one magnificent starry night. He sat in the bottom of the rig, rapt in contemplation of the sparkling sky, while his mother chatted with her neighbor. Suddenly he asked how he could find out about the stars, and she replied that people could study all about them in college. He then and there resolved to go to college, and never had a moment's doubt about it, although the members of his immediate family went no farther than the common school.

In spite of his inferiority feelings, K was not cut off from some measure of recognition in high school. His dependable and sympathetic qualities impressed themselves upon those who came into close daily contact with him, and he was made an officer of his high-school class. He was respectful toward his teachers and good in his studies.

College was an entirely different affair. His personal worries multiplied during the transition period. Lacking funds, he sought a scholarship. The only one tenable from his district to the state university was in ceramic engineering, and after looking up "ceramic" in the dictionary, he applied and was selected for admission. The work proved to have no particular interest for him, and his social life was even less satisfying. He was met at the college town by the members of a church group who lived together in a dormitory (some friend had written them), and he, though never devout, stopped with them during the first term. This marked him as a non-fraternity man. He waited tables in a fraternity house, and as bad luck would have it, a former teacher wrote highly recommending him to the consideration of this particular fraternity. When a committee broke the news to him, he was utterly confused and made such a lamentable impression that it was not possible to extend him the bid. One of his odd jobs was beating carpets at a sorority house, and this turned out to be the sorority that had pledged the girl with whom he had been (and still felt) in love.

For relaxation K was forced into the domain of the kitchen maids. A servant girl struck up a friendship with him, and he had sexual relations with her. He had tried intercourse once during high-school days, and had a premature emission, a practice which often bothered him later, providing a permanent source of humiliation.

Transferring to another college, he began his work in forestry, in which he had acquired some interest during hikes with a friendly high-school teacher. Handicapped by lack of money and worried by a mounting sense of social inadequacy, his life was no more successful than before. In high-school days he envied a talkative lad who astonished the company by glibly recounting anecdotes about Napoleon. One of his relatives whom he had known as a boy left an ideal of social charm which never was attained.

K's inner uncertainties finally reached a point which led him to resolve that he ought to discover once for all whether forestry would prove to be a proper vocation. He left college and joined the government service. This was to be the great test of his ability to master himself.

So keen was his preoccupation with self-mastery that he resented every effort to influence him, and acted with unnecessary strictness in dealing with private lumbermen. He was often deprived of human relationships during his days in the field, and gradually his mind became more and more enmeshed in morbid reflections about himself.

His mind simply refused to concentrate on the technical volumes which he had brought with him to improve the solitude. Reveries which had been slowly germinating on the periphery of his attention now began to foliate. K had always wondered why his mother burned those little bits of paper. It dawned on him one day that she might really have died of tuberculosis, and that he must therefore be predisposed toward that disease. Early in his high-school days, he had begun deep-breathing exercises, though he had never freely admitted to himself or anybody else what lay behind it. He always gave the usual account of his mother's death to insurance examiners, smothering his doubts in affirmation.

This was his state of mind when America entered the war. He found himself saying that since he was going to die anyhow from a loathsome disease, he might as well die at once and get it over with. Enlisting without delay, he sought to reach an exposed position as rapidly as he could. But the government had different ideas, and assigned him to a branch of the service where his technical skill would prove useful. In his disappointment, all the old feelings of inadequacy returned. Interviewed by an officer he floundered and stumbled, neglecting to report essential facts about his training and experience. The accidental intervention of an acquaintance straightened out the matter, and secured the authority to which his record entitled him. At first he was very much embarrassed in the company of lumberjacks, but his behavior never showed his confusion. His actual record was, as usual, excellent, and his conscientious efficiency won the indorsement of everybody who knew him.

K married a rather dominating school-teacher whom he had known for some time. When things went badly, as they often did, he was partially impotent, and also showed the phenomenon which has been christened "Sunday neurosis." Every Sunday afternoon when he was at home he would find himself assailed by deep depression, and would weep quietly to himself.[2] In spite of these neurotic troubles, K was able to make an important place for himself inside a bureaucracy, when he came back from the army.

From one point of view, K's character may be summed up by saying that his overscrupulous performance of duty was an elaborate effort to demonstrate his potency, and that his longing for danger came at a time when he was willing to surrender the struggle. K's morbid moods and persistent feelings of inadequacy are self-imposed penalties for his hostilities against the environment. He possessed very powerful aggressive drives which were partly expressed in the adoption of a self-ideal which was far more ambitious than anything deemed feasible by the family. His narcissism was such that he was prevented from viewing himself as an object, and from modifying his demands upon the world for recognition, and upon himself for production, until these demands bore a closer relationship to his own skills and opportunities. The basis for his obsessive scrupulousness was laid during early childhood, when he was torn between father and mother-loyalties, and acted out within his own nature the clashes that occurred between them. His strong mother-identification is shown by his belief that he suffered from her diseases, and would die from tuberculosis as she had died. He preferred death to a reduction in his demands upon himself and the world. Such a reaction has in it the primitive demand of the child to treat the world as controllable at will by the omnipotent

[2] Abraham and Ferenczi have reported cases of this kind.

fantasy. His genital difficulties testify to the intensity of the castration conflict, and show the passive-oral regression. K deeply resented having to adjust to the world at all. His capacity for hard work was achieved against high resistance, and in part had the value of a penance. Thus when workless days came around, he was always ill at ease, and sometimes showed the spells of weeping on Sunday afternoons. To work was to prove his potency, and to supply a ritual substitute for and defense against his antisocial impulses. He was unable to emancipate himself very far from the reactions of the people in his immediate environment.

As a class the administrators differ from the agitators by the displacement of their affects upon less remote and abstract objects. In the case of one important group this failure to achieve abstract objects is due to excessive preoccupation with specific individuals in the family circle, and to the correlative difficulty of defining the rôle of the self. Putting agitator A at one end of the scale, we may place administrator K or H near the other. Agitator B was less able to displace than A, as shown by the more personal character of the reforms which interested him. K or H were so concerned about definite people, and about their own failures in relation to many of them, that emancipation was unattainable.

As a hypothetical construction from these "marginal" cases, we may suggest that another group of administrators is recruited from among those who have passed smoothly through their developmental crises. They have not over-repressed powerful hostilities, but either sublimated these drives, or expressed them boldly in the intimate circle. They display an impersonal interest in the task of organization itself, and assert themselves with firmness, though not with overemphasis, in professional and in intimate life. Their lack of interest in abstractions is due to the fact that they have never needed them as a means of dealing with their emotional problems. They can take or leave general ideas without using them to arouse widespread affective responses from the public. Tied neither to abstractions nor to particular people, they are able to deal with both in a context of human relations, impersonally conceived. Their affects flow freely; they are not affectless, but affectively adjusted. Very original and overdriving administrators seem to show a fundamental pattern which coincides with that of the agitators; the differences in specific development are principally due to the cultural patterns available for identification at critical phases of growth.

CHAPTER IX

POLITICAL CONVICTIONS

Political prejudices, preferences, and creeds are often formulated in highly rational form, but they are grown in highly irrational ways. When they are seen against the developmental history of the person, they take on meanings which are quite different from the phrases in which they are put.

To begin, almost at random, with L. He believes that the United States ought to join the League of Nations and that our government ought to lead the world toward conciliation and peace. He is a Republican in party preference, and possesses well-rationalized judgments on a number of public questions. It is for none of these reasons that his history is of special value to the political scientist. What his intimate history does disclose is an exact parallelism between his political opinions and those of his father and mother, and, besides that, a conscious anxiety on his part to conform to the parental pattern of belief and occupation. He has a strange premonition that if he goes his own way something terrible will happen. Thus L is not only a simple conformer, but a compulsive conformer.

He is the youngest of four children. The next older member was a brother who was killed when L was eight and the brother was seventeen. Since L was so much younger than the other children, he was at first petted and spoiled. He slept around with all the members of the family, but mostly with his mother. A cousin of his own age with whom he visited provided the immediate point of departure for much exaggerated sexual fantasy. The cousin initiated him into various sexual practices when L was seven. He began very early to masturbate, and the habit stayed with him as a problem until he was through college. A certain masochistic element appeared when he got erections at an early age upon being spanked by a girl playmate. He was sexually stimulated when attending to the natural wants of small children.

L developed his guilty fantasies about his sinful impulses until he began to fear that grave retribution would be visited upon him or his family on account of his secret crimes. It was at this time that his brother, who was his favorite in the family next to the mother, was killed while out on a boyish escapade. L was profoundly stirred by this. His forebodings of disaster seemed to have direct confirmation, and he soon developed whole congeries of compulsive rituals.

When L went to the bathtub, he felt that something terrible would happen to his family, and especially to his mother, unless he plunged his head under water and held it there just as long as he had the breath. He became afraid of taking a bath because of this compulsive drive to duck his head under the water. Often in the bathroom he had the same feeling that disaster could be prevented only if he succeeded in drinking all the water that gushed out of a faucet. At night he would be seized by the sudden conviction that he must bury his face in the pillow and keep it there just as long as he possibly could without suffocating. Once he swallowed a pin after long inner debate over the efficacy of this measure. Several times he hung over the edge of the roof on top of the house until he barely had strength enough to swing back to safety on top of the porch. He felt that he could permit no one to pass him on the street. Later he thought he must outstare people, and calculated that if he kept staring until seven out of ten people dropped their eyes, that all would be well.

His mother was the central figure in L's anxieties. He evolved quite independently a theory which had been anticipated many centuries before by some primitive people and philosophers. He believed that his mother had a spirit which left her body the moment any member of the family left her alone, and that this spirit was forced to undergo all sorts of trials and tests. The spirit would always come back to his mother's body before any member of the family spoke to her. In some magical fashion his own acts relieved the burden which was laid upon his mother's spirit. Even in adulthood, he found an occasional fantasy which was reminiscent of the preoccupations of those years. Not long ago he was floating on the water in a swimming pool and found himself thinking that his mother could never hold her head under water as long as he could hold his foot under water.

With all his timidity, removal to a strange environment was a severe trial. Just before high-school days his family moved to a new community, and he never quite overcame his sense of strangeness. He had always been a coward, shrinking from physical combat. One of his first memories is of sitting on a curb with an older brother, who suddenly proposed that he should fight the little brother of another boy. L began to fight, but was overcome by fear and ran away. Later he was the center of a small clique of children in his block, all of whom were very much his junior. One of his group bragged about L's physical prowess to the leader of another group, but when the challenge was issued L backed down. He was

worried by his own timidity, but seemed unable to do anything about it.

He made a handful of friends in the new environment,
but was on intimate terms with no one. With one boy he
was able to talk somewhat freely about sexual fantasies,
and L once proposed a sexual experiment to a neighbor
girl. When he was repulsed, his guilt was enormously
increased.

About this time L began to think seriously of entering
the ministry, so that he might always think "pure" thoughts
and do "pure" things. When he went to college he at first
roomed with boys from his high school, but they talked
so openly about sex that he felt the atmosphere was de-
plorable and demoralizing. Before the month expired, he
sought a new room and went into a solitary retreat. During the first year of his college life he was acutely religious and besought church services regularly. He sought
guidance from the sermons upon personal and political
questions.

Having developed the idea that he must live up to the
family ideal at any price, L felt that he could never de-
part from the opinions and customs of his parents. In
politics he was a stout Republican, and later, when in a
religious mood, he heard his preacher espouse the League.
He felt that he ought to support the League, but was
plunged into a serious conflict, because he thought his parents were against it. Greatly to his relief he discovered
that his father and mother had also been won over to the
League by a preacher, and that his lapse from orthodox
Republicanism would not bring dishonor on the family.

His father-hatred fantasies were very oppressive. They
took the form of believing that if only his father were
dead, his mother would have a much easier time of it. L's

father was suffering from a steadily advancing paralysis. At nine he dreamed that his father was in the bathtub and that around him were fat, red snakes that were bound to devour him. L who was standing by in the dream, awoke in a fright. He often dreamed that his father was away and that his mother was happy with him.

L still shows many signs of his early neurosis in some of his ceremonial acts, and in the timid conservatism of his character. The private meaning of his political convictions is clear enough, for they are self-imposed obligations to lift his load of guilt for the murderous and incestuous fantasies which he long struggled to repress. The opinions of the family were sanctioned as a kind of religion. It is interesting to see how at first he invented a large array of ceremonial practices to substitute for his own illicit impulses, and later worked off his guilt feelings through the religious patterns which were provided by society, and which were revalidated on the basis of his private meanings. The acceptance of the political convictions of the family was on a par with the acceptance of theological dogma.

Among the nonconformists to the family pattern we may choose M, whose history was taken by Stekel. M was a prominent socialist who agitated for an economic brotherhood of man, and whose most important private motive in this particular was a bitter hatred of his own brother. Most of this hatred was displaced from his brother on to capitalistic autocracy, and overreacted against by a social ideal of fraternal equality. His hatred of his own brother was not entirely disposed of by this displacement, and it was necessary to keep at a distance from him, and from many of his traits. Thus M despised music because his brother liked it, followed a style of dress at the opposite pole from his brother, and nearly walked out on the physician when he discovered that the physician had treated his own brother.

M spent the years agitating at home and abroad, spending a year and a half in prison. Thus he succeeded in gratifying his masochistic desire to be punished for his hatred by provoking society to avenge itself on him. The motivation in this personality is notably similar to that which has been more elaborately sketched in the history of A.

Another nonconformist appears in the history of an anarchist who was once a patient of Stekel. N carried his social doctrine beyond the sharing of property, insisting that wives should be in common. He took the initiative by urging his wife to cohabit with the male members of his anarchistic society, while he demanded access to the wives of others. His own wife finally fell in love with another man, and asked N for a divorce. But before arrangements could be made, she became pregnant by her new partner, who was poor, and asked N to acknowledge the new child as his own, since this child would fall heir to some money from its supposed grandfather, the father of N. He consented to this, as he had to the divorce, but his self-esteem was hurt by his wife's desertion. He had always felt elated when his wife came back to him after each of her erotic adventures, and now he was all broken up. Stekel believes that N's espousal of communal principles in theory and practice was powerfully motivated by an irrational desire to humiliate his father by playing a generous rôle with his sexual partner, and substituting the morality of generosity for his father's possessive monopoly of the mother. When his wife-mother deserted him, N's brilliant career was ruined, and he resorted to opium,

and finally secured a revenge on his father by blocking
his ambitions for a successful son.

A father-hatred (due to unrequited love) of remarkable
intensity was the basis of another career which Stekel
examined. O was the young leader of an anarchist band
whose anarchism went beyond precept to dramatic practice. O had his companions conduct some holdups to
get money to start an anarchist paper. O was an illegitimate child who was brought up and spoiled by an overindulgent mother. When he realized that he had a father
who was still living, but whose identity was never divulged,
his anger boiled up against his mother upon whose affections he no longer had monopolistic claim, and against his
unknown father, who refused him love and distinction.
For he had no doubt that his father was a rich and important personage. O displaced much of his animosity on
to remote, abstract symbols of authority, like kings and
capitalists, and devoted himself to destroying them. Much
of his affection was likewise displaced upon abstract ideals
of a fatherless fraternal society, living together without
coercion. His sadistic impulses were by no means entirely
sublimated upon remote goals and harmonious means,
for he led his companions on common robberies. O threw
a thick mantle of rationalization over his murderous impulses and his criminal acts, seeking to justify coercion
in the name of a coercionless ideal which could only be
laboriously achieved in the world.

It is the history of such cases, in which the emotions
are peculiarly intense, which leads one to conclude that
political assassins have hated their fathers with unusual
bitterness. E. J. Kempf remarks in his psychopathology,
after reviewing the historical evidence in the cases of

Guiteau, the assassin of President Garfield, and of Booth, the assassin of President Lincoln, as follows:

The writer does not hold that every case of severe affective repression in youth, due to the father's hatred or a father equivalent's, will lead finally to a parricidal or treasonable compulsion. It is only held that such affective repressions produce a revolutionary character which, if given an appropriate repressive setting during maturity, will then converge upon the parricidal act. Without the rather specific type of affective repression in his youth, he would be invulnerable to parricidal suggestions later on.[1]

Illegitimate children, especially when the identity of their father is undisclosed, carry with them the perpetual query, "Who is my father?" Indeed, the fantasy of belonging to other parents than those physically in the family is sufficiently widespread as a disguised hostile reverie against the actual parents to enable everyone to appreciate in some measure the mental state of the illegitimate child. "My father may be rich and powerful." "My father may be an aristocrat of distinguished lineage, and he is denying me all my just privileges." Such fantasies are taken up and spun out in the reveries of the victim. There is a presumption that those who suffer from this kind of social inferiority are especially numerous among those who commit acts of political violence, as Lombroso held.

P accepted violence, but of a different kind. P is a patriot who proved his patriotism by volunteering in the late war during the course of which he was distinguished for bravery in action. His deepest longing is for war to come again. He is in favor of an aggressive foreign policy since it increases the chances of war, and war he would welcome again as he welcomed it before.

P has a younger brother and an older sister. His mother

[1] Op. cit., p. 448.

died when he was six and his relations have been strained with his stepmother, who entered the family shortly afterward. His father was a very successful professional man.

P began to fall behind in his schoolwork when he was about seven years old. This brought him into disrepute at home, for his previous promise led everyone to expect much from him, and the change seemed to prove that he was "lazy." The family has nagged him ever after, hoping to stimulate him to work harder. Just why he failed to continue to cope successfully with the demands of school becomes fairly clear when his reminiscences of the period are recovered. He had loved his second-grade teacher and had been her special favorite, and both his marks and his enthusiasm were high. The third-grade teacher impressed him as stern and cruel, and he soon began to despise the sight of her. The boy's work began to crumble, for his mind was full of hostile fancies about his new teacher, and of yearning fancies for the teacher whom he had just lost.

His emotional life was further disturbed about this time by the loss of his nurse. P's stepmother discharged her as soon as she came. Now the nurse was the lad's main love, for his own mother had been ill for some years before her death. The nurse's presence gave the child that stable reassurance which is so necessary if the mind of the child is to be kept free from morbid fears. In P's case, there were strong reasons why this reassurance was necessary. An insane man lived across the street and terrified the passers-by by screaming at everyone who passed. Shortly after his mother's death P went under ether for a minor operation and was terrified that he would die. The fear of suffocation reappeared in dreams and nightmares, and he was very timid about learning to swim.

The stepmother was a disturbing element as a strange and unknown quantity in the environment, and a competitor for the affection of the father. When she discharged the nurse, P thought of her as a malignant influence. His troubles at school were exaggerated by his home changes, and his mind became preoccupied with fantasies directed against his stepmother, or some substitute.

P's father was ambitious for the boy. P remembers him as quick to reprove and slow to praise. He dreamed of his father's death, and of seeing his father in an accident. But his manifest attitude was one of respectful affection. No matter what happened in the home, he excused his father by reflecting that the stepmother was to blame. However, on the deeper level, it appeared that he held his father accountable for the death of his mother and the disappearance of his nurse.

At school P was popular because of his good physique and his docile nature. But his studies came hard. Having failed on college-entrance tests, P bolted and joined the army. The war came along just in time to give him a dignified retreat from an unbearable personal situation. He hoped that his father would think about him with pride. He was bitterly self-accusatory because of his failure to "make good," and felt a strong unconscious need of punishment. Under these conditions he entered army life with enthusiasm, and made a fine record for personal courage.

Once the war was over, his troubles began again. He succeeded in entering college, but college felt like a nursery. He felt that his army experience sophisticated him above schoolboy tasks and chatter. All his old worries returned, complicated by his longing for a new war. He had a long series of difficulties in his occupational life.

Seen against this background, his militarism is perfectly intelligible. War gave him a chance to destroy, wildly and extensively, and also a chance to work off his guilt feelings by exposing himself to death. His repressed hatreds were partly turned against himself. An interesting feature of his ideology is that his longing for personal participation in war is combined with indignation against the exploitation of backward peoples by the imperialist powers. He identifies with the "underdog."

Q, a contrast to P, is a pacifist and a socialist. His intimate history shows that relatively simple association of ideas upon which this depends. From an early age Q showed a morbid fear of blood. Later on, when he heard that western capitalism meant war and bloodshed, he experienced a profound emotional revulsion against "capitalism," "imperialism," and their associated concepts, and called himself a "socialist," "pacifist," and "internationalist."

The blood-phobia itself was a powerful factor in developing his character. By slow degrees, he was able to push the screened memories back until he recovered a simple incident which was heavily ladened with affect, and whose recollection disposed of the blood-phobia, even though it was not completely analyzed. Q's father was accustomed to shave in the kitchen on Saturday afternoon, and Q as a small child took a great interest in the proceedings. Occasionally the father cut a pimple on his face with the big razor he was using, and flinched as the blood spurted out. He immediately swabbed the cut, and presumably forgot it. But Q did not forget so quickly. He found himself much engaged in speculating about it, drawing the inference that all the reddish projections on the body are full of blood, that, indeed, the body is a reservoir of blood; and that the reddish formations are in danger of being punctured, so the blood will spurt out and run off.

Q had previously seen his father naked in the bathtub, and he thought that his father had rubbed soap over his nipples with the palm of his hand and not with the fingers, from which he concluded that the nipples must be especially tender, and whenever he washed himself, Q carefully avoided his own nipples and massaged them most delicately with the palm of his hand.

His brother had the habit of biting his finger nails until the blood came, and the family reproached him for it, prophesying that all sorts of infections might set in. Q began to expect that something disastrous would happen, and he was not altogether averse to having it happen because of his jealousy of the brother. But it came with a great shock when his brother did actually develop an infection, thus confirming his own suspicions about the necessity for stopping outflows of blood.

About this time Q was playing with his older sister, and in the course of a scuffle his hand slid down his sister's body and over her breast. Q distinctly felt a nipple catch for a moment beneath his fingers, and he was instantly terrified for fear that his sister would bleed to death. The breasts, he thought, must be partly filled reservoirs of blood, since they were soft and yielding.

During his fourth year Q's grandmother died, and he was horrified to think of what would happen to one he loved. He had seen a photograph of a reclining nude with a beatific smile and the caption "Death" beneath. From this he surmised that people were undressed when they died, and lowered naked into the ground. But he had seen worms in the ground, and the worms would attack the body. Since the nipples were prominent and therefore easy to reach, the nipples would be eaten through first.

He shuddered to think of the worms gnawing away at his grandmother's nipples, and sometimes woke up in a fright, having dreamed that the worms were biting off his own nipples.

Once Q came running into his aunt's house and discovered a small infant cousin nursing at the breast. His aunt hastily readjusted her dress. Because of the care with which the breasts were guarded from exposure by his mother, sister, and aunt, he leaped to the conclusion that they had something to do with the secret relations of men and women.

He had all sorts of trouble trying to figure out how these relations were conducted, but when he was about eight he originated a theory that temporarily solved the problem. Q figured that a man and woman must lie on the bed with their faces close together. The male would then squeeze the breasts, alternately pressing and releasing them, as if they were balloons. Then they turned over and rubbed their anuses together. Not long after, he completed his theory of procreation by imagining that children must be born through a hole in the stomach from which the blood gushed copiously. The cutting must be very painful and bloody.

Haunted by the fearful prospect of a world which might at any time knock a hole in his body and deprive him of blood, Q was a bundle of excessive timidities. He was afraid of his grandmother's cat, he ran to his mother if he saw a dog, and he was afraid that a horse would bite off his hand if he fed it. He hated to watch a ball game for fear a foul tip would hit him, and he avoided bugs, worms, and lizards like the plague. Q never put up a fight outside the house, and cried when the other boys of the neighborhood bullied him. Sometimes he was taunted as a Jew but he never fought back, much to the disgust of his father. His forebodings spread to thunder, lightning, fire, redness, and numerous articles of food.

In marked contrast to his cringing demeanor abroad was his attitude toward the older brother, ten years his senior. Time after time he would pick a quarrel and pummel the older youth, until the brother tired of the situation and gave him a sharp blow. Thereupon he went to someone for comfort. Q's father felt that the older boy might be a little rough, but that the little fellow had something coming to him. The mother was uniformly comforting, although she reproved both boys for not behaving as brothers should.

The boys were profoundly hostile to each other, although usually cordial. The older brother made himself conspicuous for his tenderness during a serious illness of Q, running errands with alacrity, and watching constantly by the bedside. When it became clear that Q would live, the older boy's devotion stopped abruptly, indicating the unconscious basis of the exaggerated reaction. He was over-reacting against a death wish against his brother as an intruder between him and the mother.

Q envied the achievements of his older brother, and often compared himself unfavorably with him. The older boy not only stood at the head of his classes, but earned his way by playing the violin. Although Q stayed at the head of his classes, he was by no means as self-supporting as his brother. The brother-hatred appeared in such dreams as:

Dream 1.—My brother is getting married. He is in a dress suit. A long line of young men in dress suits are coming up to congratulate him. As the first one reaches out his hand, he falls backward and all the others fall over one another like tenpins.

Dream 2.—My brother and I are walking down the street near home. I hear a scream. An Italian is chasing a woman with a baby who seeks refuge in a store. The Italian knocks her down. Then my brother goes into the store and tries to deal with the Italian, but is knocked down. I enter and knock down the Italian.

The brother-jealousy is of secondary significance in Q's history. The crux of the blood-phobia was a critical experience whose traumatic effects were due to the strength of the affects which were mobilized and repressed. Q slept with his father, and the blood-letting incident aroused his slumbering desire for the death of his father and his own active fear of suffering mutilation (castration). Blood derived its significance because it involved a reinstatement of the most acute phase of the conflict. To escape from it, Q fainted unless he succeeded in getting out of the sight of blood at once. It is noteworthy that Q did not at once faint when the razor cut the pimple; it was not until the elaboration of the fantasy had continued, and the affects had become greatly concentrated, that the blood came to signalize an instant and overwhelming emergency from which a kind of suicide (fainting) was the only escape.

The following terse dream expresses something of the underlying situation:

Dream 3.—I am looking down a city street which is covered with snow and lighted by street lights. The President of the United States is walking along the street and suddenly slips and falls. My attention is then called to a place farther down the street where two tumblers are leaping over a rope stretched across the street. They are leaping backward and forward with a curious mechanical motion.

The rhythmic leaping is a pictorial symbol for the pulsations of genital excitement. The President is an authority substitute for the father. When the father is out of the way, genital activity will become safe. Since the father prescribes sexual abstinence (abstinence from handling the genitals), this expresses a desire to give greater freedom to the repressed impulses of the subject's character. The repressed positive identification with the brother shows itself in opposing two tumblers instead of one to the father.

Dream 4.—A goose or ducklike creature is being chased back and forth across the road by two dogs. The creature has a red bill and head, a blue back and wing feathers, and a white breast. The white, fuzzy dogs chase the animal back and forth but do not reach it because of their overanxiety. After two round-trips the animal, which moved with a curiously mechanical motion, runs toward a man who has come to the door and jumps between his legs. The man is middle-aged and his hair is white. He is in white pajamas. He says, "My leg is the leg of weakness; my health is hell. . . . ." I am in a winter coat standing outside the house of a friend of my sister's in whom I remember having had a mild interest, but which led to nothing since she was older than I, and not very attractive. I had just delivered a valentine. The scene is illuminated by a street light, and is especially clear because snow is on the ground. The man in the picture is unknown.

The odd creature with the red bill and head symbolizes the penis. The two dogs (brothers) try to capture it, but the father protects it. However, the hope of achieving masculinity is not wholly dashed because the old man is growing weaker.

For some time the productions of Q showed that sexuality was powerfully linked with death, and that the death was to be his own rather than that of his father, or simultaneously with the death of his father. As the castration anxiety lifted, the blood fear abated, and dreams, word-associations, posture, and other significant reactions altered toward greater ease and assertiveness.

We have seen that well-rationalized theories and preferences are not alien fungi on the personality, but an important expression of the essential trends of the personality. Thus theories are at least as indicative of the individual who espouses them as of the ostensible subjects of speculation. Pessimism, for example, is common in old age, when the sexual powers decline and the individual projects upon the world the sinfulness which he feels for wanting to indulge beyond his powers, and defy his inadequacy. The mechanism of this sort of thing stands out most clearly in extreme cases, such as R. R believed that the world was going from bad to worse and that wars and rumors of wars were devastating the earth. He spent so many hours over a plan to secure the peace of the world forevermore that he developed a confusion state. He would go out in a park, find a secluded spot and weep over the troubles of the world as Jesus wept over Jerusalem. One day in passing a market he saw some chickens in a coop without any water. The cruelty of this was more than he could bear, so he went home and went to bed. His ideas were that he had been chosen to work out the salvation of the world, and that he had been endowed with unusual, indeed supernatural, understanding of men's motives, and special power to heal insanity.

R elaborated a private form of religion. He said that he was worshiping the sun as God, as a symbol of Christ and truth (actually, of masculine virility). When it became necessary for him to commune with his spirit, he was in the habit of facing the sun and repeating a litany of his invention, which ran:

To the sun, the heart of the world! It warmeth the earth with its loveliness. Glory to God! It riseth in the east, lighting the dark corners of ignorance and wickedness. Glory to God! It chaseth the darkness before it like the host of Syria before the children of Israel. Glory to God! It chaseth the darkness before it like the host of Syria before the children of Israel. Glory to God! etc., etc.

He began to chant, and then assumed an exalted, heroic pose, with his arms and head thrown back. Presently he felt that a big storm was coming that would ruin the world. The world is like a giant serpent, a serpent asleep.

R's story is not sufficiently detailed to show much about the development of those reaction patterns which disposed him to meet old age in such a way. He was the only child of a poverty-stricken family who played by himself and got on well with his books. Some local lawyers took an interest in him and helped him through school. He read law and was admitted to the bar. After making a precarious living for a number of years, he was elected to various local offices, and then to Congress. He was reputed to be an impractical dreamer, and enjoyed making rather fanciful speeches. His legislative career as recorded in the *Congressional Record* was undistinguished, containing the usual quota of pension bills and "extensions of remarks" during tariff debates. He was opposed to the annexation of the Philippines, and hostile to imperialism; in this he went along with his party, and likewise indulged a personal conviction. He practiced law desultorily, after having been defeated for the legislature, and devoted himself to study and writing. His one published volume is a vague disquisition on human affairs, which accurately reflects the indeterminate, rhetorical, and meliorative quality of his thinking. He married a woman of his own age when he was a young man. There were no children.

When the paranoid rather than the manic-depressive strain runs through the character, nebulous and all-embracing pessimism about the world is sharpened to specific accusations. Everyone who is prominent in public life is a potential object of such attacks. One might hazard the conjecture that the importance of an individual in the community's estimation may be measured by the number of "crank" letters to him and about him. One such crank, S, wrote a trunkful of letters accusing public men of graft, of being dominated by "Big Biz," and offering suggestions to government officials. He complained of being persecuted and victimized by prominent people, especially by Harry F. Sinclair, the oil man. This was attributed by him to the fact that he had written a letter to the Chief Justice of the Supreme Court calling His Honor's attention to the Teapot Dome scandal which was being ventilated in the press, and naming Mr. Sinclair as the responsible party. Since then Mr. Sinclair had prevented him from getting a job, and paid his own sister to throw him out on the street. During his divorce proceedings he wrote to the American Bar Association to protest against the "shyster lawyers" who were representing his wife, and claims that Mr. Taft and Mr. Root answered him in the papers the following day. When Mr. John W. Davis was a presidential candidate he wrote to him, describing the various attacks to which he, S, had been subjected. Mr. Davis neglected to reply and did nothing about it, so S prevented his election, and feels that Mr. Coolidge owes him something for being elected. "I wrote to Hearst and I believe that turned the trick." In this letter he divulged the fact that Mr. Davis was connected with Wall Street, and this hint was enough to arouse Mr. Hearst. In reply to the routine question, "What is going on in the world?" he answered, "More deviltry than there ever was before."

Unfortunately the history is too meager to explain S's development, except by analogy with others who have displayed the same behavior. Certainly his life-story would, if accessible, reveal the effects of a disorganizing family environment. We do know that his father was drunk much of the time, and that the children had an unhappy lot. At five S went to live with his grandparents who wanted to take him away from his drunken father. At about fifteen he came back for a while. Shortly afterward he saved his sister from being strangled to death by their father, who in a drunken tantrum had her by the neck against the wall. S became a good mechanic, but disintegrated in later life.

Another "crank" devised an ingenious theory to explain President Wilson's conduct. T says that he discovered that Mr. Wilson was not a citizen of the United States. He first made this revelation on his draft questionnaire, and when this became generally known, Mr. Wilson went to France to escape the anger of the enraged citizenry of the United States; later Mr. Wilson fell ill of a guilty conscience at new revelations that he made. Mr. Wilson was part of the Masonic conspiracy which had been hatched against him when he was very young. T's stepfather, who was a Shriner, probably furnishes the material for this delusion. As for T himself, he believed that he descended directly from Mary, Queen of Scots, and that he had fore-knowledge of the approaching end of the world. The members of the millennium are "a creed and not a denomination," and only twenty million people will be saved, over whom T will rule.

From the excerpts included, it appears that the significance of political opinions is not to be grasped apart from the private motives which they symbolize. The degree of insight into objective relationships is one thing; the extent to which "private meanings" are accreted to the "public" or "manifest" meanings is another. When we see the private meaning of public acts, the problem of interpreting the full significance of political behavior presses itself upon our attention. Are there any implications for the general theory of the political process which follow from the intensive scrutiny of individual subjective (and objective) histories? This is the question to which we next turn.

CHAPTER X

THE POLITICS OF PREVENTION

Political movements derive their vitality from the displacement of private affects upon public objects. The intensive scrutiny of the individual by psychopathological methods discloses the prime importance of hitherto-neglected motives in the determination of political traits and beliefs. The adult who is studied at any given cross-section of his career is the product of a long and gradual development in the course of which many of his motivations fail to modify according to the demands of unfolding reality. The adult is left with an impulse life which is but partially integrated to adulthood. Primitive psychological structures continue in more or less disguised form to control his thought and effort.

The state is a symbol of authority, and as such is the legatee of attitudes which have been organized in the life of the individual within the intimate interpersonal sphere of the home and friendship group. At one phase of childhood development the wisdom and might of the physical symbol of authority, typically the father, is enormously exaggerated by the child. Eder traces the significance of this for the state in the following words:

What occurs as we come more in touch with the external world, when the principle of reality develops, is the finding of surrogates for this ideal father. We discover that the parent is not all-wise, all-powerful, all-good, but we still need to find persons or abstractions upon which we can distribute these and similar attributes. By a process of fission these feelings are displaced on to and may be distributed among a number of surrogates. The surrogates may be persons, animals, things or abstract ideas; the headmaster, the dog, the rabbit, the Empire, the Aryan race, or any particular "ism."

He comments that it is upon this self-ideal that is formed the possibility of leadership, of leaders, and of the supreme leader, who is the one capable of doing all that the child once thought the physical father could do. The unconscious motivation is reflected in the sober formula of Blackstone, "The sovereign is not only incapable of doing wrong, but even of thinking wrong: he can never mean to do an improper thing; in him is no folly or weakness."[1]

There is very deep meaning in the phrase of Paley's that "a family contains the rudiments of an empire." The family experience organizes very powerful drives in successive levels of integration, and these primitive attitudes are often called into play as the unobserved partners of rational reactions. To choose another extract from Eder:

The behaviour of the elected or representative politician betrays many characteristics derived from the family. For example, during the time I filled a political job in Palestine I noticed in myself (and in my colleagues) the satisfaction it gave me to have secret information, knowledge which must on no account be imparted to others. Of course good reasons were always to be found: the people would misuse the information or it would depress them unduly and so on—pretty exactly the parent's attitude about imparting information, especially of a sexual nature, to the children. . . . .

At the back of secret diplomacy, and indeed the whole relationship of the official to the non-official, there rests this father-child affect. This also serves to explain the passion aroused in former days by any proposed extension of the franchise.

[1] See the chapter on "Psycho-analysis in Relation to Politics" in *Social Aspects of Psycho-Analysis* (London, 1924).

In the sphere of political dogma, unconscious conflicts play the same rôle which Theodor Reik discussed when he drew a parallel between religious dogma and obsessive ideas.[2] Dogma is a defensive reaction against doubt in the mind of the theorist, but of doubt of which he is unaware. The unconscious hatred of authority discloses itself in the endless capacity of the theorist to imagine new reasons for disbelief, and in his capacity to labor over trivialities, and to reduce his whole intellectual scheme to a logical absurdity. Sometimes this appears in a cryptic formula to which some sort of mysterious potency is ascribed, but which is hopelessly contradictory in so far as it possesses any manifest meaning. The celebrated doctrine of the unity of the trinity is an instance of such culminating nonsense. Words lose their rational reference points and become packed with unconscious symbolism of the ambivalent variety. The description of sovereignty found in Blackstone refers to nothing palpable, and functions principally as an incantation. Much solemn juridical speculation, since so much of it is elaborated by obsessive thinkers, ends thus. Deep doubts about the self are displaced on to doubts about the world outside, and these doubts are sought to be allayed by ostentatious preoccupation with truth.

Defiance of authority is defiance of the introjected conscience, and involves a measure of self-punishment. We have seen how a powerful need for self-punishment is the stuff out of which martyrs and sensational failures are made; but of more general importance is the rôle of the sense of guilt in supporting the *status quo*. Deviation from accepted patterns becomes equivalent to sin, and the con-

[2] "Dogma und Zwangsidee," *Imago*, XIII (1927), 247–382.

science visits discomforts upon those who dare to innovate. Radical ideas become "sacrilegious" and "disloyal" in the view of the primitive conscience, for they tend to represent more than a limited defiance of authority. They put the whole structure of the personality under strain. The childish conscience is easily intimidated into preserving order on slight provocation; it knows little of the capacity to consider the piecemeal reconstruction of values. "Radicalism" is felt as a challenge to the whole system of resistances which are binding down the illicit impulses of the personality, rather than as an opportunity for detached consideration of the relation of the self to the rest of reality. There is little boldness in political thinking which is not accompanied by an overdose of defiance, for even those who succeed in breaking through the intimidations of their infantile consciences must often succumb in some measure and "pay out." Much of the struggle, the fearful *Sturm und Drang* of the emancipated thinker, is his unconscious tribute to the exactions of the tribunal which he erected within himself at an early age, and which continues to treat innovation as *ipso facto* dangerous. The non-obsessive thinker is one who can coolly contemplate revisions in the relations of man to reality unperturbed by his antiquated conscience. Often readjustments of human affairs which are proposed are driven to absurdity because the original mind is compelled to transform his mere departure from the conventional into a defiance of conventionality. When one perceives the operation of this powerful self-punishment drive, and the secondary efforts to free one's self from feelings of guilt for defying the authorized order, it is possible to remain understandingly tolerant of the eccentricities of creative minds. To put the point a bit sharply,

it is safe to say that the adult mind is only partly adult;
the conscience may be four years old. The conscience,
the introjected nursemaid, reacts undiscriminatingly to
change, and construes it as rebellion.

The organization of motives which occurs in adolescence possesses direct significance for the interpretation
of political interests.

The physical and mental storm of puberty and adolescence often culminates in the displacement of loves upon
all humanity or a selected part of it, and in acts of
devotion to the whole. It is here that the fundamental
processes of loyalty are most clearly evident as they relate to public life. S. Bernfeld has written extensively on
the psychology of the German youth movement. He comments on the very different lengths of puberty, and distinguishes between the physical and the psychological
processes. When the psychological processes outlive the
·physical ones, certain characteristic reaction types arise.
Dr. Bernfeld believes that the discrepant type prevails
most characteristically in the youth movement, and he
enumerates its characteristics. The interests of this group
are turned toward "ideal" objects like politics, humanity,
and art. The relation to these objects is productive, since
the youth tries to produce a new form of politics or art.
There is always a great deal of self-confidence present, or
many symptoms of a repression that has failed. This is
expressed in the high opinion of one's self and the low
opinion one holds of his companions. An outstanding
individual, the friend or master, is loved and revered.
Often this love for a friend is extended to the whole group.
The sexual components of the personality do not concentrate on finding objects, but in creating a new narcissistic
situation. Bernfeld distinguishes this secondary narcissism

from infantile narcissism on the ground that it is accompanied by deep depression reminiscent of melancholia. The reason lies in the formation of an ideal self that attracts a great part of the libido and enters into contrast with the real ego, a process which is particularly characteristic of the complex or discrepant type which he found in the youth movement.[3]

Political life seems to sublimate many homosexual trends. Politicians characteristically work together in little cliques and clubs, and many of them show marked difficulties in reaching a stable heterosexual adjustment. In military life, when men are thrown together under intimate conditions, the sublimations often break down and the homosexual drives find direct expression. A German general has gone so far as to declare that one reason why Germany lost the war was that the command was shot through with jealousies growing out of homosexual rivalry. Dr. K. G. Heimsoth has prepared a manuscript describing the rôle of homosexuality in the volunteer forces which continued to operate against the Poles and the communists after the war. In the case of certain leaders, at least, the reputation for overt homosexuality was no handicap; indeed, the reverse seemed to be true. Franz Alexander has suggested that one reason why homosexuality is viewed with contempt in modern life is the vague sense that complex cultural achievement depends on an inhibited sexuality, and that direct gratification tends to dissolve society into self-satisfied pairs and cliques. The observations of Heimsoth throw some doubt

[3] Succinctly described in "Über eine typische Form der männlichen pubertät," *Imago*, IX (1923), 169 ff. On the homoerotic elements see Hans Blüher, *Die deutsche Wandervogelbewegung als erotisches Phänomen*, and his more elaborate volume cited in the Bibliography.

on the wisdom of this "vague sense."[4] The prominence of alcoholism and promiscuity among like-sex groups has often been observed, and both indulgences appear to be closely connected with homosexual impulses.[5]

Political crises are complicated by the concurrent reactivation of specific primitive impulses. War is the classical situation in which the elementary psychological structures are no longer held in subordination to complex reactions. The acts of cruelty and lust which are inseparably connected with war have disclosed vividly to all who care to see the narrow margin which separates the social from the asocial nature of man. The excesses of heroism and abnegation are alike primitive in their manifestations, and show that all the primitive psychological structures are not antisocial, but asocial, and may often function on behalf of human solidarity.[6]

Why does society become demoralized in the process of revolution? Why should a change in the political procedures of the community unleash such excesses in behavior? Reflection might lead one to suppose that since important decisions are in process of being made, calm deliberation would characterize society. Evidently a reactivating process is at work here; there is a regressive tendency to reawaken primitive sadism and lust. The conspicuous disproportionality between the problem and the

[4] I was kindly permitted to see this manuscript which is not yet published.

[5] See Sandor Rado, "Die psychischen Wirkungen der Rauschgifte," *Internationale Zeitschrift für Psychoanalyse,* XII (1926), 540–56; A. Keilholz, "Analyseversuch bei Delirium Tremens," *ibid.,* pp. 478–92; and Stekel's volumes.

[6] For a sketch of the unconscious processes involved in warfare see S. Freud, "Zeitgemässes über Krieg und Tod," *Imago,* IV (1915–16), 1–21; Ernest Jones, *Essays in Psycho-Analysis;* William A. White, *Thoughts of a Psychiatrist on the War and After.*

behavior necessitates an explanation in such terms. Federn published a sketch of the psychology of revolution in his pamphlet *Die vaterlose Gesellschaft* in 1919. When the ruler falls, the unconscious triumphantly interprets this as a release from all constraint, and the individuals in the community who possess the least solidified personality structures are compulsively driven to acts of theft and violence. An interview which Federn gave to Edgar Ansel Mowrer in 1927 on the occasion of the Vienna riots reviews in somewhat popular form some of his conceptions.

VIENNA, AUSTRIA, July 20.—"Distrust of father was the chief cause of the Vienna riot," said Paul Federn, onetime president of the Psychoanalytical Society. From a psychoanalytical standpoint all authority is the father, and this formerly for Austria was incorporated in the imposing figure of Emperor Franz Josef. But during the war the father deceived and maltreated his children, and only the material preoccupations of life and the joyous outburst when at the close of the war the old authority broke asunder prevented Austria from having a revolution then.

The state again built up the old ruling caste and began to hope for restoration, and therefore an abyss opened between Vienna, which under socialist leadership is trying to replace the traditional father principle by a new brotherhood, and the Austrian federal state, which had returned to a modified father idea. Trust in father is the child's deepest instinct. Vienna first respected the Austrian republic, but gradually this belief was undermined by the continual misery, by newspapers preaching fanaticism and by legal decisions which virtually destroyed the people's belief in the new father's justice.

Accordingly there occurred a spontaneous manifestation which unconsciously drove the disillusioned and furious children to destroy precisely those things on which the paternal authority seems to rest—namely, records and legal documents.

Why the peaceful Viennese should suddenly be transformed temporarily into mad beasts is also clear to the psychoanalysts. Had the police offered no resistance the crowd would soon have dispersed and no harm would have been done. But once the police fired blood flowed and the mob reacted savagely, responding to the ancient fear of castration by the father which is present in all of us unconsciously in the face of the punishing authority. Therefore, fear grew along with the violence, each increase leading to new violence and greater fear, as appeasement can only follow a complete outbreak and as the inhabitants were widely scattered in their houses it took three days before the last hatred could fully get out.

One further point can only be explained by psychoanalysis. The social democratic leaders are at heart revolutionary, but they did not wish this demonstration. They realized that revolution in little Austria today would be suicidal, and, therefore, at a given moment called out the republican guard with orders to interfere and prevent violence. The guard arrived much too late.

Why did not the leaders send out the guard at 6 a.m. when they knew the demonstration was beginning? They say they "forgot." This is a flagrant example of unconscious forgetfulness. The socialists forgot to take the only step which could have prevented something which they consciously disapproved, but unconsciously desired.

The Vienna riots were in the deepest sense a family row.[7]

Eder speculates about the unconscious factors in the well-known tendency of certain political alternatives to succeed one another in crude pendulum fashion.

I think it was Mr. Zangwill who once said that it is a principle of the British Constitution that the King can do no wrong and his ministers no right. That is to say, the ambivalency originally experienced toward the father is now split; the sentiment of disloyalty, etc., is displaced on to the King's ministers, or on to some of them, or on to the opposition. . . . . Modern society has discovered the principle of election, and the vote to give expression to the hostile feelings toward their rulers. Psychoanalytically an election may be regarded as the sublimation of regicide (primary parricide) with the object of placing oneself on the throne; the vote is like a repeating decimal; the father is killed

[7] *Chicago Daily News,* July 20, 1927.

but never dies. The ministers are our substitutes for ourselves. Hence the political maxim of the swing of the pendulum.

Alexander and Staub have undertaken to explain the unconscious basis of the crisis which is produced in the community when criminals are permitted to go with no punishment or with light punishment. The study of personality genesis shows that the sublimation of primitive impulses is possible on the basis of a kind of primitive "social contract." The individual foregoes direct indulgences (which have the disadvantage of bringing him into conflict with authority), and substitutes more complex patterns of behavior on the tacit understanding that love and safety will thereby be insured. When another individual breaks over and gratifies his illicit impulses directly on a primitive level, the equilibrium of every personality is threatened. The conscious self perceives that it is possible to "get by," and this threatens the whole structure of sublimation. The superego tries to maintain order by directing energy against the ego, perhaps subjecting it to "pricks of conscience," for so much as entertaining the possibility of illicit gratification, and seeks to turn the ego toward activities which reduce temptation. This may involve the reconstruction of the environment by seeking to eliminate the "non-ideal" elements in it, and may be exemplified in the panicky demand for the annihilation of the outsider (who is a criminal) for the sake of keeping the chains on the insider (who is a criminal). Every criminal is a threat to the whole social order since he reinstates with more or less success an acute conflict within the lives of all members of society. The success of the superego depends upon imposing certain ways of interpreting reality upon the self. When reality grossly refuses to conform to the "ideal," the energies of the self are divided, and an acute crisis supervenes. The superego undertakes to reinforce its side of the contradictory ego trends by punishing the ego, and by forcing the projection of this situation upon the outer world. Certain aspects of the outer world become "bad" because they are connected in private experience with the pangs inflicted by the taskmaster within, the conscience. A strong conscience may enforce this "distortion" of reality upon the self to such a degree that the self acts on quite fantastic assumptions about reality. These are most acutely manifested in such phenomena as confusion states, hallucinations, and delusions, all of which are forms of deformed reality. When reality becomes "ominous," violent efforts to change may appear futile, and safety is sought in physical flight, or in physical passivity and autistic preoccupation. Since our conceptions of reality are based upon little "first-hand" experience of the world about us, the superego usually has a rather easy time of it.

Political movements, then, derive their vitality from the displacement of private affects upon public objects, and political crises are complicated by the concurrent reactivation of specific primitive motives. Just how does it happen that the private and primitive drives find their way to political symbols? What are the circumstances which favor the selection of political targets of displacement?

Political life is carried on with symbols of the whole. Politics has to do with collective processes and public acts, and so intricate are these processes that with the best of intentions, it is extremely difficult to establish an unambiguous relationship between the symbols of the whole and the processes which they are presumed to designate. To the common run of mankind the reference points of political symbols are remote from daily experience, though they are rendered familiar through constant reiteration. This ambiguity of reference, combined with universality of use, renders the words which signify parties, classes, nations, institutions, policies, and modes of political participation readily available for the displacement of private affects. The manifest, rational differences of opinion become complicated by the play of private motives until the symbol is nothing but a focus for the cumulation of irrelevancies. Since the dialectic of politics is conducted in terms of the whole, the private motives are readily rationalized in terms of collective advantage.

Politics, moreover, is the sphere of conflict, and brings out all the vanity and venom, the narcissism and aggression, of the contending parties. It is becoming something of a commonplace that politics is the arena of the irrational. But a more accurate description would be that politics is the process by which the irrational bases of society are brought out into the open. So long as the moral order functions with spontaneous smoothness, there is no questioning the justification of prevailing values. But when the moral order has been devalued and called into question, a sincere and general effort may be made to find a reflectively defensible solution of the resulting conflict. Politics seems to be irrational because it is the only phase of collective life in which society tries to be rational. Its very existence shows that the moral order, with all its irrational and non-rational sanctions, is no longer accepted without a challenge. A political difference is the outcome of a moral crisis, and it terminates

in a new moral consensus. Politics is the transition between one unchallenged consensus and the next. It begins
in conflict and eventuates in a solution. But the solution
is not the "rationally best" solution, but the emotionally
satisfactory one. The rational and dialectical phases of
politics are subsidiary to the process of redefining an emotional consensus.

Although the dynamic of politics is to be sought in
the tension level of the individuals in society, it is to be
taken for granted that all individual tensions are not removed by political symbolization and exertion. When Y
hits a foreman in the jaw whom he imagines has insulted
him, Y is relieving his tensions. But if the act is construed by him as a personal affair with the foreman, the
act is not political. Political acts are joint acts; they depend upon emotional bonds.

Now people who act together get emotionally bound
together. This process of becoming emotionally bound is
dependent on no conscious process. Freud said that he
was made clearly aware of the emotional factor in human
relations by observing that those who work together extend their contact to dining and relaxing together. Those
with whom we work are endowed with rich meanings on
the basis of our past experience with human beings. Since
all of our motives are going concerns within the personality, our libido is more or less concentrated upon those
with whom we come in touch. This reinforces the perception of similarities, and supplies the dynamic for the
identification process. Even the negative identification is
a tribute to the extent to which the affective resources
of the personality become mobilized in human contact.

People who are emotionally bound together are not
yet involved in a political movement. Politics begins when

they achieve a symbolic definition of themselves in relation to demands upon the world. The pre-political phase of the labor movement as sketched by Nexo in his *Pelle the Conqueror* is an able characterization of what the facts may be. The workers had plenty of grievances against their employers, but individuals took it out in sporadic acts of violence, and in frequent debauchery. It was not until a new "set" of mind was achieved with the appearance of socialist symbols, and their adoption, that the tension found an outlet in political form. When J hits a foreman on the jaw because the foreman swore at him, J is not acting for the working classes; but after J becomes a socialist, his acts are symbolically significant of the expanded personality which he possesses. Acts cease to be merely private acts; they have become related to remote social objects. The conception of the self has new points of reference, and points of reference which interlock with those of others.

It is of the utmost importance to political science to examine in detail, not only the factors which contribute to the raising and lowering of the tension level, but the processes of symbolization. In regard to the former aspect of the problem, data will have to be taken from specialists of many kinds, but in regard to the latter problem, the student can come into ready contact with the raw material. The stock in trade of realistic politics is the analysis of the history of "pressure groups," ranging from such associations as the Fabian Society through political parties to conspirative organizations. What are the conditions under which the idea is itself invented, and what are the conditions of its propagation? That is to say: What are the laws of symbolization in political activity?

I wish to call attention to certain possibilities. Several social movements will be found which represent a desire on the part of an intimate circle to perpetuate their relationship at the expense of society. It is worth remembering that Loyola and the other young men who founded the Jesuits were in long friendly relationship before they hit upon their famous project. Not only that: they were anxious to remain in some sort of personal relation through life, and they invented many expedients before they hit on the final one. What we had here was a friendly group which desired to preserve their personal connections before they knew how they could actually do it. It is less true to say that institutions are the lengthened shadow of a great man than that they are the residue of a friendly few.

Other social movements will be found to have adopted their project from a lone thinker with whom they have no direct connection. The process here is that one member of the group, with whom the others are identified, is impressed by the scheme, and interprets and defends it to the others. He gets a hearing because of his emotional claim on the others, and he may whip the doubters and waverers into line by wheedling or by threatening to withdraw affection.

The formation of a radiating nucleus for an idea is especially common among adolescents, and among those who function best in single-sex groups. Thrasher has described gangs which had a mission in his book on *The Gang*, and the literature of youth study is full of instances of two's, three's and quartettes which have sworn undying fealty to one another, and to a project of social reform. When the idea is embraced later in life it not infrequently appears among those who have shown pronounced evi-

dence of emotional maladjustment. Much social and political life is a symptom of the delayed adolescence of
its propagators, which is, of course, no necessary criticism
of its content.

The psychology of personal, oratorical, and printed
persuasion by means of which support is won for particular
symbols has yet to be written. William I. Thomas long
ago commented on the quasi-sexual approach of the re-
vivalist to the audience. Some orators are of an intimate,
sympathetic, pleading type, and resemble the attempts
made by some males to overcome the shyness of the female. Other orators fit into the feared yet revered father-
pattern; others are clowns who amuse by releasing much
repressed material; others address the socially adjusted
and disciplined level of the personality. Thus the relationship between the speaker and the audience has its
powerful emotional aspects, which are not yet adequately
explored. There are some who excel in face-to-face relations, but who make a poor showing out on the platform.

The processes of symbolization can be studied with particular ease when widespread and disturbing changes occur in the life-situation of many members of society.
Famine, pestilence, unemployment, high living costs, and
a catalogue of other disturbances may simultaneously
produce adjustment problems for many people. One of
the first results is to release affects from their previous
objects, and to create a state of susceptibility to proposals.
All sorts of symbols are ready, or readily invented, to
refix the mobile affects. "Take it to the Lord in prayer,"
"Vote socialist," "Down with the Jews," "Restore pep
with pepsin," "Try your luck on the horses"—all sorts
of alternatives become available. The prescriptions are
tied up with diagnoses, and the diagnoses in turn imply
prescriptions. "A sinful world," "Wall Street," "a col-

lapse in the foreign market"—all sorts of diagnoses float about, steadily defining and redefining the situation for the individuals affected. Political symbols must compete with symbols from every sphere of life, and an interesting inquiry could be made into the relative polarizing power of political and other forms of social symbolism. Certainly the modern world expects to fire the health commissioner rather than burn a witch when the plague breaks out.

The competition among symbols to serve as foci of concentration for the aroused emotions of the community leads to the survival of a small number of master-symbols. The mobilization of the community for action demands economy in the terms in which objectives are put. The agitation for the control of the liquor traffic passed through many phases in America until finally legal prohibition became the chief dividing-line. To prohibit or not to prohibit grew into the overmastering dichotomy of public thought.

Symbolization thus necessitates dichotomization. The program of social action must be couched in "yes" and "no" form if decision is to be possible. The problem of he who would manipulate the concentration of affect about a particular symbol is to reinforce its competitive power by leading as many elements as possible in society to read their private meanings into it. This reinforcement and facilitation of the symbol involves the use of men of prestige in its advocacy, the assimilation of special economic and other group aims, and the invention of appeals to unconscious drives. Propaganda on behalf of a symbol can become a powerful factor in social development because of the flexibility in the displacement of emotion from one set of symbols to another. There is always a rather considerable reservoir of unrest and discontent in society, and there is nothing absolutely fixed and predestined about the particular symbol which will have attracting power.

The analysis of motives which are unconscious for most people, though widespread, gives the propagandist a clue to certain nearly universal forms of appeal. The moving pictures which have been produced by the communist government in Russia are often remarkable examples of the use of symbols which not only have their conscious affective dimension, but which mobilize deep unconscious impulses. In one film, for instance, it is the mother who suffers under tsarism and fans the flames of revolt. Analysis has disclosed the general, and presumably universal, meaning of the attachment to the land. The boy-child's wish for union with the mother, for all-embracing care and protection, undergoes some measure of sublimation in social life. Eder remarks that it finds expression in attachment to the earth, the land, the mother-country, home. The *Heimweh* of the Swiss, the pious Jew's desire for burial in Palestine, and a host of similar manifestations are instances of this emotional tie whose significance for state loyalty is large.

At first sight it might appear questionable that political science can ever profit from the disclosure of motives which are supposed to operate in the unconscious of every human being. If these motives are equally operative, how can they throw any light on differences in political behavior? And are we not able to point to conditions of a more localized and definite nature which suitably explain why the Republican party loses out when the farmer loses his crops? Or why there is revolution in 1918 and not in 1925?

The mere fact that motives are more or less universal does not mean that they are always activated with the same intensity. They may block one another, until some exciting condition disturbs the adjustment and releases stores of energy. Indeed, the exploration of unconscious motivation lays the basis for the understanding of the well-known disproportionality between responses and immediate stimuli, a disproportionality which has been the subject of much puzzled and satiric comment. Farmers do vote against the Republicans when the crops fail through adverse weather conditions, although reflection would tend to minimize the possibility that the party in power exercises much authority over the weather. Oversights in personal relations which seem very slight do actually give rise to huge affective reactions. The clue to the magnitude of this notorious disproportionality is to be found in the nature of the deeper (earlier) psychological structures of the individual. By the intensive analysis of representative people, it is possible to obtain clues to the nature of these "unseen forces," and to devise ways and means of dealing with them for the accomplishment of social purposes.

Modern democratic society is accustomed to the settlement of differences in discussion and in voting. This is a special form of politics, for differences may also be settled with a minimum of discussion and a maximum of coercion. In its modern manifestation, democracy and representative government have enthroned "government by discussion," that is, "government by public opinion." President Lowell some time ago pointed out that public opinion could only be said to exist where constitutional principles were agreed upon. Differences must be treated as defined within an area of agreement. Democratic and representative institutions presuppose the existence of the public which is made up of all those who follow affairs and expect to determine policy in discussion and by measures short of coercion. The public has a common focus of attention, a consensus on constitutional principles, and a zone of tolerance for conflicting demands respecting social policy.

When debate is admissible, some standards of right are tacitly admitted to be uncertain. The zone of the debatable is not fixed and immutable, but flexible and shifting. Questions rise and debate proceeds; and presently the resulting solution is no longer discussible. It has become sanctified by all the sentiments which buttress the moral order, and any challenge is met by the unanimous and spontaneous action of the community in its defense. In the presence of a challenge, the public may be dissolved into a crowd, by which is meant a group whose members are emotionally aroused and intolerant of dissent.

What light does the study of the genesis of personality throw on the factors which determine which symbols are debatable? What is the mechanism of the process by which the moral patterns are broken up, discussed, and eventually reincorporated in more or less modified form into the moral consensus of the community?

The growth of emotional bonds among individuals of diverse cultural and personal traits is the most powerful solvent of the moral order. A valuable treatise could be constructed on the theme, "Friendship versus Morality." It is well-known that governments are continually handicapped in the impersonal application of a rule by the play of personal loyalties. Robert E. Park has stressed the importance of curiosity in the field of interracial relations. In no small measure this is very primitive curiosity about the sexual structure and behavior of odd-looking folks. When personal ties are built up, exceptions are made in favor of the friend; what, indeed, is the constitution among friends?

The mechanism is clear by which issues once settled are presently non-debatable. Growing individuals incorporate the end result into their own personalities through the process of identification and introjection. Once a part of the superego of the rising generation, the moral consensus is complete. Where no. dissent is tolerated and dialectic is impossible, we are dealing with a superego phenomenon. Certain symbols are sacrosanct, and aspersions upon them produce the crowd mind and not the public.[8]

Even this brief sketch of political symbolization has shown ample grounds for concluding that political demands probably bear but a limited relevance to social needs. The political symbol becomes ladened with the residue of successive positive and negative identifications, and with the emotional charge of displaced private motives. This accumulation of irrelevancy usually signifies that tension exists in the lives of many people, and it may possess a diagnostic value to the objective investigator. The individual who is sorely divided against himself may

[8] The distinction between the crowd and the public is best developed in the writings of Robert E. Park. Freud undertook to explain the crowd on the theory that an emotional bond was forged by identification of the individual with a leader, and by a process of partial identification through the perception of this similar relationship to the leader. He set out from the observation that when people are interacting upon one another they behave differently than when they are alone. The loss of individuality represents a relinquishment of narcissistic gratification which can only come when libido is directed outward toward objects. Freud's theory applies strictly to a special case of crowd behavior only. Crowd states may also arise when interlocking partial identifications occur on the perception of a common threat. Crowd behavior often arises before anybody assumes a "leading" rôle, and rival leaders are "selected" by the crowd.

seek peace by unifying himself against an outsider. This is the well-known "peacefulness of being at war." But the permanent removal of the tensions of the personality may depend upon the reconstruction of the individual's view of the world, and not upon belligerent crusades to change the world.

The democratic state depends upon the technique of discussion to relieve the strains of adjustment to a changing world. If the analysis of the individual discloses the probable irrelevance of what the person demands to what he needs (i.e., to that which will produce a permanent relief of strain), serious doubt is cast upon the efficacy of the technique of discussion as a means of handling social problems.

The premise of democracy is that each man is the best judge of his own interest, and that all whose interests are affected should be consulted in the determination of policy. Thus the procedure of a democratic society is to clear the way to the presentation of various demands by interested parties, leaving the coast clear for bargain and compromise, or for creative invention and integration. The findings of personality research show that the individual is a poor judge of his own interest. The individual who chooses a political policy as a symbol of his wants is usually trying to relieve his own disorders by irrelevant palliatives. An examination of the total state of the person will frequently show that his theory of his own interests is far removed from the course of procedure which will give him a happy and well-adjusted life. Human behavior toward remote social objects, familiarity with which is beyond the personal experience of but a few, is especially likely to be a symptomatic rather than a healthy and reflective adjustment.

In a sense politics proceeds by the creation of fictitious values. The person who is solicited to testify to his own interest is stimulated by the problem put to him to commit himself. The terms in which he couches his own interest vary according to a multitude of factors, but whatever the conditioning influences may be, the resulting theory of his interest becomes invested with his own narcissism. The political symbol is presumably an instrumental makeshift toward the advancement of the other values of the personality; but it very quickly ceases to be an instrumental value, and becomes a terminal value, no longer the servant but the coequal, or indeed the master. Thus the human animal distinguishes himself by his infinite capacity for making ends of his means.

It should not be hastily assumed that because a particular set of controversies passes out of the public mind that the implied problems were solved in any fundamental sense. Quite often the solution is a magical solution which changes nothing in the conditions affecting the tension level of the community, and which merely permits the community to distract its attention to another set of equally irrelevant symbols. The number of statutes which pass the legislature, or the number of decrees which are handed down by the executive, but which change nothing in the permanent practices of society, is a rough index of the rôle of magic in politics.

In some measure, of course, discontent is relieved in the very process of agitating, discussing, and legislating about social changes which in the end are not substantially affected. Political symbolization has its catharsis function, and consumes the energies which are released by the maladaptations of individuals to one another.

But discussion often leads to modifications in social

practice which complicate social problems. About all that can be said for various punitive measures resorted to by the community is that they have presently broken down and ceased to continue the damage which they began to inflict on society.

Generalizing broadly, political methods have involved the manipulation of symbols, goods, and violence, as in propaganda, bribery, and assassination. It is common to act on the assumption that they are to be applied in the settlement of conflicting demands, and not in the obviation of conflict. In so far as they rest upon a philosophy, they identify the problem of politics with the problem of coping with differences which are sharply drawn.

The identification of the field of politics with the field of battle, whether the theater be the frontier or the forum, has produced an unfortunate warp in the minds of those who manage affairs, or those who simply think about the management of affairs. The contribution of politics has been thought to be in the elaboration of the methods by which conflicts are resolved. This has produced a vast diversion of energy toward the study of the formal etiquette of government. In some vague way, the problem of politics is the advancement of the good life, but this is at once assumed to depend upon the modification of the mechanisms of government. Democratic theorists in particular have hastily assumed that social harmony depends upon discussion, and that discussion depends upon the formal consultation of all those affected by social policies.

The time has come to abandon the assumption that the problem of politics is the problem of promoting discussion among all the interests concerned in a given problem. Discussion frequently complicates social difficulties, for

the discussion by far-flung interests arouses a psychology
of conflict which produces obstructive, fictitious, and irrelevant values. (The problem of politics is less to solve
conflicts than to prevent them; less to serve as a safety
valve for social protest than to apply social energy to the
abolition of recurrent sources of strain in society.

This redefinition of the problem of politics may be
called the idea of preventive politics. The politics of
prevention draws attention squarely to the central problem
of reducing the level of strain and maladaptation in society. In some measure it will proceed by encouraging
discussion among all those who are affected by social
policy, but this will be no iron-clad rule. In some measure it will proceed by improving the machinery of set-
tling disputes, but this will be subordinated to a comprehensive program, and no longer treated as an especially
desirable mode of handling the situation.

The recognition that people are poor judges of their
own interest is often supposed to lead to the conclusion
that a dictator is essential. But no student of individual
psychology can fail to share the conviction of Kempf
that "Society is *not* safe . . . . when it is forced to
follow the dictations of one individual, of one autonomic
apparatus, no matter how splendidly and altruistically it
may be conditioned." Our thinking has too long been misled by the threadbare terminology of democracy versus
dictatorship, of democracy versus aristocracy. Our problem is to be ruled by the truth about the conditions of harmonious human relations, and the discovery of the truth is
an object of specialized research; it is no monopoly of people as people, or of the ruler as ruler. As our devices
of accurate ascertainment are invented and spread, they

are explained and applied by many individuals inside the social order. Knowledge of this kind is a slow and laborious accumulation.

The politics of prevention does not depend upon a series of changes in the organization of government. It depends upon a reorientation in the minds of those who think about society around the central problems: What are the principal factors which modify the tension level of the community? What is the specific relevance of a proposed line of action to the temporary and permanent modification of the tension level?

The politics of prevention will insist upon a rigorous audit of the human consequences of prevailing political practices. (How does politics affect politicians? One way to consider the human value of social action is to see what that form of social action does to the actors. When a judge has been on the bench thirty years, what manner of man has he become? When an agitator has been agitating for thirty years, what has happened to him? How do different kinds of political administrators compare with doctors, musicians, and scientists? Such a set of inquiries would presuppose that we were able to ascertain the traits with which the various individuals began to practice their rôle in society. Were we able to show what certain lines of human endeavor did to the same reactive type, we would lay the foundation for a profound change in society's esteem for various occupations.

Any audit of the human significance of politics would have to press far beyond the narrow circle of professional politicians. Crises like wars, revolutions, and elections enter the lives of people in far-reaching ways. The effect of crises on mental attitude is an important and uncertain field. Thus it is reported that during the rebellion of

1745–46 in Scotland there was little hysteria (in the technical pathological sense). The same was true of the French
Revolution and of the Irish Rebellion. Rush reported
in his book *On the Influence of the American Revolution
on the Human Body* that many hysterical women were
"restored to perfect health by the events of the time."
Havelock Ellis, who cites these instances, comments that
"in such cases the emotional tension is given an opportunity for explosion in new and impersonal channels, and
the chain of morbid personal emotions is broken."[9]
The physical consequences of political symbolism may
be made the topic of investigation from this point of view:

> When the affect can not acquire what it needs, uncomfortable
> tensions or anxiety (fear) are felt, and the use of the symbol or
> fetish, relieving this anxiety, has a marked physiological value in
> that it prevents the adrenal, thyroid, circulatory, hepatic and
> pulmonic compensatory strivings from becoming excessive.[10]

Political programs will continually demand reconsider-
ation in the light of the factors which current research discloses as bearing upon the tension level. Franz Alexander
recently drew attention to the strains produced in modern
civilization by the growing sphere of purposive action.
He summed up the facts in the process of civilized development in the following way: "Human expressions of instinct
are subject to a continual tendency to rationalization, that
is, they develop more and more from playful, unco-
ordinated, purely pleasure efforts into purposive actions."
The "discomfort of civilization" of which Freud recently
wrote in the *Unbehagen der Kultur* is characteristic of the
rationalized cultures with which we are acquainted. Life
is poor in libidinal gratifications of the primitive kind

[9] *Studies in the Psychology of Sex*, I, 231.
[10] Kempf, *Psychopathology*, p. 704.

which the peasant, who is in close touch with elementary
things, is in a position to enjoy.[11] Modern life furnishes
irrational outlets in the moving picture and in sensational
crime news. But it may be that other means of relieving
the strain of modern living can be invented which will have
fewer drawbacks.

Preventive politics will search for the definite assessment, then, of cultural patterns in terms of their human
consequences. Some of these human results will be deplored as "pathological," while others will be welcomed
as "healthy." One complicating factor is that valuable
contributions to culture are often made by men who are
in other respects pathological. Many pathological persons
are constrained by their personal difficulties to displace
more or less successfully upon remote problems, and to
achieve valuable contributions to knowledge and social
policy.[12] Of course the notion of the pathological is itself
full of ambiguities. The individual who is subject to
epileptic seizures may be considered in one culture not
a subnormal and diseased person, but a supernormal person. Indeed, it may be said that society depends upon
a certain amount of pathology, in the sense that society
does not encourage the free criticism of social life, but
establishes taboos upon reflective thinking about its own
presuppositions. If the individual is pathological to the
extent that he is unable to contemplate any fact with
equanimity, and to elaborate impulse through the processes of thought, it is obvious that society does much to
nurture disease. This leads to the apparent paradox that
successful social adjustment consists in contracting the

[11] Franz Alexander, "Mental Hygiene and Criminology," *First International Congress on Mental Hygiene.*

[12] For an appreciation of the rôle of the pathological person in society
see Wilhelm Lange-Eichbaum, *Genie-Irrsinn, und Ruhm,* and Karl Birnbaum, *Grundzüge der Kulturpsychopathologie.*

current diseases. If "health" merely means a statistical report upon the "average," the scrutiny of the individual ceases to carry much meaning for the modification of social patterns. But if "health" means something more than "average," the intensive study of individuals gives us a vantage ground for the revaluation of the human consequences of cultural patterns, and the criticism of these patterns.[13]

If the politics of prevention spreads in society, a different type of education will become necessary for those who administer society or think about it. This education will start from the proposition that it takes longer to train a good social scientist than it takes to train a good physical scientist.[14] The social administrator and social scientist must be brought into direct contact with his material in its most varied manifestations. He must mix with rich and poor, with savage and civilized, with sick and well, with old and young. His contacts must be primary and not exclusively secondary. He must have an opportunity for prolonged self-scrutiny by the best-developed methods of personality study, and he must laboriously achieve a capacity to deal objectively with himself and with all others in human society.

This complicated experience is necessary since our scale of values is less the outcome of our dialectical than of our other experiences in life. Values change more by the unconscious redefinition of meaning than by rational analysis. Every contact and every procedure which discloses new facts has its repercussions upon the matrix of partially

[13] Something like this is no doubt the thought in Trigant Burrow's very obscure book on *The Social Basis of Consciousness*.

[14] This point was forcibly made by Beardsley Ruml in his speech at the dedication of the Social Science Research Building at the University of Chicago. See *The New Social Science*, edited by Leonard D. White, pp. 99–111.

verbalized experience, which is the seeding ground of conscious ideas.

One peculiarity of the problem of the social scientist is that he must establish personal contact with his material. The physical scientist who works in a laboratory spends more time adjusting his machinery than in making his observations, and the social scientist who works in the field must spend more time establishing contacts than in noting and reporting observations. What the instrumentation technique is to the physicist, the cultivation of favorable human points of vantage is for most social scientists. This means that the student of society, as well as the manager of social relations, must acquire the technique of social intercourse in unusual degree, unless he is to suffer from serious handicaps, and his training must be directed with this in mind.

The experience of the administrator-investigator must include some definite familiarity with all the elements which bear importantly upon the traits and interests of the individual. This means that he must have the most relevant material brought to his attention from the fields of psychology, psychopathology, physiology, medicine, and social science. Since our institutions of higher learning are poorly organized at the present time to handle this program, thorough curricular reconstructions will be indispensable.[15]

What has been said in this chapter may be passed in brief review. Political movements derive their vitality from the displacement of private affects upon public objects. Political crises are complicated by the concurrent reactivation of specific primitive motives which were or-

[15] I have suggested that those who write human biography should be included among those who require this comprehensive training. See "The Scientific Study of Human Biography," *Scientific Monthly*, January, 1930.

ganized in the early experience of the individuals concerned. Political symbols are particularly adapted to serve as targets for displaced affect because of their ambiguity of reference, in relation to individual experience, and because of their general circulation. Although the dynamic of politics is the tension level of individuals, all tension does not produce political acts. Nor do all emotional bonds lead to political action. Political acts depend upon the symbolization of the discontent of the individual in terms of a more inclusive self which champions a set of demands for social action.

Political demands are of limited relevance to the changes which will produce permanent reductions in the tension level of society. The political methods of coercion, exhortation, and discussion assume that the rôle of politics is to solve conflicts when they have happened. The ideal of a politics of prevention is to obviate conflict by the definite reduction of the tension level of society by effective methods, of which discussion will be but one. The preventive point of view insists upon a continuing audit of the human consequences of social acts, and especially of political acts. The achievement of the ideal of preventive politics depends less upon changes in social organization than upon improving the methods and the education of social administrators and social scientists.

The preventive politics of the future will be intimately allied to general medicine, psychopathology, physiological psychology, and related disciplines. Its practitioners will gradually win respect in society among puzzled people who feel their responsibilities and who respect objective findings. A comprehensive functional conception of political life will state problems of investigation, and keep receptive the minds of those who reflect at length upon the state.

CHAPTER XI[1]
THE PROLONGED INTERVIEW AND ITS OBJECTIFICATION

The empirical material assembled in this book has appeared in the course of prolonged interviews with individuals under unusually intimate conditions. This method of the prolonged interview has now had a history of some thirty years in the form devised by Freud, but so far there are very few efforts to objectify the events which transpire there. Otto Rank has written a series of studies of the "interview situation" which is the most important effort so far made to characterize the distinctive features of the method. But the empirical material which is so far reported does not rest upon the verbatim recording of what happens, except in a few specimen instances of highly pathological cases, and attempts are only now being made to record some of the principal physiological changes in the subject.

It will be remembered that Freud learned to predict the future course of reminiscence by watching word slips, random movements, and many other acts which were formerly dismissed as chance occurrences. He also found that he could abbreviate the laborious efforts of the patient to recall the traumatic (the original) episode by proposing various interpretations. It is at this point that the cautious physician and psychologist have picked serious quarrels with psychoanalytical findings. They allege

[1] Modified and expanded from "The Psychoanalytic Interview as a Method of Research on Personalities," in *The Child's Emotions*, pp. 136–59.

that the patient produces the kind of material which the analyst suggests is to be brought forth, and that the whole process is one of putting a rabbit in the hat which you triumphantly extricate later on. They have seized upon the schisms in the analytical fold, and declare that you eventually dream about anima figures if you are analyzed by Jung, that you relive birth traumas if you are analyzed by Rank, and that you welter in a galaxy of anal, oral, and urethral symbols if you are deeply analyzed by Freud. You talk about inferiority feeling if you work with Adler, and about castrative anxiety if you work with Freud.

One might suppose that after thirty years of labor there would be in existence a body of documents which could be consulted by a group of competent specialists who were trying to reconcile their differences and doubts about what actually goes on in the analytical interview.[2] At the present time the interview situation is poorly reflected in the notes taken by the analyst at the expiration of each period (if and when he takes them). Nobody knows what processes distort the reporting practices of different listeners, and nobody knows the value of the published scraps. Since one of the avowed purposes of therapeutic analyses is to bring the person to stand on his own feet and to stop leaning on others, or upon symptom indulgences, personal relations are usually broken off at the end of the interview. This obviously impedes the possibility of following up the subsequent history of the personality, and of ascertaining the stability of the supposed therapeutic results. The case-history documents available

[2] See Harold D. Lasswell, "The Problem of Adequate Personality Records: A Proposal," *American Journal of Psychiatry*, May 1929. Also Appendix B of *The Proceedings of the First Colloquium on Personality Investigation*.

in good institutions have the advantage of representing the combined product of several people who are in touch with the subject, and who may be supposed to operate as a check upon one another. But these documents are usually short, and betray the psychopathological slant of the ones chiefly responsible. And these documents are typically incomplete in reporting the whole personality of the subject on account of the clinician's interest in the more circumscribed disease phenomena displayed.

When John Brown reports an episode in which he was told that his nose would be cut off if he didn't quit handling himself, how do we know what importance to assign to the alleged reminiscence? Are we to accept this as a historical statement? Are we to construe it as a fabrication which, however, shows what he wanted to have happen, or supposed would happen, if he disobeyed orders? Are we to interpret it as a sign of his fear of the interviewer, couched in the language of the past, because this mode of exercising the imagination has been trained into him? Are we to interpret this as a sign of his hatred of the interviewer, on the theory that a self-punishing fantasy is a defense of the conscience against a murderous impulse of the unadjusted portion of the self? Are we to accept it as an effort to win the approval of the interviewer by reporting the kinds of things which he has learned to suppose the interviewer wants to hear, a supposition which is based upon a private study of psychoanalytical literature? Are we to accept it as an "original trauma" and to expect an immediate or eventual decrease in the neurotic anxiety which the individual shows? Are we to look upon it as a screen reminiscence for a genuinely traumatic episode in which the threat was made, not against his nose, but against his penis? Or is it a screen for a prohibited impulse which was once activated, and which seized upon a past episode and gave it the significance of a threat?

These are a few of the specific questions which can be raised about the proffered material, and the scientific problem is to devise more convincing demonstrations of the available theories, or more conclusive refutations, than we now have. What are some of the criteria of a "traumatic episode"? If the reminiscence is accompanied by much affect (excitement), there is a presumption of its authenticity. And how is affect measured? We depend at the present time upon the observer's judgment of the variations in the voice, and shifts in posture, or the twitches and jerks of the body. This can be augmented under experimental conditions by taking a continuous record of variations in blood pressure, respiration, galvanic reflex, etc.—all of which offer some indication of excitement.[3] We are thus able to improve our assessment of the possible significance of the reports, speculations, and general fantasies of the subject. It may be that in due course we shall be able to differentiate on a physical basis between "suppressions" and "repressions," and that we shall be able to follow through the transformations from beginning to end of the interviewing process.

Our judgment of the "traumatic episode" is also influenced by the subject's certainty. If the subject reports that he believes what he remembers, this has some value in raising a presumption. This is especially true if the subject has fought against the idea, but it has spontaneously continued to appear and plague his associations. But a re-

[3] We are now engaged upon studies of this kind at the Personality Laboratory in the Social Science Research Building at the University of Chicago. Harry Stack Sullivan is conducting a series of researches on expression changes, with particular reference to schizophrenia, which are of the greatest importance.

ported sense of certainty is flimsy stuff, unless this certainty survives for some time. We know that individuals try to escape from anxiety feelings by a flight into explanations, and that they are ready to volunteer or to accept all kinds of interpretations of their behavior rather than to continue to endure anxiety. This is the basis for the credulity of the neurotic, and explains why everything from mysterious "glandular unbalances" to "astral perturbations" are accepted from time to time as completely adequate explanations of personal troubles. So the subject's reported certainty must survive even disparaging suggestions and prolonged self-scrutiny, and become emancipated from affect, if it is to be taken very literally.

Another criterion is the consistency of the reported episode with all the other relevant facts. There must be something wrong about the report that K was brutally punished by his father at a time which was some years after the parent's death.[4]

The obstacles which lie in the path of a research program which calls for objective records of as much as possible of what transpires in the interview situation are not to be minimized. The bulk of a verbatim report of an hour's conversation per day over several months is almost overwhelming. But historians are accustomed to plow through whole libraries of pages about Napoleon or Bismarck, and from the standpoint of a comprehensive theory of personality development any personality is almost as good as any other, although high elaboration and distinguished achievement are advantages.

There are some points in favor of applying this technique of personality study to people who are normal, at least in the sense that they are suspected of normality by

[4] The topic of reliable criteria will be dealt with in detail in the reports upon experiments in progress.

themselves and others. There is a moral to be learned from some of Freud's early mistakes when he assigned critical significance to certain childhood experiences which later investigation showed were very common. The clinical caricature is invaluable for the high relief in which certain tendencies of the normal are revealed. Indeed, "normality" is more difficult to understand than disease, from one point of view, since it involves a complicated integration of many tendencies, a flexible capacity to snap from one mood, preoccupation, and overt activity to another, as the changing demands of reality require. Normality is complexity and integration, and it ought to be approached as directly as possible as a control on the pathological.

The main advantage which the normal subject hopes to glean from the analytical interview is a judgment of the importance of this, in comparison with other, psychological methods. Records being as they are today, only one who has been through the mill can talk with much assurance about what happens, and if he has a critical mind, he isn't too sure then. The analytical interview is a discipline in self-scrutiny. The subject learns to exploit a new method of using the mind, which he tries to cultivate and to correlate with the logical methods to which he is partly accustomed in ordinary adult life. The new technique of using the mind is the free-fantasy technique, whose chief function is to produce new material for logical consideration.

The interview necessitates the reactivation of the individual's struggle with his antisocial impulses. This happens be the subject sick or well, for every individual possesses more or less active and powerful antisocial drives. Every personality displays some pathology in the form of remainders of the Oedipus phase of growth. The socially adjusted portion of the personality takes up the battle again against the unsublimated drives, and a considerable amount of neurotic anxiety is generated in the process. The problem is to encourage the subject to face these unadjusted remnants frankly, to bring them to the full focus of waking consciousness, and to discharge their bound energy. This comes to pass in the roundabout way of recapturing the original episodes in which the neurotic solution was invented. The work of reminiscence is the preliminary to liberation and understanding.

The interview substitutes the talking-out for the acting-out of personality drives. One learns to recover the critical points in one's past history by watching the present for clues to the full meaning of the present situation, and this includes the inspection of reminiscences. A reminiscence is always relevant to a present situation, and serves the double rôle of annotating the present and reporting the past. The interview experience is long and arduous, and the subject learns very slowly to deal with himself as an object in a world of objects, and to free his judgment more and more from the distorting effects of primitive psychological structures.

The analytical situation is so arranged as to facilitate this process of self-inspection. The provocations to act out rather than think out are reduced by simplifying the sensory present. The subject lies in a relaxed position, and is better able to observe those stiffenings of the body, those variations in respiration, those oscillations of visceral tension, those impulses to scratch and finger which escape ordinary attention, but which are indicative of the meanings put in the current situation. The sensory environment remains substantially constant, and the interviewer handles the situation on a rather fixed routine. The subject is temporarily encysted from the demands of professional and conventional tasks, but the interviewer is present to prevent the individual from dissipating his energy in musings which are quickly forgotten. The interviewer is a prod to associate freely, and a spur to the critical consideration of the material supplied by the freely moving fancy. The necessity for verbalization brings the acts of fantasy into clearer focus than usual, which is a necessary preliminary to moments of sustained logical reflection. Since the interviewer permits the subject to disregard the usual amenities of society, and to let his fantasies fly for the sake of finding where they land, regressive responses are permitted to appear. That is, the individual is not required to adjust to a conventional world of adult reality, but is permitted to reactivate earlier forms of dealing with the world. In the world of adult reality, the multiple tendencies of the individual are canalized into conventionally acceptable forms, and the most maladapted drives may display themselves in unobtrusive variations on the pattern. When conventional reality is no longer present, and the individual is encouraged to watch his partly forming responses, rather than to co-ordinate, condense, ignore, or suppress them, these tendencies spread forth diffusely in imagination and reminiscence. When this process continues far enough, the individual achieves a high degree of insight into the genetic development of his current preoccupations and traits.

Since the analytical process is a period of strain for the subject, it may be wondered why it is bearable. Fortunately for the investigator, there are many advantages to the participant which sustain and fortify his conscious purpose to persevere until understanding has been substantially deepened. The analyst treats every manifestation of the personality, no matter how trivial, with respectful interest. This is exaggerated unconsciously by the subject, who greatly overestimates the personal affection which the interviewer has for him. Some of the energy of the personality is always free to begin new object attachments, and this energy is concentrated upon the interviewer. The subject is permitted to talk at length about himself, and when the interviewer listens attentively and patiently, the subject identifies himself with the listener on the basis of a common attitude of interest in a beloved object. The interviewer's ascendancy in technical knowledge (his authority) resembles the authority of the adults who were once supposed to possess unlimited knowledge. The day-by-day solicitude tends to reinstate the emotions of the early family situation in which the child could play irresponsibly, under the watchful, responsible care of the adult. The subject relaxes the effort to keep baudy, disloyal, mean, and revengeful thoughts from welling into this mind. The frank expression of these thoughts in ordinary social life would bring down punishment upon his head, or mark him out as a victim of mental disorder. The subject is enabled to welter in unsocial or antisocial ravings and imaginings, and the process of developing these symptoms in the presence of another person becomes an absorbing part of his daily, weekly, and monthly existence. The subject intensifies his warm emotional interest in the one who exempts him from society's code of reticence. This is a mark of the analyst's tremendous power, and also of the analyst's special interest in the subject. The free-fantasy procedure even exempts the individual from abiding by the ordinary forms of logic and grammar. He is also able to enjoy the pleasure of impressing someone else with the brilliance of his language. From time to time, new insight comes into old habits and worries, and the zest of intellectual comprehension is added to the other pleasures.

At first sight the teaching or research interview might seem to sacrifice the most powerful motive upon which the interviewing procedure has relied, namely, that of securing relief from disturbing symptoms. The individual who is suffering from some crude pathological disturbance, like a functional gastro-intestinal disorder, psychological impotence, obsessive ideas and compulsions, comes to the interviewer as a weak person seeking aid of a stronger. If he has been shuttled from one internist to another perhaps receiving derisive looks and contemptuous preachments, the objective interest with which the psychotherapist treats his symptoms produces a keen conscious and unconscious gratification. Even the symptoms are beloved parts of the self, and like the ugly ducklings, they are sometimes treated with special affection (Ferenczi). The hope of being relieved of the annoying symptoms, which is consciously present in many pathological cases, is supported on the unconscious level by an old infantile attitude which expects the interviewer to work miracles. Even some of the antisocial impulses of the personality may welcome the therapeutic situation. These antisocial tendencies are themselves not entirely gratified in the symptoms, for the nature of a symptom is a compromise between these antisocial tendencies and the socialized impulses of the self. Nunberg has pointed out that the unsocialized portions of the personality may support the misguided hope that the outcome of therapy will be the boundless and unlimited gratification of their demands. There is also evidence of the existence of a compulsion to confess (Reik) to antisocial tendencies, which are rejected by the socialized self, and thus to gratify an unconscious need of punishment.

Now the sense of being sick and the desire to get well are not entirely absent from any normal person. No one is entirely free from remnants of his adjustive problems, and no one is entirely satisfied with himself. At the beginning of the interview, this motive may appear in consciousness as nothing more substantial than the innocuous belief that any increase in self-knowledge will enable one to deal even more satisfactorily with personal problems as they arise.

Among the other motives which play into the analytical situation, and enable the subject to go through with it, may be mentioned a few very primitive ones. Life has meant the blocking of many impulses by authorities whose power cannot be successfully defied on the spot. Hatreds can only express themselves under these conditions with some prospects of success when they seek to overcome the superior by trying to take his power into one's own personality by copying him. That is to say, the individual seeks to identify himself with the one who possesses superior knowledge in the analytical situation, and by becoming like him, to secure independence, and thus to annihilate him as an intimidating and obstructive external object. There may be a desire to secure a weapon by means of which other people may be eviscerated, and deprived of their power to outstrip the individual. On the conscious level, these motives are partly visible in excessive aspirations for self-mastery and control. This taking-in and biting-off of the analyst's power is also rooted in some of the earliest reaction patterns which the infant displays toward objects. The sheer pleasure of talking, and giving and withholding information is also present.

As the subject withdraws attention from the original symptoms or motives, concentrates on the game of dilating upon the past, and indulges in prohibited delights, the analytical situation becomes an orgy of illicit pleasure.

Emotions are released from old channels and find new objects of crystallization, especially in the person of the analyst. The interviewer who permits this "transference" is now in a position to aid the subject in coming to grips with the underlying unsocialized impulses of the personality. The behavior of the subject has by this time given a host of clues to the history of his emotional growth. The analyst continues to stimulate the individual to scrutinize his associations, to state honestly the wayward wishes flit across his mind, or which lurk half-seen in the marginal recesses of attention. Back and forth, bit by bit, there is reconstructed the subjective history of a life. To put it metaphorically, old sores run anew, smoldering embers of jealousy and lust flame once more, and ancient wounds yawn again. Reminiscence reguilds the faded tapestries of the past, and restores to the full glare of consciousness the cobwebs of the mind which house the spiders of malevolence and lechery. Primitive meanings, once appropriate to a situation, and later projected unintentionally into the adult world, are recovered and criticized in the light of their appropriateness to society. Regressive reliving, which is powerfully supported by narcissism and the repetitive compulsion, is observed and overcome.

It should not be supposed that the secrets of the mind are exposed for the asking. The method of repression is a primitive means by which the feeble, nascent self seeks protection from impulses which, if tolerated, if not shut out with unreflecting violence, would overrun it (Alexander). When the self becomes strong and stable, primitive impulses can be permitted to develop farther in consciousness without imminent danger that they will pass over into action by controlling the motor apparatus. Now the critical, reflecting, deciding self must not be crippled by an unduly strong conscience. The structure which we know as the conscience is begun in early childhood, and is formed by the incorporation into the self of the orders and commands which are administered by authority. When the self is weak, as during these formative years, the conscience relies on crude methods to protect its hard-won ascendancy over the antisocial drives in the personality. It visits penalties of anxiety upon the self whenever there are any signs of leniency toward these impulses. The conscience keeps its summary, sadistic quality long after, and neurotics are properly said to suffer from an excess of conscience. Blind denial of the existence of fundamental trends in the personality must be supplanted, and the *obiter dicta* of the conscience subjected to the criticism of the more mature and experienced self. An obstacle to this procedure is furnished by those energies of the personality which are specialized in resisting the antisocial impulses which have been repressed and denied direct and undisguised access to consciousness. Any lowering of resistance subjects the individual to acute anxiety, as the conflict between the socialized and the unsocialized drives is reinstated. All sorts of subterfuges are hit upon to obviate the necessity for enduring this anxiety and bringing the hidden into consciousness, where it can lose its charge. The overcoming of this resistance to taking up the battle again is a major process in the prolonged analysis.

The recapitulation of the drives which the individual has experienced throughout his life is the process which lends unique value to the psychoanalytic interview record. The literature of psychoanalysis is full of sample fantasies which are assigned to places in the hypothetical sequence of personality growth. Over twenty years ago Freud wrote some preliminary remarks on character types,

especially stressing the rôle of certain excretory pleasures in the development of some psychological structures.
The sucking, biting and anal retention interests of the
infant and young child have been the subject of theoretical
treatment by several analysts, among whom Abraham is
the most important. Ferenczi has sketched a comprehensive theory of the rise of genital interests on the part of
the child, and this has been amplified in various directions
by Reich. The differences between male and female development have been sketched by Sachs, Deutsch, and
Horney.

It is not within the necessary limits of this discussion to
go farther into the nature of the hypotheses which have
been proposed by these various investigators. We will
be able to formulate them more precisely when we have
succeeded in objectifying what happens in the course of the
interview, and this is to be achieved along the lines previously sketched. Some day we can state hypotheses more
definitely which can be taken and tested by non-analytical
methods. Some of these conceptions can be confirmed or
eliminated by the direct observation of children of all age
groups. It is quite possible, however, paradoxical though
it may sound, that the best way to study some phases of
infancy and childhood will be to study the adult. There
is some reason to believe that the superior expressive
power of the adult, whether in words or in drawing, may
render explicit many states which are beyond the scope
of one who merely looks at movements. If we find that
the subjective reconstructions during the adult analysis
check closely with the results secured by modified analytical and behavioristic procedures applied directly to older
children, we will have more confidence in the material
which purports to relate to very early experience. We may

also test out as far as possible the "historicity" of the reminiscences produced at different phases of the analysis. It should be said in passing that the analysis of children requires important revisions in the externals of the technique, as Anna Freud has shown.

I want to stop at this point to comment upon the significance of the fact there should be such a thing as the psychoanalytic method of dealing with the genesis of personality. How does it happen that at the end of the nineteenth century there appeared in Western European civilization this remarkably intricate procedure? Why do we regard it as worth while to spend months or even years in constant introspection?

Viewed in the large, I suppose this is the most spectacular sign of the value crisis in our civilization. Here is an effort to stimulate the individual to the reconstruction of values, not on the basis of imposed authority, but through prolonged scrutiny of the self as a process. The processes of the human personality are subjected to the same patient, arduous, and minute inspection which has proved so successful when applied to the objects of the physical world by the naturalist, astronomer, and microscopic specialist. The end result of a long and successful analysis is an individual who is able to interpret his relation to the world in terms of a few master-symbols. These symbols take on meaning because they have been acquired in the course of a long apprenticeship under the exacting eye of another. These symbols define for the individual in comprehensive terms his relation to unfolding reality. They permit in favorable instances added smoothness of adjustment, and offer a means of relief from disproportionate feelings of futility, despondency, persecution, and omniscience.

The appearance of a system of communicable master-symbols for the definition of one's relation to the universe is anything but a novel phenomenon in the culture history of mankind. At one time a leading question was, "What is God's will for me?" The belief was that this could be made manifest after the reading of Holy Writ, reverent supplication, and sudden revelation. Our Western civilization has sapped at the pillars of this structure of thinking. We are committed to the persistent querying of the world of change, and the problem is always "*How* does it change?" How do the routines of the seeable, smellable, touchable, audible, tasteable universe actually work? In what characteristic order do the subjective events of the mind follow one another? In what order do subjective and objective events occur? And no matter how many intermediate links in the sequence have been named there always remain new intermediate and new all-embracing frames of reference to be identified and placed in orderly relationship.

Values are sought to be defined, not on the authority of another, but in the act of scrutinizing processes. We place enormous value upon the quest for sequences, and discover our new values in the act of broadening or deepening our understanding of change. If you tell a sophisticated carrier of Western culture that God reveals his wisdom after the reading of a printed passage, he will be less impressed by what is put in than by what is left out of the account. What relation is there between what is read and what is decided? Can you set up controlled repetitions for the sake of testing the predictive value of these generalizations? Are there other words which can be read but which will result in the same decisions when the reader has the same pecuniary stake in acting a certain way? And so on and on.

It is worth noticing that the symbols supplied by analysis are not "ought" words but "process" words. You are not told to die for your country; you are told to face all the values which you can find in the situation. This does not, however, eliminate the "arbitrary" character of decisions actually reached. The decision comes with all the shock of revelation, of inevitability, of unexpectedness; the individual may only control decisions by rehearsing the pertinent values until he finds himself in the clutches of a judgment. This willingness to accept uncertainty, to scrutinize intermediate terms and pertinent values, is an outcome of the analytical discipline.

Such a procedure grew up in a civilization whose values have been in confusion since the medieval cosmology broke down. President Masaryk, serious thinker and scholarly writer, began his sociological work with a study of suicide, which he found to be a rough index of the value strains in culture. When emotional bonds are forged with exponents of life-patterns of different design, the mental stage is set for both creative originality and destructive disintegration. The individual must assume the load of working out his own scheme of values, and many are disorganized in the attempt.

The validation of the prolonged interview as a contributor to our dependable knowledge about life depends upon objectifying its processes; the achievement of its implications for the reconstruction of the hierarchy of individual values is an impressionistic and often turbulent experience.[5]

[5] The best technical discussions of the nature of the analytical situation are in the writings of Freud, Rank, Ferenczi, Nunberg, and Alexander.

CHAPTER XII[1]

THE PERSONALITY SYSTEM AND ITS SUBSTITUTIVE REACTIONS

So far in this book human behavior has been interpreted in terms of various "tendencies" which such behavior is supposed to manifest. Suppose we call into question this type of psychological explanation. What, after all, is a "tendency"? It postulates a relationship between events, one of which is taken as the terminal situation, and others of which are treated as relative approximations to the type situation. Terms like "wishes," "desires," "instincts," "impulses," "drives," and "motives" are all employed in this sense.

For purposes of analysis, tendency interpretations may be divided into five main classes, depending on the nature of the relationship which is postulated between the approximate and the terminal situation. First, personality events may be interpreted as approximations toward, or realizations of, goals (terminals) which are communicated by the subject. We may believe a man who tells us that he is running for a train when we see him dashing along the street toward the railway station.

Second, personality events may be interpreted as degrees of approximation to subsequent events which are actually observed. Mr. C's solicitude for the health and welfare of the needy ones of the district may be construed in the light of his subsequent campaign for Congress.

[1] Expanded from an article with the same title which appeared in the *Journal of Abnormal and Social Psychology*, January, 1930.

Third, personality events may be treated as degrees of resumption of terminal situations of a type which have already been observed. Lying in bed after waking up in the morning, whenever there are difficulties to cope with, may be interpreted as a reactivation of an earlier psychological impulse to lie still and be waited on.

Fourth, personality events may be construed as approximations to "normal" terminal events which are observed for the biological or cultural category of the individual. Thus heterosexuality may be postulated as a tendency of a human being, although he consummates no heterosexual adjustments.

Fifth, personality events may be interpreted in terms of end situations which are "extreme" for the members of the species or the culture. Thus the acts of man may be viewed as degrees of approximation to murder, suicide, and incest.

Each sense in which the tendency conception is used is valid and useful for certain purposes, and is exposed to characteristic liabilities to error. Thus if we accept the man's statement that he is running to catch a train, we may be wrong; he may be running to the woods beyond to escape the constable.

The reactive type of statement is an alternative (I should prefer to say a supplement) to tendency generalizations. When we make a reactive statement, we specify quite definitely the antecedent-consequent relation to which reference is made. The specific stimulus-response description of the events which elicit the knee jerk, or call out an avoidance reaction to yellow cloth, illustrates what is meant here. Of course the stimulus-response style of thinking is not nearly as exhaustive, and the tendency style of thinking is not nearly as ambiguous in actual application, as might appear at first glance. The stimulus-response statement of how to elicit the knee jerk which is usually given may be predictively valid in eight cases out of ten; but there are "exceptions" which show how wide is the context of factors which it would be necessary to include in the picture, were it nearly complete. And when the stimulus-response mode of thinking is extended from such relatively stable and touchable situations to those which involve complex central (subjective) events in the sequence, it becomes in reality a disguised form of tendency interpretation.

The chief possible virtue of tendency conceptions is in introducing some sort of order in complex phenomena. If the observer tries to enumerate all the body movements, all the electronic gyrations, all the nuances of social adjustment which are thinkable in a given constellation of personality events, he is likely to become lost in aimless classification, and to prove barren in the invention of procedures which are calculated to elicit particular aspects of the whole which may be of high predictive value. The human mind is able to operate with a very small number of categories with which to introduce order into events, particularly when these are, for the most part, still defined qualitatively. Clarity of thought demands economy in the orienting frames of thought.

How a tendency simplification may lead to fruitful research for predictively valuable particulars is shown in the case of Freud, in contrast to Janet. Janet made remarkably clear classifications of the psychopathological facts as he saw them, and although his terms and categories were abundant, his work was comparatively sterile of novel procedures for the modification of human personalities. Even his classificatory pursuits were hampered by his little-criticized assumptions. His notion that dreams were passing confusions which were traceable to diminished psychological tension in sleep deprived dream material of all significance as classifiable data, and he almost completely ignored it. Freud, who tended to operate with a few bold tendency simplifications, brought into the range of observation whole categories of data which have high predictive value.

When tendency simplifications are used until vast numbers of instances accumulate of their supposed operation, "subtendencies" (such as the variations of the manifestations of the Oedipus constellation) multiply apace until the problems of rendering one tendency consistent with the expressions of another one carry scientific speculations into the logical molds of legalism and dogmatic theology. If the subtendencies are not modified, and long lists of special tendencies are added, terminological difficulties likewise arise in applying the unwieldy list. The long inventories of supposed instincts are less at fault because they imply an unwarranted assurance about the innate propensities of man than because they are "too numerous to mention," and introduce confusion rather than orienting principles in the field of study.

Although the prediction of one set of tangible reactions from another is the aim of scientific formulation, this by no means implies, then, that the reactive style of thinking is the one best calculated to guide the attention of the thinker to the selection of the most fruitful hypotheses ("if" predictions). Indeed, especially valuable results have been secured in the personality field by the pattern of thinking which views a cross-section of facts as an expression of a few tendencies.

But a reactive style of thinking which operates with a few simplifications might prove useful in the study of human personality at the present time, since both the psycho-analytical and the "itemistic" psychologies have a plethora of particulars with which they are familiar, but suffer from certain crippling viewpoints inherent in their early starting-points. Psychoanalysis is well accustomed to the use of a few orienting terms, but since these are stated in "tendency" form, there is much lack of emphasis upon rendering the objective marks of their manifestation pre-cise. The inventory psychologies though accustomed to precision are accustomed to overlooking the woods for the trees.

Can the personality be viewed as a system, and can we think of it in a few terms which can be gradually ob-jectified, and which indicate the principal varieties of personality manifestation? If the personality is a true system, interferences which are introduced at various points ought often to produce substitutive reactions at many remote parts of the personality. Personalities may be compared from one cross-section to another, and from one personality to another, by exposing them to similar interferences, and by examining the substitutive reaction sequences which emerge.

For the purpose of summing up the personality at any given period, we may consider it to be a constellation of the following action patterns: object orientations, ad-justive thinking, autistic reveries, somatic reactions.

The object orientations of the individual are describ-able as various degrees of assertiveness, provocativeness, or submissiveness toward sexual and non-specifically sex-ual objects in the environment. In extreme instances the individual may be abusive, insulting, domineering toward superiors, colleagues, clients, and subordinates in his pro-fession, and toward his wife or mistress in intimate life;

or he may be cowed in his work and timid in his sexuality; or he may show extreme variations between his professional and private levels of behavior. These are the differentiating reactions upon which it is hoped to throw some light by the examination of the personality system in its principal manifestations.

Adjustive thinking has to do with the relationship of the individual to reality. It issues in socially relevant acts, which on the creative level mean contributions to science, art, administration, and philosophy. Autistic thinking is highly egocentric, but adjustive thinking when it dwells upon the relationship of the self to its surroundings is able to treat the self as an object among objects.

Autistic reveries are non-adjustive to reality. They may be divided into several classes of which morbid-suicidal, pessimistic, megalomanic, denunciatory, and persecutory reveries are particularly common. In exaggerated form they become the most conspicuous feature of the personality, and various clinical names are used to distinguish them. Common, and representative, themes are suggested by these quotations: "I'm a hopeless sinner"; "The world's going to the dogs"; "I'm the slickest guy in the world"; "The President is the Judas of mankind"; "The President is using death-rays on me." Autistic thinking flourishes in greater or less abundance in every personality whose history is taken for any length of time.

The somatic reactions at any given cross-section of the personality are striped muscle movements and tensions; heart and circulatory reactions; gastro-intestinal responses; skin adjustments; organic sexual behavior; respiratory, pupillary, and urogenital adaptations; inner glandular action on the biochemical balance of the blood; heat production (fever and certain metabolic alterations not included before); electrical conductivity; and immunological responses. Under the same environing conditions individuals show wide variations in physical behavior, and when these manifestations show certain gross deviations from norms, though no organic lesion can be shown to be present, the presumption is that the energy of some mental process has been converted into somatic form. This notion of hysteria (and what may be called hysteroid reactions) was classically formulated by Freud. Every individual who is closely scrutinized shows, from time to time, tendencies to urinate excessively (though no adequate physical explanation is apparent), to refrain from passing feces, or to suffer pains in the back or neck.

The comparisons which may be made among personalities on the basis of the nature of the substitutive reactions which arise when they are subjected to similar conditions may be illustrated on the gross level by citing some "experiments" which society has tried. Mr. A is a member of the city council in one of our large cities. On two occasions, when he was defeated for re-election, he developed autistic reveries to such an extent that he was confined in a sanitarium under the care of a psychiatrist. Thus Mr. A met a deprivation in the sphere of his orientation to social objects (political activity) by developing exaggerated autistic reveries (depressive preoccupations). The case of A may be thrown up against that of Mr. B. When Mr. B lost out in his campaign for re-election to the legislature, he began to worry about his health, and although the physicians could find no adequate physical basis for his trouble, he developed a host of gastro-intestinal disturbances which incapacitated him from regular professional life. His substitutive reaction was somatic. Another man, a Mr. C, was defeated and spent most of his time writing a subsequently well-recognized book on political theory. His substitutive reaction was in the sphere of consecutive, theoretical, adjustive thinking. It will be remembered that one of our driving administrators, J, had his administrative duties curtailed and immediately took the wife of another for his mistress showing that his object orientation in the world of affairs was a substitute for his object orientation in the sexual field.

From this point of view, we are able to examine the relative function which political activities and preoccupations play in the personality integration of the individual. For one it is an alternative to mental disorder, for another it is an alternative to physical disease, for another an alternative to aggressive sexuality.

Now it is of interest and importance to observe that the study of the life-histories of these men showed that their mode of meeting the world had become organized rather early. The man who developed somatic symptoms had shown a physical upset after losing a contest for the presidency of his class in college, and also in adolescent and preadolescent deprivation situations. Alexander traced the basis for the personality splitting in J to very early childhood.

I want now to indicate how the prolonged interview throws much light on personality development, and lends itself to consideration from the point of view outlined here. If the analyst is "insulted" by the subject in the course of a day's interview, the subject may the next day report somatic trouble, or morbid reveries, or unusual kindliness toward an annoying person, or a burst of creative work. The interviewer, taking such facts in juxtaposition to others, may be able to predict the kind of substitutive reactions which this person is likely to show in a whole range of social situations, and to predict retrospectively the

form of reaction which was manifested at different levels
of development. The trained psychoanalyst watches the
subject like a hawk for clues of this kind; the possibility
of removing his "hunches" from the realm of art into the
area of dependable knowledge depends upon the objectification of his observations, and upon the development of
specifically experimental methods.

A method by which some certainty is to be introduced
in personality records is by testing the coincidence of
observations taken through time by observers who occupy
specified positions in relation to the subject. Very important applications of this procedure have been made to
child study by several child psychologists, more particularly by Florence Goodenough and Dorothy Thomas. A
set of categories were set up to describe various acts,
such as "smiling," "physical contact with other child," and
"physical contact with object." The definiteness of each
term was then tested by having two independent observers
make the same number of observations at fixed intervals
during a prescribed period. The results showed which
categories were ambiguous, and which categories were sufficiently clear to justify their inclusion in behavior studies.
It was discovered, for example, that "smiling" behavior
showed much less definiteness than "physical contact with
another child." This procedure makes it possible to measure the error of a measuring procedure and is strictly
comparable to the calibrating process common to the physical sciences in determining the relative reliability of
measurements made by a particular instrument. The social scientist is compelled to rely on the use of his eyes,
and the problem is to standardize the use so that objective
results can be secured.[2]

[2] Dorothy Swaine Thomas and Associates, *Some New Techniques for
Studying Social Behavior.*

Such methods of devising and testing categories for the observation of behavior need urgently to be developed for the study of courtroom, legislative, committee, mass meeting, and other types of behavior in situations of immediate political interest. It is possible to record the differential reactions of participants, and to distinguish that which is inherent in the rôle performed (chairman), and that which is the individualized penumbra of the act (individual gesture).

These objective categories and recording practices can be extended to the study of behavior wherever dominating and submissive behavior is found. The gap between the studies of children and the study of personalities in complicated adult political situations can be filled in with the idea of finding reliable criteria of the stability of political reactions. Some early studies have been made which suggest that types of dominating behavior are isolable at very early ages. Charlotte Bühler detected children who dominated through pressure of activity, despotic behavior, and "leadership" behavior. Her monograph reproduces photographic illustrations of what she means by the terms employed.[3] An outgrowth of her work is the experimental study by Marjorie Walker at the Minneapolis Institute of Child Welfare (under direction of Anderson and Goodenough). An observational study by Mildred Parten at the same place showed that in uncontrolled play activities the dominating or submissive rôles might be strikingly monopolized by individual children.[4]

[3] "Die ersten sozialen Verhaltungsweisen des Kindes," *Quellen und Studien zur Jugendkunde*, Heft 5.

[4] Referred to by John E. Anderson, "The Genesis of Social Reactions in the Young Child," *The Unconscious: A Symposium*. These researches are abstracted in William I. Thomas and Dorothy S. Thomas, *The Child in America*.

By methods which are less objective but much better than simple impressionism, there have been a number of "political types" observed in later development. Karl Reininger kept a careful record of the behavior of his pre-puberty schoolboys, and brought out very clearly the functional distinction between the "leader" and the "specialist." The specialist might temporarily guide the group in some activity for which he was particularly competent, but the leader kept him within limits and reassumed the direction as soon as the special activity was over. Reininger has many shrewd observations to offer about the bearing of what he saw on the whole range of social psychological theory, and his monograph is a beautiful example of how a circumscribed empirical study can be given meaning and distinction against a broad theoretical background.[5] Hildegard Hetzer watched the spontaneous groupings of children in play groups, and shrewdly distinguished organizers, specialists, and social leaders from one another.[6]

At a still later level is the study which Viktor Winkler-Hermaden made of the psychology of youth-movement leaders. These leaders are recruited from youths who are not much ahead of their groups in age, and in a well-balanced and penetrating chapter he contrasted the "ruler," "teacher," and "apostle."[7]

Special studies of dominating and submissive types in various situations ought to be made with some reference to the reaction-type classifications for the age period which are made by competent students. Since puberty-adoles-

[5] *Über soziale Verhaltungsweisen in der Vorpubertät*, "Wiener Arbeiten zur pädogogischen Psychologie" (herausgegeben von Charlotte Bühler and Viktor Fadrus), Heft 2.

[6] *Das volkstümliche Kinderspiel*, Heft 6, in the same series as the above.

[7] "Psychologie des Jugendführers," *Quellen und Studien zur Jugendkunde* (herausgegeben von Dr. Charlotte Bühler).

cence is of so much importance, the categories which are proposed in the literature ought to be examined by the special investigator. H. Hoffman gives a modified list of the puberty types described by Spranger and Croner in one section of his general book on character formation.[8] Suggestions on various distortions of development which lie behind certain forms of dominating and submissive behavior are to be found in August Aichhorn's lectures on *Verwahrloste Jugend*.[9] This is the most valuable book to a student of youth which has yet been explicitly devoted to the subject by an analyst. Aichhorn reports in his eighth lecture the results of an extremely important experiment which he made with the most aggressive and uncontrollable boys under his supervision (he has served for many years as the head of a home for homeless boys). The whole group was put together, and the staff members were instructed never to interfere with them, short of stopping permanent injury. These "hard-boiled" youths broke up the furniture, mauled one another, and wore out several attendants before they gradually tamed down. After having learned that they could not taunt the environment into punishing them, and into justifying their own suspicions of it, they went through a process of character re-education. The behavior of the group is reported in graphical form, and representative instances of what occurred are recited in the text of the lecture. Several specific genetic hypotheses are set up to explain particular

---

[8] *Das Problem des Charakteraufbaus*, pp. 68–80. See E. Spranger, *Psychologie des Jugendalters*, and Else Croner, "Die Psyche der weiblichen Jugend," *Schriften zur Frauenbildung*, Heft 6.

[9] *Internationale Psychoanalytische Bibliotek*, Band XIX.

kinds of behavior on the part of the boys with whom Aichhorn has had intimate touch.[10]

Will we be able to predict from objective studies made of preadolescent boys who dominate their play groups that one set of them will stand a high chance of dominating play and work groups in adolescence? Can we thus isolate rather stable developmental sequences for various trait constellations which are of direct importance to the student of politics? Can we achieve a composite picture for a given culture by studying overlapping age groups for a two-year period? Certainly the way is becoming clearer to an effective relationship between political science and the disciplines associated with the study of the growing individual.

One of the difficulties which lie in the path of successful collaboration with psychiatrists and child psychologists is that the political scientists have not themselves made it entirely clear just what the adult differentials are whose genetic history they would like to understand. What are the questions about the specifically political life of the individual which the political scientist would like to have included in any master-inventory of possible facts about the intensively studied individual?

The following classification of political attitudes is intended to have suggestive value rather than formal completeness. The first section of this classification refers to the political preferences and expectations or forebodings of the individual investigated. Some individuals cherish a fraternal and some a paternal ideal. The anarchist, so-

[10] See especially p. 278. Harry Stack Sullivan is tracing out the developmental history of various forms of personality in his forthcoming volume on *Personal Psychopathology*.

cialist, and democrat talk the language of equality among a family of brothers; the monarchists preserve a father.[11] A series of other ideological distinctions are perhaps sufficiently clear from the terms used.

CLASSIFICATION OF POLITICAL ATTITUDES

SECTION A. POLITICAL VIEWS

I. Preferences

Paternal ideal
Fraternal ideal

Strong central authority
Weak central authority

Revolutionary ideal
Counter-revolutionary or reactionary ideal

Cataclysmic change
Evolutionary change

Indulgent toward coercion, secrecy, ruthlessness
Insistent upon persuasion, openness, scrupulousness

Emancipatory, defensive, expansive ideal for group
World-unity ideal

II. Expectations and forebodings

Small political change can have great results
Small political change can have some results of value
Little of value can be accomplished by politics
Revolutionary changes imminent, eventual, contingent

It is probably in relation to political practices, as distinguished from political views, that the intensive study of the individual has the most to offer. I have included a list of questions in Appendix B which are intended to suggest the sort of thing which is directly pertinent to the interest of the political scientist in this regard. How has the individual acted as a subordinate when confronted by superiors of various kinds (in the army, in school, in frater-

[11] Paul Federn commented in his pamphlet that a democratic state must depend upon a democratic family life.

nity organizations, in business, in party clubs, in propaganda organizations, in administrative hierarchies, and the like)? How has the individual acted as a superior when confronted by subordinates of various kinds? Besides considering the behavior of the person as subordinate or superior, we may inquire into his attitude toward individuals who have not been members of his various organizations, but who have been possible helpers or obstacles. Thus he may have approached strangers for money, or sought to win diplomatic support from another organization against a common menace. His tactics may be classified according to the means employed and the measure of success attained. Special attention may likewise be devoted to the behavior of the individual, not toward particular persons, but toward publics, which are necessarily anonymous. Summarizing:

SECTION B. POLITICAL PRACTICES

I. As subordinate
 Confronted by superiors who are
 A. Strong, brutal
 B. Masterful but rather objective
 C. Weak
 Reaction (conscious)
 1. Does not assume a friendly mask (exterior) even though he sees it would be an advantage (seeks to escape, becomes stubborn, surly, assaultive, joins anti-authoritation acts engaged in by associates, continues to contemplate revenge long after)
 2. Does not see or press up own individual advantage because of attachment or intimidation (deference without conscious hostility, pronounced affection, intimidated sacrifice of associates to curry favor, overgratitude)
 3. Combines friendly mask with conscious acts of hostility (plays up qualities admired by chief, whether imitative of chief or expressive of the chief's repressions)
 4. Irrational elements in adaptation at a minimum

II. As authority
Confronted by subordinates who are
A. Strong, hostile, dangerous rivals
B. Strong and objective
C. Weak
Reaction
1. Does not refrain from taking up a hostile front even when it is recognized to be inappropriate
2. Takes apparently friendly line while pursuing hostile purposes
3. Does not take strong-enough measures to secure efficiency or respect (too indulgent of mirrors of self or of those who work out frustrations)
4. Objective (inflicts narcissistic wound when advantageous, reassures when useful, develops abilities of subordinates, thwarts when dangerous)
III. In dealing with possible helper or obstructor who is outside organization (most effective tactics chosen and range of tactics)
Appeals to logical standards
Appeals to sentiment
Non-violent and violent coercion
Inducement (tangible advantage)
IV. In dealing with public
Types of tactics chosen, success

Forms of expression, thought, and interest may be singled out for special consideration. What is intended here is sufficiently apparent from the captions:

SECTION C. FORMS OF EXPRESSION, THOUGHT, INTEREST
I. Forms of expression
(Includes all symbolizing forms: political editorials, novels, poems, paintings, cartoons, plastic media, plays, acting)
Most effective style
Analytical and dialectical
Persecutory (sarcastic, denunciatory)
Enthusiastic

    Humorous

    Commanding

    Range of style wide or limited

II. Mode of thought

    Quick or slow to suggest policies or tactics

    Almost totally uninventive

    Systematically collects data prior to judgment

    Impressionistic improvisation

    Welcomes suggestion and criticism before decision

    Impatient of suggestion and criticism before decision

    Anxious to justify decision to those about or to world

    Indifferent about justifying decision

    Stubbornly holds to decision

    Oscillates in decision

    Much influenced by facts and arguments (or little)

    Much influenced by appeals to sentiments (or little)

    Much influenced by personal inducements (or little)

    Much influenced by coercion (or little) (note that influence may be negative as to direction)

    Genuine pursuit of general interest in exercise of discretion, or not

    Elated by victory or depressed

    Genuine or narrow in sharing credit

    Deeply depressed by defeat or satisfied in defeat

    Interested in programs and values

    Interested in processes and methods

    Long-run or short-run objectives

    Aims at immediate or eventual political action

    Presses through to a decision capable of being tested

    Conclusions or decisions vague

    Ideal of responsible personal participation

    Consistency between opinion and practices

    Self-consciousness of own techniques

    Conforms or not to family pattern (exaggerated, adoption of opposite, ...)

III. Political interest

    Formulated early and persists through life

    Formulated early, lies dormant, reawakened

Aroused early, disillusioned
Aroused late

By this time it is perhaps superfluous to comment that every fact is defined from the point of view of an observer, and that the problem is to specify as definitely as possible the angle of observation of the recorder. Trait lists are meaningless unless they can be filled in by a fact-collecting process which surveys the various situations with respect to which it is of possible relevance. It is very obvious to the psychopathologist that the man who is "aggressive" at work may be "timid" in sexuality. All too frequently personalities are supposed to be "aggressive" when a certain number of raters have agreed on it, without stopping to consider whether the raters have a chance to become acquainted with the behavior of the individual in many situations. The multiplication of ratings by persons who are in a poor position to judge the subject (even by "intimate" friends who do not, however, act as sexual partners) adds nothing but a spurious specificity to the data. The interviewer who listens to the intimate life of the individual through many weeks and months is in a very strategic position to become acquainted with details of individual reactions which even intimates have not seen. A "rating" must be taken with special reference to the history of the relations of the rater and the rated. It may be that we shall presently find that the ratings of analysts in dealing with certain types of people who can be easily identified do not substantially deviate from those of "intimates" or even rather casual acquaintances of certain kinds. Such knowledge will enable research to proceed with more certain pace toward the time when we shall know what to look for and how to elicit what we want with the maximum of economy. The specialist who interviews a man for an hour may be able, during the course of what appears to be an ordinary social relation, to find the tell-tale signs which detailed research has shown to be invariably, or almost invariably, connected with particular impulse systems and developmental histories. As Bjerre so well put it:

As soon as our intercourse with a certain person is no longer governed by common interests, but by a desire to acquire a knowledge of his inmost being, we immediately abandon the formal content of his utterance and begin unconsciously to seek for whatever indication of his inner life appears in his speech independently of, or even in spite of, his conscious will.[12]

What is achieved is a correlation of the results of "casual" contact and "intensive" study, a correlation which is the common target of a converging attack upon the understanding of the human personality.

Some day we shall know how to validate the saying of the old physician which is on the title-page of this book: "From him who has eyes to see and ears to hear no mortal can hide his secret; he whose lips are silent chatters with his fingertips and betrays himself through all his pores."

[12] See his excellent methodological chapter in *The Psychology of Murder*.

CHAPTER XIII

THE STATE AS A MANIFOLD OF EVENTS

Implications have continually been drawn in the fore-going pages about the bearing of the intensive study of individual personalities upon the meaning of the political process as a whole. Since the psychopathological approach to the individual is the most elaborate procedure yet devised for the study of human personality, it would appear to raise in the most acute form the thorny problem of the relation between research on the individual and research upon society. We are therefore justified in devoting more extended attention to the theoretical problem involved than we have yet taken occasion to do.

It may be asserted at the outset that our thinking is vitiated unless we dispose of the fictitious cleavage which is sometimes supposed to separate the study of the "individual" from the study of "society." There is no cleavage; there is but a gradual gradation of reference points. Some events have their locus in but a single individual, and are unsuitable for comparative investigation. Some events are widely distributed among individuals, like breathing, but have no special importance for interpersonal relations. Our starting-point as social scientists is the statement of a distinctive event which is widely spread among human beings who occupy a particular time-space manifold.

Subjective events occupy definite positions in the flow of events, and the problem of explanation is the problem of locating stable relations. Since subjective events are

not open to direct observation, but are inferred from movements, the observer, O, must infer the existence of subjective terms in the sequence by imagining what he would
experience under all the similar circumstances which he
can survey and compare to his own experience. Reduced
to its simplest terms, the observer's procedure is that of
isolating a subjective event which he wishes to investigate,
and of searching for the "externals" which will make the
conditions of its occurrence clearly communicable to others.
These externals are sometimes fairly clear, and can readily
be stated in precise, "touchable" form. The sensation of
"roughness" can be predicted to follow the application of
certain objects to specified parts of the skin. A transition
from a rough to a smooth object may also produce "flinch-
ing," which can be somewhat definitely described, and
which accompanies and (perhaps) initiates some of the
subjective events.

When any observer undertakes to talk about the state,
he may choose specific subjective experiences, such as a
sense of loyalty to a community, and say that all who have
this experience (and/or certain others) under specified
conditions make up the state. Such specified conditions
may include the act of testifying to it when asked by an
intimate friend, or when warned that the community is
in danger. The concept of the state may be amplified by
searching for the external circumstances which precipi-
tate the appearance of the subjective events which are
characteristic of stateness.

Such a method of defining the state absolves us from
"superindividual" constructs. The locus of the subjective
events is still individual. The group is not a superindividual phenomenon but a many-individual phenomenon. The
time-space abstraction of the "group" is just as "real"

or "unreal" as the time-space abstraction called the "individual." They are both equally real or unreal, and they stand and fall together.

The state has duration. It is a time-space frame of reference for individual events. Particular individuals may pass on, but if the overwhelming majority of those who occupy a certain geographical area continue to experience the subjective events of the type chosen as critical for the state, the state endures. The state is thus independent of any one individual, but it ceases to exist when enough individuals change their minds or die without procreating.

I have not yet defined the particular events which are to be treated as the marks of the state. In the sea of subjective events we must choose certain typical ones. Now definitions of this kind can be developed most advantageously when we proceed, not by a method of rigorous exclusion, but of relative emphasis. Suppose we tentatively begin by saying that the distinguishing experience is that of communal unity, when it is manifested by the use of coercion against outside and inside disturbers of the communal order. Imagine an observer is overlooking a primitive village. He sees a band of young men whose behavior he interprets thus: They are wearing painted stripes, brandishing spears, and having left the village, they engage in fighting a band of young men from a neighboring village. Is this evidence of the existence of the state? The facts are insufficient to justify a decision. Closer observation may show that these young men all live in one quarter of the village and that other young men are idling about. When the "warriors" come back, they are only cheered by those who live in one section. Those who live there may prove to be members of one family, some of whose young men have avenged a private wrong in which the village as a whole has no part. The system of claims and expectations which is the essence of the communal order is not at stake. The communal order must be involved if the state is involved.

Robert H. Lowie[1] has shown that the term "state" may properly be used to designate even the most primitive communities, and that the common distinction between a prestate and a state period of cultural development is a distortion of the facts. The simplest peoples known, the Yurok of northwestern California, the Angami of Assam, and the Ifugao of northern Luzon, all have a sense of belonging to a social unit larger than a kin group, and act in overt defense of this order. The theft of property of one kin group, when committed by a fellow-villager, is mulcted by a traditional fine, but the theft, when committed by a marauding outsider, is punished by death. In the case of adultery, warring families inside the village are merely engaged in adjusting the size of the penalty; it is universally assumed that some penalty is due.

The marginal cases notoriously play havoc with definitions. The statement made before that the distinguishing mark of the state is the experience of communal unity, when it is manifested by the use of coercion against outside and inside disturbers of a communal order, is too narrow to cover a small but extremely interesting series of facts. There may be no use of coercion against outsiders, for the war pattern may be entirely absent from the community, although violence against insiders who threaten the communal system of claims and expectations appears to be universal.

The view so far proposed rests upon a frank acceptance of social "parallelism "[2] Hans Kelsen has subjected

[1] *The Origin of the State.*

[2] Not to be confused with mind body parallelism, which is not accepted.

the theories of parallelism of psychological states (common emotion and the like) to a sharp, and in many ways devastating, criticism. He says that "common emotion, common volition and common idea can never mean anything more than a description of the coincidence in consciousness of a number of individuals." But

if one really wished to consider the state as consisting of a community of consciousness such as this, and as a matter of fact, such a realistic, empirical psychological meaning is often attributed to what is called the collective will or the collective interest of the state, then, in order to avoid inadmissible fictions, one would have only to be consistent enough really to consider the state as formed only by the contents of those whose consciousness had shown the necessary agreement. One would be bound to realize that community of will, feeling or thought, as a psychological group manifestation, fluctuates tremendously at different times and places. In the ocean of psychic happenings, such communities may rise like waves in the sea and after a brief space be lost again in an ever-changing ebb and flow.[2a]

In this keen dialectic Kelsen has been led astray by a failure to recognize the time dimension of the events referred to by such a concept as the state. Subjective facts are located in time in relation to one another when viewed from the standpoint of any observer. The concept of the state involves similar events in relation to one another within a duration. The concept of the state includes this idea of a temporal frame, and can best be grasped as a relational system (a manifold) in which a certain frequency of subjective events is maintained. Thus the state is not abolished when some individuals sleep or occupy themselves with the banalities of existence, unless

[2a] Cf. Kelsen, *Der Soziologische und der juristische Staatsbegriff;* "Der Begriff des Staates und die Sozialpsychologie," *Imago,* VIII (1922), 97–141; "The Conception of the State and Social Psychology," *International Journal of Psycho-Analysis,* V (1924), 1–38.

the state is defined with reference to a duration of a few seconds or hours or days. But there is no reason whatever for choosing such a transitory frame of reference. It is just as valid to use a year as a minute, or a decade as a year, for the time dimension. Thus the state can be treated in what Kelsen speaks of as an "empirical psychological" sense. It is a durable empirical fact just so long as a certain frequency of subjective events occurs. If Kelsen agrees that contents of consciousness are "empirical," he is bound to see them in a world of duration, and he has no authority to prescribe that the state must refer to subjective events as a "knife-edge instant."

The state, then, is a time-space manifold of similar subjective events. Kelsen is incorrect in alleging that the acceptance of the parallelism of psychological phenomena as a fundamental fact destroys the state as a permanent institution.

Mere parallelism of psychological events does not give us the state, for a distinguishing type of subjective event must be selected if we are to characterize the state, the family, and other social groups. Kelsen is entirely correct in criticizing those theories of the state which invoke parallelism but neglect to specify the particular "contents of consciousness," "since not every and any group manifestations formed upon the parallelism of psychic processes is able to constitute that community."

That subjective event which is the unique mark of the state is the recognition that one belongs to a community with a system of paramount claims and expectations. This recognition of belonging does not necessarily imply an indorsement of this state of things. The essence of the state is this recognition, and the individual may indorse or deplore the fact without abolishing it. One need not be sentimentally bound to the order; it is enough if the order is noted.

This unique experience is never found unassociated with other subjective events. The recognition is usually amplified by pride in belonging to the state, and by a determination to enforce the order upon one's self and others. One's recognition of the order is usually accompanied by an idealization of one's participation in it, by an idealization of the order itself, and by a condemnation of deviations from it. All this is frequently expressed as the "sense of justice" which is the foundation of certain theories of law and the state.

The subjective event which marks the state is usually manifested in various "externals." Thus the use of coercion is well-nigh universal. The externals may be broadened to include behavior which may be treated as a substitute for coercion. Ordering and obeying relationships which function in a coercive crisis may continue when peace comes. There may be an apparent "elaboration backward" of processes antecedent to coercion in foreign and domestic affairs, and this may obviate a resort to the *ultima ratio*. The regulation of the use of coercion, and the maintenance of a certain degree of mobilization during non-crisis periods, devolves upon "leaders," who may preside over initiations, goods distribution, and general ceremonials. The process by which "heads" are selected may involve electoral colleges, elections, and agitations.

It is worth observing that in the description of political processes terms are employed which often carry no "subjective" connotations on their face. But in fact every term unavoidably carries subjective implications, and if these be ignored, there is danger that social theory will hypostatize "patterns" or "traditions" as extra-subjective entities, endowed with distinctive energies and amenable to special laws.

Often the subjective "burr" on the pattern is so dim that the subjective need scarcely ever be made explicit. Many generalizations can be made by disregarding the subjective element and focusing attention upon the transformations through which the associated patterns pass. Linguistics has achieved notable success by this method. Phonetic arrangements are named as objects of investigation and the fact discovered that those sounds which occur in certain relationships presently alter in regular ways.

It is theoretically possible to make a rough scale of descriptive conceptions according to the relative fulness or thinness of the subjective element in the pattern. To express this symbolically, the complexity of the S to the E (subjective to external) varies between nearly 100 and nearly 0. The contemporary prominence of what is called "social psychology" is due to the effort to draw attention to the consideration of patterns in which the S factor is large.

The failure to stress the subjective dimensions of the events referred to as "processes," "patterns," or "customs" is not only due to the circumstance that the S is often negligible, but that the objective element may often appear with other subjective elements. John B may rise when the national anthem is played, but he may do so "automatically" with his mind mostly preoccupied with the sore on his heel. The particular S which is meant when the full pattern of patriotic ceremonialism is discussed may thus be supplanted by another S with the same E. Thus the act becomes an entirely different phenomenon, and may erroneously be classed with patriotic ceremonialism in the full sense.

This point has far-reaching consequences for political science. The accurate comparison of behavior patterns depends upon comparison of the whole pattern. It must not be automatically inferred that S exists where E is found. The nature of the subjective factor can be inferred from extending the observation in several directions. It may be lengthened (John B may complain of a sore heel after the anthem). It may be more intensively scrutinized within the same period (John B may be seen to shift his weight from one foot to another, and to frown when one heel touches the floor).

Descriptive political conceptions are undergoing a continuous redefinition in the life of society, and unless the student of political processes is on the alert to test his descriptive conceptions in the light of changing reality, he will operate with falsifications and not with simplifications. "Voting," to choose an instance, is a concept of the greatest complexity. It does not alone consist in the dropping of ballots into urns or boxes or hats, or in the punching of buttons on a machine. These external elements, the E's, in the concept of voting are not the heart of the matter. What count especially are the subjective terms in the constellation of which these externals are a part, and a highly variable part at that. How seriously do people take the responsibility of collecting information about the personalities and issues with which they are confronted and judging these matters in the light of a conception of the public interest? Voting is an entirely different matter when individuals are coerced into casting ballots a certain way and when they are free, leisured, and interested. To call the casting of ballots under all circumstances "voting" is to deprive the term of most of its significance.

It is highly probable that the phenomenon which is loosely called voting in Chicago is today quite different from what is was fifty years ago; it is radically true that the phenomenon called voting in London is something different from voting in Cook County.[4] How are we to decide what meaning to assign to particular aspects of the political process as we observe them at different times and places? The ocean of subjective happenings which are related to external movements of a kind often associated with politics is ever changing, and it cannot be described by inventory methods. Not inventory but sampling is essential if empirical definiteness is to be attached to a term.

Speaking very generally, two modes of procedure are possible. The first is to begin with the externalities which are a rather fixed feature of a pattern of social behavior with which the investigator is familiar, and to proceed to find out how the subjective features of this pattern change. One may study "balloting" or "modes of punishment" and the like from this point of view. Throughout Western European culture there prevails such relative homogeneity of pattern that research may proceed directly from this starting-point.

The field ethnologist, who deals with cultures of a drastically different kind, must often use another avenue of approach. A set of external movements like "balloting" may not be sufficiently widespread to permit comparison. The ethnologist must proceed by stating to himself the subjective fact whose presence he would like to detect (such as a desire to participate earnestly in deciding com-

[4] Perhaps the most important part of the Merriam and Gosnell study of *Non-Voting* is the symposium of conversational scraps which suggest what balloting actually means to various classes and sections of a modern metropolitan community.

munal problems), and participate as fully in the daily life of the people as he can, in the hope that presently he will divine such a subjective viewpoint and its characteristic modes of expression. It is true that there are some movements of man whose significance is practically universal, but these are too few to enable the utter alien to dispense with a long period of participation in the day-to-day life of the people. What happens is that the observer presently begins to recognize the subjective fact behind the movements of the body, but this primitive judgment of his is a diffused judgment, based upon a mass of subtle particulars which he may long be unable to isolate in his own thinking and to point out to others; indeed, this process is never complete, or we should have a complete understanding of human life.

Obviously both points of departure for research have their advantages. The American student of social patterns in Western Europe has thousands of subtle meanings established in common with Frenchmen, Germans, or British. This is an enormous time-saving asset. If anyone undertakes to use the ethnologist's approach to a familiar culture, the results are likely to strike the participant in that culture as perfectly obvious and hardly worth the effort.[4]

The whole aim of the scientific student of society is to make the obvious unescapable, if one wishes to put the truth paradoxically. The task is to bring into the center of rational attention the movements which are critically significant in determining our judgment of subjective events, and to discover the essential antecedents of those patterns of subjectivity and of movement. For all the

[4] Such criticism has been directed against the pioneer venture of the Lynds, *Middletown*.

people who are startled to find that they have spoken
prose all their lives, there are many to emulate the rustic
who "know'd it all the time" when scientific facts are
stated about human nature. That which is known implicitly and based upon diffused, unverbalized experience
must be made explicit if new ways of dealing with the
world are to be invented.

The work of investigation may eventuate in statements
of the subjective constellations which find expression in
particular cultural forms, or in the description of the
subjective constellations which are connected with forms
which are universal for all men. The frame of reference
of the social scientist is the culture; the frame of reference of the human psychologist is the species.

What is known as the "quantitative method" provides
a valuable discipline for the student of culture because it
directs his attention toward the discovery of events which
are often enough repeated to raise a strong presumption
that a particular sequence does actually exist. These
events must be so defined that similar events can be identified by other workers. This necessitates an operational
definition of the concept, which is to say, terms must be
used to specify the position of the observer in relation to
the configuration which it is proposed to describe.[5]

The impatience among students of culture with the slow-
footed quantitative approach is partly due to the diffuse,
implicit nature of the experiences upon which is based
the judgment about a subjective event outside one's self,
and the resulting bias of the student of culture against
exaggerating the significance of items in the pattern. The
statement that "his life-experience has been hued with

[5] An able discussion of the operational concept is in P. W. Bridgman,
The Logic of Modern Physics.

melancholy" is a generalization which presupposes a knowledge of a prodigious number of facts. Or the statement that "the prestige of public office is greater in Germany than in any country" depends upon possible observations as numerous as the sands of the sea. Any proposition in Bryce's *Modern Democracies* or in Masaryk's analysis of Russian civilization refers to tremendous ranges of data. Of course, the experience of any observer is puny beside the Gargantuan proportions of the facts, and able inquirers always proceed upon a sampling basis. They get in touch with men of every income group, every religious, every racial, and every provincial group; they study the manifestations of the culture in painting, literature, mathematics, legislation, administration, and physical science.

The procedure of a Bryce was quantitative in the sense that many observations were accumulated before inferences were fixed, but it was not quantitative in the special mathematical sense of the word. The student of culture is often alienated by the quantitative approach, because the quantitative method necessitates the simplification of the number of facts taken into account; the impressionistic-quantitative approach of the student of culture gets an undivided reaction to the whole and makes simplification afterward, perhaps revising and indeed oscillating at frequent intervals.

There is more in common between the student of culture, and especially of alien culture, and the student of the individual by prolonged-interview methods than might appear at first sight. The ethnologist confronting the manifestations of an alien culture and the psychopathologist confronting the alien manifestations of the unconscious secure unique training in their research for meanings in details which escape the attention of the naïve man. Both form their idea of the subjective events from a multitude of signs, which may be spread over months of intimacy, and both are somewhat inclined to disparage the search for simple external facts which can be relied upon to indicate a specific subjective content.

The psychopathologist possesses the most elaborate known means of exploring the manifold subjective events which may be associated with external movements. Besides the conscious subjective experience there is a rich unconscious life which he is especially proficient in exposing. Thus our movements are not alone the outcome of simple conscious processes; they are said to be "overdetermined" by a variety of factors.

This concept of overdetermination is not unknown to popular common sense. We know that John B is proud of being an American, and that he wants to fight for his country; we comment slyly that John B's best girl likes the uniform, and this is one reason why he volunteers. And more than that. We know that action is not always the outcome of experiences that point in the same direction. We may know that John B. is anxious to stay on the job a month longer and to get a promotion, and that going into the army at a given moment means sacrifice. Thus his mind is partly divided against itself. What psychopathological methods do is to disclose yet wider vistas, and to expose the operation of factors which cannot be readily seen. Thus a deep longing for death may be a contributing factor to heroism.

The psychopathological approach is embarrassing less in the specific content of its revelations than in the wealth of meaning which it discovers behind what is at first glance but a simple pattern. The rôle of a particular sub-

jective experience and of a movement cannot be fully
appraised apart from the total context at which it functions, and this method discloses a wider context than common sense is aware of.

Now the multiplicity of human motives has always been
a source of embarrassment to people who wanted to manage men or merely to understand them. The clumsy machinery of judicial administration has been worked out
along certain lines in the hope of introducing some degree of uniformity into adjudication by limiting the consideration of the motives which operate in a particular
case. The judge is thus supposed to limit himself to the
determination of the existence of a particular state of facts,
and to act in a particular way if these facts can be established according to a prescribed procedure. The movement toward the standardization of the discretion of public
officers expresses itself in this general pattern of thought:

An act is prohibited by the state.
Certain prescribed "externals" shall establish the fact of the
act having been committed.
The actor shall be dealt with in certain specified ways.

This crusade against the subjective element in the mind
of the public officer is in some measure determined by the
desire of the judge or civil servant to avoid responsibility.[6]

The psychopathological approach precipitates something
very like a panic among those who have tried to box the
manifestations of human life into conventional common-
sense categories. A dozen motives seem to bloom where
but one was found to bud before.

Let us see what this does for political theory. The prolonged study of individuals enables us to discern the de-

[6] Alexander and Staub have commented on this in *Der Verbrecher und
seine Richter*. But it is principally due to the suspicion of the public
officer.

tails of the process by which the political pattern, as we meet it in adult life, comes to be achieved by individuals.

When X runs for office or passes judgment, his behavior is overdetermined by motives, conscious and unconscious, which were organized in successive patterns during infancy, childhood and youth. The recognition of belonging to a communal order never functions in isolation, and the comparison of life-histories shows that this is implanted in the child on the basis of meanings which he has elaborated in his struggle, first against inhibitory factors in the environment, and presently, when he has introjected the demands of the environment, against his own antisocial impulses.

The early restrictions which the environment imposes upon a child are important in that they are met by reactions on his part which predispose him to meet subsequent limitations in certain ways. These early restrictions are imposed upon the child by inflicting pain or by distracting attention to pleasurable stimuli. Inhibition is thus established in the organism by *force majeur* on the part of the environment, since the infant is simply overpowered or outgeneraled by the environment.

Thus far in his development the growing individual has not become socialized in the sense that he has become self-regulating in relation to objects in the environment. The infant learns "sphincter morality" (in the phrase of Ferenczi), but this involves no emotional relationship to objects. His pleasures remain on his own body (autoplastic), and the environment is an instrument for removing bodily tensions in the simplest manner. Gradually the child begins to look for gratification by lively erogenous activities upon the body of another. This outward push of activity is again limited and frequently blocked by *force majeur.* In the place of sexual relations to objects there now appears a new form of relation, and the child socializes himself by incorporating the practices of those about him.

It will be remembered that emotional bonds are established in two ways: by object choice (for sexual acts) and by identification. Identification, Freud writes, is the original form of emotional tie with an object. It can become a substitute for a libidinal object tie, and it may arise with every new perception of a common quality shared with some other person who is not an object of the sexual instinct. This latter is partial identification. The qualities of the object are copied (introjected). The energy for the identification is said to be supplied by aim-inhibited sexual instincts. The name of the state, the ceremonial acts of deference toward ceremonial symbols—all this and much more is characteristically a feature of the child's growth.

Characteristic, that is to say, frequent, but not invariable. Children are always brought in relation to a system of interferences and indulgences (ways of raising children), and they always perceive an order of some kind. But in some cases when a nation lives subjected to a state, the recognition of the state relation may be accompanied by resentment.

The state pattern itself prevails when many people take it as more than a mere state of affairs, and the idea is reinforced by "irrelevant meanings." Some individuals impose motivations upon others through the state pattern. These individuals, whether despots or enthusiasts, may be termed "radicles," the active ones who serve as radiating centers for the preservation and amplification of the state pattern.

Freud treats the state as an emotional unity.[7] The members of the state identify themselves with an abstract object (the idea of the state) and are bound emotionally by the partial identification which arises in perceiving an analogous relationship to the object. Kelsen has objected to this conception of the state as a real subjective unity by arguing that identification is a process between individuals, and that each member of a state cannot be thought of as having entered into personal relationships with every other member. Even if his narrow construction of identification were well founded, the state could still be treated as a real subjective unity on the basis of interlocking identifications. A has identified with B and B with C, and one of the features of B which the child A would typically take over (introject) would be the name and other symbols of the state.

Indeed, it is the interlocking character of identifications which reasonably insures the incorporation of the state symbol into the child's conception of himself. There is such a process as negative identification, the rejection of patterns which are connected with hated persons. The child is usually exposed to many adults and contemporaries, and if they all associate themselves with the state, the child is almost certain to reject only those patterns which pertain exclusively to the hated individuals. This is the fundamental reason for the staying power of patterns once accepted in a group.

It has been customary in the psychoanalytical literature on social and political processes to describe the state as a universal father-substitute. We are at length in a position to discuss the problems raised by such a generalization.

[7] See his sketch of social psychology in *Massenpsychologie und Ich-Analyse*.

The distinctive contribution of the psychopathological approach is the plurality of individual meanings which it discloses. It is an anticlimax to discover that the appearance of diversity is, after all, spurious, and that those who insist upon the strenuous simplification of human motives are justified. The point which I wish to insist upon is that the data revealed by the psychopathological procedure are far more significant for political and social science than this single-track generalization would lead one to suppose.

The special value of the psychopathological approach is that it represents a supermicroscopic method of utilizing individual instances for the study of culture patterns. If we begin with a political pattern and view it against the private histories of actual people, we find that this pattern takes on variable meaning from one individual to another, but that broad groupings of associated meanings are possible of ascertainment. Any subjective event which is frequently associated with a political pattern is important. Valid generalizations depend upon multiplying cases which are selected from different groups in the culture, and which are studied by methods capable of disclosing subjective contexts. This is the point where quantitative procedures can be made profitable to the student of culture, whose attention is riveted on patterns whose subjective element is important.

But are these studies likely to lead to anything valuable if subjective events are so variable that any subjective event may be associated with any other subjective event? Why not terminate the investigation at the outset by saying that the general law of probabilities can be relied upon to predict the frequency with which any two of a number of specified subjective events may be expected to occur together? Is not our empirical inquiry likely to terminate in an inventory of subjective states and their frequently accompanying movements, thus foredooming any effort to discover more-frequent-than-chance simultaneities, antecedents, and successions? If you look long enough, won't you find every subjective event associated with every other one?

A great many facts tend to substantiate this point of view. It is true that many imposing psychological schools of thought have arisen, run swiftly for a time in narrow channels, and then stagnated in a shallow pool of "faculties" or "instincts," mere inventories of patterns which are abstracted from all concrete events and which are therefore capable of being combined in any event in nearly infinite combinations. The search for specific connections slacks down, and the psychological mill pond is only stirred when somebody throws a stone in the pool in the form of a new theory of specific causation, which troubles the waters until it is found that the specific event is found to occur with only chance frequency. In this sense the only contributors to psychology are those who are sufficiently naïve, or sufficiently unscrupulous, to exaggerate the rôle of a specific type of experience. So we have psychologies based on "fear" or "love" or "imitation," or we have a long string of separate terms, "subfears," which multiply as the range of concrete observation widens, and the failure of the selected factor to explain everything is made manifest, or disguised.

Thus a history of psychology could be written by taking "completed" systems, analyzing the functional equivalence of the categories applied, and reducing every new system to a collection of synonyms for the terms of preceding systems. This hypothetical history of psychological theories would show how an inquirer, much impressed by certain experiences, would seize upon certain terms to describe them, and how, confronted by more and more empirical realities, he would modify the distinctive meaning of his explanatory conceptions out of existence. A history of psychoanalytic terminology, such as Rank has sketched in his treatment of genetic psychology, might be raw material for such a comparison.

Would nothing remain but dictionaries of synonyms, all rather dubious contributions to the grist of linguistic research? It might be that our projected history would show that each psychological system left a permanent legacy behind it in the form of a significant "mechanism" which had not previously been stressed. Now the whole world of "causation" is implicated in any event, and the whole number of significant mechanisms which may be discerned in the "mind at a moment" is infinite. So our hypothetical volume might conclude by accepting the assumption that some events can be brought about by more than chance frequency, subject to the reservation that experimental confirmation is never reliable as to the future. The critical configurations may never "reappear." We commonly say that the probability of an event's future repetition is greater if it has been oft repeated in the past. But there is no means of demonstrating that the future contains analogous configurations to the elapsed. The probability of the future repetition of an event is "no probability." If events appear to be predictable, this is so because our knowledge of contingencies is limited, and our sequences of similar configurations may still be treated as special instances of "no sequence." The stable is a special case of the unstable, to put the ultimate paradox. The discovery of aggregates of mechanisms whose rearrangement in short periods would enrich the apparatus of social control is the dream (the mirage?) of psychology.

Whether these objections will be well founded depends on the outcome of the test, and are incapable of dialectical resolution. It may be pointed out that the search for generalized mechanisms rests on no firmer logical foundations than the search for subjective sequences, since mechanisms are likewise aspects of the world of events, and as such are subject to the same "no probability" laws of recurrence.

It should be repeated that the aim of life-history investigation is not to arrive at such thin generalizations as the statement that the state is a universal father-imago (symbol). What matters to the student of culture is not the subjective similarities of the species, but the subjective differences among members of the same and similar cultures. The life-history configuration is precisely the one which has special meaning for the study of culture, and has its own valid place as an object of investigation in the world of events.

We may at this point briefly retrace the steps which have been taken in this monograph. The psychopathological approach has been examined in its historical setting, and the distinctive value of the free-fantasy method of using the mind has been illustrated. Its importance, likewise, for the understanding of political types has been shown with special reference to the agitators and the administrators.

The general formula for the developmental history of the political man employs three terms:

$$p \left.\right\} d \left.\right\} r = P$$

p equals private motives, *d* equals displacement on to public objects, *r* equals rationalization in terms of public interest. *P* signifies the political man, and $\Big\}$ means "transformed into."

The political man shares the *p*, the private motives
which are organized in the early life of the individual,
with every man, and the *d*, the displacement on to public
objects, with some men. The distinctive mark of the *homo
politicus* is the rationalization of the displacement in terms
of public interests. Political types may be distinguished
according to the specialized or the composite character of
the functions which they perform and which they are de-
sirous of performing. There are political agitators, administrators, theorists, and various combinations thereof.
There are significant differences in the developmental history of each political type.

The hallmark of the agitator is the high value which
he places on the response of the public. As a class the
agitators are strongly narcissistic types. Narcissism is
encouraged by obstacles encountered in the early love relationships, or by overindulgence and admiration in the
family circle. Libido is blocked in moving outward toward
objects and settles back upon the self. Sexual objects
which are like the self are preferred, and a strong homoerotic component is thus characteristic. Among the agitators
yearning for emotional response of the homoerotic kind
is displaced upon generalized objects, and high value is put
on arousing emotional responses from the community at
large. The oratorical agitator, in contradistinction to the
publicist, seems to show a long history of successful impostorship in dealing with his environment. Agitators differ appreciably in the specificity or in the generality of
the social objects upon which they succeed in displacing

their affects. Those who have been consciously attached to their parents and who have been successful impostors ("model children") are disposed to choose remote and general objects. Those who have been conscious of suppressing serious grievances against the intimate circle, and who have been unable to carry off the impostor's rôle successfully, are inclined to pick more immediate and personal substitutes. The rational structure tends toward theoretical completeness in the former case. The object choices for displaced affects depend on the models which are offered when the early identifications are being made. When the homoerotic attitude is the important one, the assaultive, provocative relation to the environment is likely to display itself; when the impotence fear is active, grandiose reactions figure more prominently.

As a group the administrators are distinguished by the value which they place upon the co-ordination of effort in continuing activity. They differ from the agitators in that their affects are displaced on less remote and abstract objects. In the case of one important group this failure to achieve abstract objects is due to excessive preoccupation with specific individuals in the family circle, and to the correlative difficulty of defining the rôle of the self. Very original and overdriving administrators show a fundamental pattern which coincides with that of the agitators. The differences in specific development are principally due to the culture patterns available for identification at critical phases of growth. Another group of administrators is recruited from among those who have passed smoothly through their developmental crises. They have not overrepressed powerful hostilities, but either sublimated these drives, or expressed them boldly in the intimate circle. They display an impersonal interest in the task of organization itself, and assert themselves with firmness, though not with overemphasis, in professional and intimate life. Their lack of interest in abstractions is due to the fact that they have never needed them as a means of dealing with their emotional problems. They can take or leave general ideas without using them to arouse widespread affective responses from the public. Tied neither to abstractions nor to particular people, they are able to deal with both in a context of human relations, impersonally conceived. Their affects flow freely; they are not affectless, but affectively adjusted.

The psychopathological method was also employed to discover the significance of political convictions, for it is evident that beliefs are expressive of a rational and logical "manifest" content, and that they symbolize a host of private motives. In this connection there was passed in review the history of a compulsive conformist to the pattern of the family, and the histories of several nonconformists. The private meaning of militarism and pacifism, and of the pessimism and censoriousness of old age, were explored.

Attention was then turned from the case-history fragments to the problem of drawing out the implications of intensive personality study for the theory of the collective political process.

Political movements derive their vitality from the displacement of private affects upon public objects. The affects which are organized in the family are redistributed upon various social objects, such as the state. Political crises are complicated by the concurrent reactivation of specific primitive impulses. One might suppose that when important decisions are in process of being made society would deliberate very calmly; but the disproportionality between the behavior of man during wars, revolutions, and

elections, and the requirements of rational thinking is notorious. Evidently a reactivating process is at work here;
there is a regressive tendency to reawaken primitive sadism
and lust.

Political symbols are particularly adapted to serve as
targets for displaced affect because of their ambiguity of
reference, in relation to individual experience, and because of their general circulation. Although the dynamic
of politics is the tension of individuals, all tension does
not produce political acts. Nor do all emotional bonds
lead to political action. Political acts depend upon the
symbolization of the discontent of the individual in terms
of a more inclusive self which champions a set of demands
for social action.

Political demands are of only a limited relevance to
the changes which will produce permanent reductions in
the tension level of society. The political methods of coercion, exhortation, and discussion assume that the rôle
of politics is to solve conflicts when they have happened.
The ideal of a politics of prevention is to obviate conflict
by the definite reduction of the tension level of society by
effective methods, of which discussion will be but one.
The preventive point of view insists upon a continuing
audit of the human consequences of social acts, and especially of political acts. The achievement of the ideal of
preventive politics depends less upon changes in social
organization than upon improving the methods and the
education of the social administrators and the social scientists.

The empirical material utilized in the book was brought
together in the course of prolonged interviews with individuals under unusually intimate conditions. At the present time there are no satisfactory records of what actu-

ally happens under these interview conditions, and it is important for the future of personality study to improve the methodology of these procedures. The objectification of what transpires in the interview can be secured by arranging for a verbatim transcript of what goes on, and by recording the physical changes which occur.

Effective personality research depends upon viewing the personality reactions as a system, and upon perfecting the procedures by which the substitutive reactions of this system may be exposed. Broadly speaking, the personality may be treated as a system of object orientations, adjustive thought, autistic reveries, and somatic reactions. The problem is to introduce interferences into the system, and to reveal the substitutive reactions for comparison and further analysis. Every "fact" about personality events is to be defined from the standpoint of a specified observer, and a major problem for the future is to check the "facts" of the observer in the prolonged interview against the "facts" of observers in other situations. Personality research can be made more valuable for political science when the adult reactions are clearly seen which chiefly interest the political scientist (see Appendix B).

What, in general terms, is the relationship between research upon the individual and upon society? There is no cleavage; there is but a gradation of reference points. Events which are of collective interest always have an individual locus, and these events may be studied in their relation to the sequence of events "within the individual" or in relation to the events "among individuals." The distinctive event which serves as the orienting frame for political research is the recognition of belonging to a community with a system of paramount claims and expectations. This event, when distributed with sufficient frequency among the individuals who occupy a given territory during a specified time period, define the state, which is thus a manifold of events. Research which studies the order of events "within the individual" or "among individuals" is equally relevant to the understanding of the state; the difference is a difference of starting-point and not of final result.

When the state is seen as a manifold of events the conditions of whose occurrence are to be understood, the theoretical foundation is laid for both the intensive and the distributive inquiries upon which the politics of prevention can be built. In particular will it be possible to profit as the years pass, and as psychopathology widens the range of its investigations, and increases the dependability of its methods.

AFTERTHOUGHTS: THIRTY YEARS LATER[1]

Since the publication of *Psychopathology and Politics* the psychoanalytic movement has undergone many transformations.[2] Three great European centers of origin and dissemination—Vienna, Budapest, Berlin—were at least temporarily obliterated by the Nazi upsurge. The mildly receptive climate in Moscow, where high officials could at first send their children to an analytically oriented experimental school, turned cold and froze out psychoanalysis. The United States became the principal refuge and creative center of dynamic psychiatry. The change was accompanied by many modifications of emphasis within the "orthodox" school. "Splinter groups" increased as Horney and Reik, for example, began to take independent intellectual or organizational directions.

2

Political science has participated in the general acceleration of scholarly and scientific activities in the United States. *Psychopathology and Politics* was itself an expres-

[1] The present comment has been revised from a paper called "Psychopathology and Politics: Twenty-Five Years After" read at the San Francisco meeting of the American Psychological Association in 1955. A symposium on applications of psychoanalysis was planned by R. Christie, Franz Alexander, Else Frenkel-Brunswik and me. In the end Doctor Frenkel-Brunswik did not present a paper.

[2] I shall not undertake to review the history. On some points see my discussion of "The Impact of Psychoanalytic Thinking on the Social Sciences" in L. D. White, ed., *The State of the Social Sciences* (1956).

sion of the initiative taken by Charles E. Merriam and
others to widen and deepen the empirical and systematic
range of all disciplines having a common concern with
man.[3] The study of politics, government, and law was
deeply affected by the "Chicago school" so that it presently
became the most distinctive feature of the "American
school."[4] As with all developments this was not accomplished without stout defensive maneuvers and counter-
attacks, especially from scholars whose philosophy did
not include adequate provision for learning from empirical study, especially of themselves.

3

It may still seem strange to think of applying psychoanalysis to the investigation of politics. Psychoanalysis
began as a branch of psychiatry and was initially oriented
toward the therapy of disordered individuals. Political
scientists are only incidentally interested in explaining or
curing individual symptoms (functional paralysis, for
example). They have usually shared the historian's interest in noting the presence or absence of mental illness or
defect among the powerful.[5] Long before Freud it was
common to describe the psychopathology of kings, gen-

[3] Professor Merriam was the leading academic figure whose initiative led
to the formation of the Social Science Research Council. He began by organizing conferences to reconsider the position of political science. Beardsley Ruml
of the Laura Spelman Rockefeller Memorial Fund supplied vision and dollars.

[4] See the surveys of world political science under the auspices of UNESCO
where the American empirical and psychological approaches are shown to be
rather unique. *Contemporary Political Science: A Survey of Methods,
Research and Teaching* (1950). George E. G. Catlin was a vigorous pathfinder
in the re-assessment of political studies and an early recognizer of the significance of what he called the "Chicago School."

[5] For a compendious bibliography see W. Lange-Eichbaum, *Genie-Irrsinn
und Ruhm* (1928).

erals, judges, and other public figures. As medicine advanced, new disease entities were isolated, and new categories were rather promptly applied to the symptoms of historical personages. Hence when the discovery of epilepsy was first in favor physicians found epileptic politicians galore. And everybody who knew what Kraepelin meant by dementia praecox or paranoia and who had heard of Ludwig of Bavaria promptly pinned a label on the king. As early as the opening years of the nineteenth century, American physicians contributed to the discovery of an inverse relationship between the incidence of neurosis and such social crises as war or revolution.[6]

What confers importance upon psychoanalysis is that Freud devised a tool aimed at more than the diagnosis and treatment of psychotics, neurotics, and disordered characters. Psychoanalysis is a comprehensive theory of the development of human personality and therefore brings the "healthy" as well as the "sick" within its scope. Psychoanalysis is also a distinctive method of observation in which are combined "free association" and "interpretation." By means of the method, psychoanalysts are able to investigate the direction and strength of "unconscious" factors, and to locate critical situations along the career line of an individual in which these unconscious factors are shaped. Psychoanalysis has brought into political science, as into all studies of man, a method of investigating the unconscious substratum of personalities and situations.

4

In what sense is the *Psychopathology* an application of psychoanalysis to politics? To put it negatively: the book

[6] Dr. Richard Rush, *On the Influence of the American Revolution on the Human Body*

is the work not of a professional practitioner of psycho-analysis but of a professional student of political behavior. Hence the psychoanalysts have grounds for disclaiming whatever they disapprove of. Thirty years ago psycho-analysis was so new that the literature of the subject con-tained very few explicit applications to politics.[7] No tra-dition had been established of publishing in this field, however ardent the individual analyst might be about polit-ical philosophy or practical politics. By contrast, system-atic students of government had a long tradition of active concern with theories of human nature in society and hence of human nature in politics. Referring only to British thinkers, it is enough to recall John Locke, Thomas Hobbes, and Jeremy Bentham among the "classics" and Graham Wallas among contemporaries.[8]

We can say that the book is an "application" in at least these senses. The author was exposed to a training analysis from psychoanalysts (and from physicians or psychol-ogists heavily indebted to Freud); he brought together the case fragments available in the literature and examined the articles and books—few in number—dealing directly with psychoanalysis and politics; he discussed theories of the interrelationship with specialists and read the existing corpus of psychoanalytic literature (and the appraisals of psychoanalysis made by former associates of Freud and by exponents of other "schools"—Kraepelinian psychiatrists,

---

[7] The bibliography noted specific discussions of politics and psychoanalysis by Oskar Pfister, Hanns Sachs, Otto Rank, A. J. Storfer, Karl Abraham, Ludwig Jekels, Leo Kaplan, Ernest Jones, Viktor Tausk, Hans Blüher, Sieg-fried Bernfeld, Paul Federn, L. Pierce Clark, Aurel Kolnai, Joel Rinaldo, William A. White, Barbara Low, William Boven, Emil Lorenz, J. K. Friedjung, Herman Swoboda, Wilhelm Reich, and a few others.

[8] Graham Wallas did not refer to Freud in *Human Nature in Politics* (1908). In *The Great Society* (1914) the only allusion is a footnote (p. 141). Wallas objects to the proposition imputed to Freud that all love between human beings is sex feeling.

Watsonian behaviorists, Pavlovian reflexologists, McDoug-
alian instinctualists, Wertheimerian perceptualists, Stern-
ian personalists, Angellian functionalists [to mention a
few]).

The *Psychopathology* may be called an application in a
further and perhaps more debatable sense. The author obtained some of the case material directly by means of life-
history interviews with politically active persons. The interviews elicited free associations from the subjects, thus
obtaining a body of material more amenable to "depth"
interpretation than was obtained by traditional methods
of interviewing and participant observation. The interviews were with subjects who said they were willing to live
up to the psychoanalytic rule of "speaking out everything
that crosses your mind," and who were provided with opportunities to associate freely to dreams, slips of the
tongue, gestures, gross body movements—and to the interviewer.

The "prolonged interview" was conducted with subjects
who had highly diverse motivations. Some were referred
by physicians who although too busy to take the individual
as a patient were willing to cover the interviewer with their
medical responsibility. The situation proceeded substantially as in the ordinary therapeutic interview. In some
other cases therapy was an unimportant motive. The principal incentive might be the opportunity to get better acquainted with the technique of free association (and to
receive psychoanalytically oriented interpretations). Hence
the relationship was substantially that of the orthodox
training analysis. Some subjects were willing and able to
talk about themselves but they could not—or would not—
engage in free association. Others wanted to talk about
their professional career in politics with minimum disclosure of their intimate histories. Such a subject might

give little information about his sexual life and could not lift the amnesia of pre-Oedipal years.

5

While it would be a mistake to exaggerate the distinction, a useful contrast can be drawn between two modes of applying psychoanalysis—or indeed any other psychological innovation—to the study of politics. The take-off point of one is the theoretical system. The other emphasizes the observational standpoint, the specific procedures by which theoretical systems are linked to a field of observation. The *Psychopathology* was the outcome of an attempt to apply and adapt a procedure rather than to propose a formally exhaustive body of applications of a comprehensive system of theory.

The choice was deliberate. At one time I thought of making a systematic exposition of the theory of psychoanalysis and suggesting as many implications for politics as I could think of. But the theory was in rapid flux. A movement of ideas was under way that presently resulted in the "ego" theory which added so much to the instinctual and super-ego dimensions of the personality system.[9] More important, however, was the fact that I was more impressed by the observational procedures innovated by Freud than by the theory or its then available results. The "unconscious," for instance, was in Plato; Plato's "unconscious" was populated by the same congeries of repressed sexual and destructive drives that reappeared in psychoanalysis.

The most distinctive innovation of Freud appeared to be the prolonged interview, with its reliance upon both free

[9] A landmark was Anna Freud, *The Ego and the Mechanisms of Defense.*

association and interpretation for scientific and therapeutic purposes. The method seemed to contain within itself the seeds of its own correction. No matter how literary, mythological, and Grecian the terms employed in analytic theory, it was obvious to me that they were capable of operational definition in the context of the interview situation itself.

6

My primary purpose in the *Psychopathology*, in the light of these considerations, was to disseminate provisional findings obtained by the use of the psychoanalytic method of observation. Since the theory was incomplete, the essential aim was to contribute to the sophisticating of the political-science audience to the challenge of a new and evolving standpoint for the study of human nature in politics.

Psychoanalysts and social scientists had not yet become fully alive to the point that it is impossible to examine a case from a psychodynamic point of view without making an important contribution to knowledge. Hence the case histories taken by psychoanalytically oriented clinicians were not centrally abstracted in a way that brought out their significance for the social process. It was necessary to travel from clinic to clinic and from physician to physician in order to find out whether they could recall, or produce records of, politically active persons. Enough instances were assembled to sustain my initial characterization of various political "types" (or, more conveniently, "rôles").

However open to modification in detail the findings may be, I think that the *Psychopathology* was on the right track, for instance, in seeking to connect the playing of a political rôle with the whole personality system as it is found at any cross-section of adult life; and further, in attempting to connect the personality of the adult with the developmental sequence through which the person has passed.

In many ways the most distinctive impact of the social and psychological sciences is the ceaseless confrontation of conventional patterns with their functional significance. In the special realm of politics this calls for the study and restudy of every conventional feature of what are commonly called "politics," "government," and "law." The object of the exercise is to arrive at an appraisal of any specific detail or of the total institution in terms of its importance for man. Or, to put it another way, the purpose is to reveal the significance of any institutional practice or personality trait for human values. To the extent that this task is accomplished the scientific scrutiny of man contributes to the potential enlightenment of all.

Strictly speaking, we are going beyond "official" categories when we perceive the "agitator," "administrator," "theorist," or related rôle-player in public life. Our formal system of government does not elect individuals to the post of "agitator" or "theorist"; and the jobs which are called "administrative" are not necessarily held by "administrators" as we describe them. As indicated in the *Psychopathology*, such "types" are characterized by an inner tie with particular activities. When we describe agitators, administrators, and theorists in terms of an inner bond with categories of action, we have already gone beyond the simple identification of an "office" with a "generalized rôle." A step has been taken in the direction of separating conventional slots in the social system from fully elaborated appraisals in functional terms.

To describe a personality system comprehensively at any cross-section in time is to discover the pattern of value demands (and specifications) of the person, and to describe the mechanisms chiefly relied upon by the person in seeking to maintain internal order within the changing configuration of external environments. The value demands are selective in regard to outcome; the mechanisms are selective in terms of the style by which outcomes are sought. Any conventional perspective or operation within a total system of personality is functionally described when we can say how much the specific pattern is valued within the whole system, and how representative the style is.

7

Today I find it advantageous to use a standard list of categories for the purpose of designating the preferred outcomes—the values sought by persons or groups.[10] Wherever a component of choice enters, an individual seeks to maximize preferred outcomes and to minimize dis-preferred outcomes. He seeks to do this within the limits of the capacities available to him. We speak of a zero or low range of choice—which we call coercion—when factors are present that operate upon the human being as though he were an inanimate object, as at the time when a desperately wounded and helpless soldier is taken prisoner, or killed. The degree of coercion is also high when the only available alternatives are disadvantageous in terms

[10] See especially Lasswell and A. Kaplan, *Power and Society: A Framework for Political Inquiry* (1950). Recent applications: Lasswell, "The Normative Impact of the Behavioral Sciences," *Ethics*, 67, 1957, 1-42; M. S. McDougal and Lasswell, "The Identification and Appraisal of Diverse Systems of Public Order," *American Journal of International Law*, 53, 1959, 1-29.

of the preferences of the individual, as when he must surrender or accept the overwhelming probability of being
destroyed.

In human affairs the demand to coerce is the phenomenon with which we are most concerned as professional
students of politics. This is the distinctive characteristic of
the social value that we call power. It is the most rewarding object of "functional" as distinguished from "conventional" study in the political and legal sciences.

The demand to impose, which is a synonym for the demand to coerce, has been recognized since the study of
politics began as a distinctive field of inquiry. More accurately, political thinkers have generally dealt with power
relations *within* a territorially bounded community context
or *among* such contexts. The only exceptions have been
closely related contexts, such as the nomad tribes who
move through the jungle and have no clear territorial demands; or social formations which, though contiguous to
others, largely confine themselves to interacting with their
own members (ghetto-like religious societies, for instance).

When we examine community contexts in which human
beings interact with one another, it is always possible to
find at least a few situations in which adults coerce one
another (and pre-adults). In all these settings it is feasible
to discover *relative* power even when the degree of power
may seem small in the context of larger groupings. Power
relations in the relative sense can be found in every group-
ing, no matter how small (the pair, the trio, and so on).

Comprehensive investigations of power relationships
must make clear *which* context is being studied for how
long. Even in very small social settings it may be important
to make the distinction between conventional and functional conceptions. The members of a small colonizing
venture may agree that y is supposed to be under the

orders of x. Everyone may be equally aware that y is the originator of policy ideas and that x is timid and indolent, so that x performs a formal "rubber-stamping" role for y. So long as forms of "authority" are not flouted, effective "control" may remain in the hands of y without any disruption of "legal order" followed by the emergence of a "naked power" system or a new legal order.

8

We cannot arrive at a clear delimitation of the power value in a given social context without making explicit its connection with all the other categories of value with which a scientific observer characterizes the total context. (The point of using an exhaustive category list is to make it easier to make valid comparisons from one context to another. If the category list is not treated as exhaustive it is impossible to know what may have been omitted in the description of each context.)

It is convenient to identify some value-shaping and -sharing activities as "wealth." They culminate in transactions (gifts, barter, exchange) by which claims to assets capable of producing more wealth are open to transfer or claims are transferrable for the obtaining of goods or services that may be consumed. When claims to assets are transferred by the use of coercion the relationship has become one of power in addition to one of wealth.

Besides power and wealth we have identified six categories of value: respect, affection, skill, enlightenment, well-being, rectitude. In each instance valued outcomes are shaped and shared; and they culminate in potential transfers of claim to further development or to enjoyment.

Although I did not examine the data provided by psychoanalytic interviewing from the standpoint of the systematic value analysis here outlined, the information can be made more widely comparable in this frame of reference. So far as the power value is concerned the *Psychopathology* adopted substantially the same conception here outlined. When we examine the unconscious component of the "agitator" we perceive that the "demand for response" is intelligible as a drive to obtain prompt indulgence from large audiences in terms of values such as affection and respect. Indeed, some "enthusiastic" agitators are so seductive in their approach that it would be a mistake to think of them as "power-centered personalities," if we restrict this designation to the rather extreme cases in which the personality is intensely focused upon coerciveness.

Some "agitators" are greatly involved in the condemnation of others. To condemn is to apply a standard of responsibility (of "right and wrong") and to declare and denounce alleged nonconformity. Psychoanalytic research clearly indicates the importance of standards of responsibility (of rectitude) to the self-appraisal of the politicians in question. These persecutory agitators are "driven by guilt"—by severe condemnations of the self—and seek to obtain relief by such mechanisms as the projection upon others of adverse characterizations in terms of rectitude.

Although "administrators" were treated as less demanding than agitators of gratification from particular people, it was obvious that the predilection of some "bureaucrats" for red tape was connected with the struggle to keep their destructive impulses under control. In these cases the demand to coerce was very close to full expression and therefore suggests a closer affinity with power-centered than with more permissive types.

Because of my absorption with relatively active persons in conventional government and politics, I came almost incidentally upon the intimate histories of individuals who were primarily oriented toward business. It was quite obvious that some party politicians were almost wholly oblivious to any opportunity other than money-making. They fed their private businesses with government contracts, and devised clever ways of combining pay-offs and legality. An examination of their personality structure suggested that they were strongly motivated toward consolidating their personal security and that of the family. Besides affection and respect, they attached great importance to well-being—toward attaining health, safety, and comfort in old age.

The sketch of the "theorist" gave weight to enlightenment (and skill) values, and reported that the individuals in question had met many frustrations in early life. In a few instances power motivations were close to the surface and took the indirect form of attachment to an active politician whom the subjects hoped to influence.

9

Unless the summary statement is supported by a vast amount of detailed data it cannot be said that we have learned much when we say that x is more strongly oriented toward one value than toward another, and that fully conscious perspectives are not the same as the value demands, expectations, or identifications that lie near the surface. I propose to provide a fairly precise indication of how the technique of psychoanalysis can be employed to provide the research worker with knowledge of the value system of his object of study, and to enable the interviewer to benefit from the proceedings by improving the effective insight at his disposal.

First, however, it will be economical to make a point about the nature of the "mechanisms" which analytic work has brought to light. By mechanism we refer to the patterning displayed by the fundamental elements of an act (or sequence of interaction). The elements are the units of which all acts are composed, units whose arrangement accounts for formal differences among them.

In classifying the basic components of an act, from the standpoint of a scientific observer, we characterize the event sequence constituting the act as (1) symbols, (2) signs, and (3) movements and materials. Movements and materials are the "physical events" familiar to every natural scientist. They can be assigned operational indexes of the kind used to measure mass and energy. Signs, on the other hand, are more complex because they include two components: body movements and an inferred pattern of subjective events (symbols) insofar as they are indexable by testimony. "Testimony" typically means words; and the words tell "what the sign is about." A symbol is a subjective event, and the "outside" observer must select the pattern of verbal references or other signs that he will accept as an operational index.

The distinctions among symbols, signs, and movements enable us to refer with as much precision as desired to any specific mechanism. Some mechanisms, for example, occur in acts in which bodily events are conspicuous, as in the case of paralyses or any conversion having a "psychosomatic" origin.[11] One category of mechanisms is

---

[11] See A. G. Wolff, ed., "Life Stress and Bodily Disease," *Proceedings of the Association for Research on Nervous and Mental Disease*, 29, 1950; F. Dunbar, *Emotions and Bodily Changes*, 4th ed. (1954). Concerning gesture: R. L. Bird-

distinguished by the degree of elaboration achieved by signs. This is true of "pressure of speech," "stereotyped gestures," and the like. Finally come the mechanisms whose principal complication is symbolic in the sense of "subjective."

Psychoanalysis was particularly successful in discerning the great variety of symbol mechanisms (a term used more broadly by Freud than it is used here). Projection, introjection, condensation: these are faint reminders of the whole.

In describing symbol events it is useful to draw subdistinctions among symbols of "identification," "demand," and "expectation." The "I," "me" events are "primary ego" identifications; and the symbols of other egos may be included with a primary ego to comprise a "self." Some symbol references are to non-self egos; these are "other selves."

The demand symbols are "preferences" and "volitions" for outcome events (values). These may be classified according to power, wealth, respect, affection, skill, enlightenment, well-being, rectitude. We find that each value is in some degree demanded by the "self as a whole" and also on behalf of each "sub-self," such as the family, political party, nation, and so on.

The "expectations" are the matter-of-fact references (excluding the symbols of identification).

We must distinguish events that are "fully conscious at the full focus of waking awareness" from those that are "marginally conscious," "preconscious," and "unconscious." Furthermore, it is essential to take note of the phases through which an "act" may run to completion and the modes of interference or facilitation that occur.

whistell, *Introduction to Kinesics*, Foreign Service Institute, Department of State (1952) ; M. Krout, *Autistic Gestures* (1935).

10

Without going further into these mechanisms at the moment it may be possible to show how a systematic "value" approach to the interaction between psychoanalytic interviewer and interviewee can provide both data for the scientist and effective insight for the subject.

Let us begin by looking at what goes on during an interview from the value standpoint. As we shall see, the same basic categories must be given distinct operational indexes from the point of view of each observer-participant. The interviewee, it will be recalled, has agreed to speak out whatever crosses his mind.

Suppose that an interviewee begins — as therapeutic cases often do—by complaining of a physical symptom. In terms of the "manifest content" the interviewee is obviously concerned with the well-being value.

This is by no means the universal beginning. One person may get under way by complaining of his difficulty in the sphere of love. He may comment upon no difficulty with the sexual organs, and dilate exclusively upon the difficulty of loving and being loved. Another interviewee may take off with complaints in the sphere of respect relations, alleging that he is continually being denied recognition. Or the problem may be one of skill: "I am hopelessly clumsy at work or at play." Enlightenment may be the source of concern: "I am confused about myself and the world." Economic difficulties may be put in the foreground; or frustrated political ambition. The interviewee may be "depressed" (which we call a negative well-being reference) because of a "vague and damning sense of guilt" (a negative rectitude reference).

The foregoing samples (from direct experience) show the interviewee presenting himself to the interviewer as "deprived" rather than "indulged" in terms of each value standard applied (to self by self).

References to the self are not wholly adverse. Even at the beginning the predominating presentation may be favorable, often in the form of direct evaluation. The picture is likely to be complicated, not simply by negative references to an "other," but by the portrayal of the "other" as "wrongfully" imposing deprivations (or indulgences) upon the self.

It is worth pausing to underline the point that regardless of the categories employed by the interviewer, or the technique employed to keep the stream flowing productively, every case history is of potential significance for the understanding of man and society. Depth interviews of the kind provide "inside accounts" of what it is like to live in the various social settings to which an individual is exposed from early infancy to the date of interview. For the purposes of research we use such categories as the following to describe social settings:

Communities.[12] This term refers to contiguous interacting units with distinctive cultures. They vary from "modern" and "ancient civilizations" or "folk societies" to significant regions such as the Southern States, or lesser entities.

Classes.[13] Within a community people can be classified according to upper, middle, or lower share of power, wealth, and all other social values.

[12] The most daring attempts to apply psychoanalytic and related conceptions to the impact of culture upon personality are to be found in the work of Margaret Mead, G. Gorer, H. V. Dicks, J. Rickman, W. LaBarre, G. Bateson, J. C. Moloney, A. Kardiner (among others). Consult M. Mead, "The Study of National Character," in Lerner and Lasswell, *The Policy Sciences: Recent Developments in Scope and Method* (1951). See E. Fromm, *Escape from Freedom;* J. Whiting and I. Child, *Child Training and Personality: A Cross-Cultural Study* (1953).

[13] The interplay of class and personality has figured in the writings of such distinguished sociologists as Karl Mannheim and Talcott Parsons.

Interests.[14] Groups that are too small for classes, or that cut across class or even community lines, are interests.

Personalities.[15] Everyone has an environment of personality systems which are characterizable by value-orientation, specific practice interpretations, and mechanisms.

Crises.[16] This term refers to high or low levels of "stress toward action." The four preceding categories are repeated here on the assumption that on the "first time through" the classification was according to some "normal" or "frequent" level.

11

For the study of "politics from within" it is obvious that these social settings are of great importance, and that every psychoanalytic interview discloses a constellation of formative factors that, while presumably constant within limits for each context, are changing at various rates. It is a matter of keen regret that psychodynamically oriented specialists have been slow in organizing a procedure for reporting at least many of the most pertinent features of every case. Had these collections been available during the last thirty years—to reiterate a complaint in the *Psychopathology*—

[14] Concerning various interests and personality: O. Sperling, "Psychoanalytic Aspects of Bureaucracy," *Psychoanalytic Quarterly*, 19, 1950, 88-100; H. Zink, "A Case Study of a Political Boss," *Psychiatry*, 1, 1938, 527-33; F. Alexander and F. Staub, *The Criminal, the Judge and the Public* (1931); J. Frank, *Law and the Modern Mind* (1930).

[15] George, A. L. and J. L., *Woodrow Wilson and Colonel House: A Personality Study* (1956); Adorno et al., *Authoritarian Personality* (1950); R. M. Lindner, *Rebel Without a Cause* (1944); R. E. Lane, "Political Character and Political Analysis," *Psychiatry*, 16, 1953, 387-398; J. R. Rees, ed., *The Case of Rudolf Hess, A Problem in Diagnosis and Forensic Psychiatry* (1948); G. M. Gilbert, *Nuremberg Diary* (1947).

[16] The topic of war has attracted the most psychoanalytic attention. For example: R. Waelder, E. Glover, E. F. M. Durbin and J. Bowlby, Money-Kyrle, W. A. White, I. D. Suttie. For current discussions see the journal *Conflict Resolution*.

our knowledge would be far more full and reliable concerning the impact of civilizations, classes, interests, and personality types upon one another at various levels of crisis.

As such knowledge grows in representativeness and depth, social psychiatry comes to play a more valuable rôle in appraising the human consequences of all social formations. Freud succeeded in posing questions which can be answered only when adequate institutions of self-survey are in operation. For instance, the founder of psychoanalysis was apprehensive of the future of man in society. It is true, certainly, that Freud himself lived an exceedingly "bourgeois" life despite his long struggle to overcome a recalcitrant neurosis. No matter how murderous or incestuous the impulses that erupted from his unconscious, Freud held them in check by the steady fortification of his ego structure. But Freud's apprehensions sprang from the expectation that other men and women might not be able to wage a successful struggle for self-mastery. Hence mankind must, in all probability, look ahead to outbursts against the "intolerable" burden of culture.[17]

As a countervailing consideration we may draw, not only upon Freud's private victory as a widely emulated model, but upon the clarification of human development which has been expedited by the shock and the productivity of psychoanalysis. The more intensively we analyze the "self system" the more apparent it becomes that the true unit in the social process is *not* the biological entity comprised of man the organism. Rather each unit is a person-to-person context.

Most revolutionary innovators, like Freud, find it almost impossible to accept fully some of their most brilliant

[17] *Civilization and Its Discontents* remains one of the most arresting of Freud's political and sociological essays.

discoveries. It is not surprising to find that Freud continued to talk about "man" versus "society" rather than to
recognize that it is always a case of "man in society"
versus (or with) "man in society." From the earliest days
of birth—if not, indeed, during prenatal months—social
influences play upon and modify each physical organism,
so that each organism moves through time carrying the
latest "modified-by-society" into the next opportunity to be
modified, and to influence others in return.[18]

12

The significance of this conception is exemplified by the
train of events in the interview situation, with its ceaseless
to and fro of "signs" which mediate "symbol" events between the two immediate participants. A few pages above
I called attention to some features of the interview seen
from the standpoint of an interviewer who was classifying
the self-references (and some other references) uttered
by the interviewee. Let us shift the frame of reference
slightly and consider an interviewer who is noting the significance for him—as interviewer—of the events in the
situation.

Clearly a dominant value for the interviewer is skill;
and the interviewee can run through the gamut from interviewer indulgence to interviewer deprivation. All compe-

[18] I am writing as one who regards the "sociologizing" of psychoanalysis as
a development that is helping to prune Freud's legacy of mistakes. Among
European analysts in America Karen Horney played an important transition
rôle. The native American, Harry Stack Sullivan, made the Washington
School of Psychiatry of the W A. White Foundation a center for the study
of interpersonal relations. For the present state of research upon the therapeutic process and the therapeutic community see M. Greenblatt, D. J. Lev-
inson, R. H. Williams, eds., *The Patient and the Mental Hospital* (1957) and
A. H. Leighton, J. A. Clausen, R. N. Wilson, eds., *Exploration in Social Psychiatry* (1957).

tent analysts are keenly sensitive to the ways in which their skill may be tested and often frustrated by the defensive maneuvers of the unconscious "defenses" of the personality system of the interviewee.

Psychoanalysts are subject to indulgences and deprivations in terms of affection. An interviewee may arouse the love of the interviewer and confront him with the "costs" of denying spontaneous expressions of affection in order to assist the subject to overcome his peculiar problems.

Interviewers are often exposed to moral problems; for example, the obvious suffering that some interviewee patients go through can arouse deep guilt feelings. These are typically more subtle and difficult to cope with than an outspoken denunciation uttered by the patient.

There are problems connected with curiosity (enlightenment). Interviewers may touch upon matters of great interest and some importance for understanding an aspect of world affairs; but the interviewer voluntarily endures frustration by not following up the allusion.

I have referred to feelings of guilt. Typically these are complicated by anxiety and other surviving features of the interviewer's neurosis (or even psychosis). Some interviewees exert unmistakably adverse effects upon the well-being of the interviewer.

Interviewers are often confronted by the prospect of economic loss, not only from "service" cases, but as a maneuver by patients and sponsors. Indulgences, too, are forthcoming; and one test of the interviewer's level of skill and rectitude is whether he distinguishes between "symptoms" and realistically acceptable contributions.

Respect values are chronically at stake for the interviewer, especially when the interviewee is of higher social position and betrays "unconscious" devaluations of lower-class people.

Many interviewers are heavily enough involved with politics in the conventional sense to feel threatened when interviewees attack their party program or the ideology of the "capitalistic system."

The latter allusion to politics is a conventional meaning. An interviewer has ample occasion to be the target of power, and to exercise power in the functional sense of coercion. This is especially obvious in the context of a mental hospital, for instance, where the physician has more potential power over the patient than over a volunteer subject on the outside.

The important point is that the interviewer-interviewee relationship, like all social interactions, is a continuing process of value indulgence and deprivation by each participant of the other, and of each self by the self. As has been indicated above, the indulgences or deprivations "of the self by the self" are often more intense than the plus or minus responses directed toward an "other," or immediately received from an "other."

The latter point does not, however, imply that the "individual" faces "society"; for the components of the self that indulge or deprive the self are the imprints of past experience interacting with others.

13

It must be apparent by this time why the study of politicians (and of politics in general) by methods largely inspired by psychoanalysis has made but modest progress to date. There are thousands of political rôles. It is a vast social audit to discern these rôles in the conventional or the functional sense. And it is a vast task to ascertain the degree in which these rôles are played by power-oriented personalities. It is a huge undertaking to demonstrate the developmental sequence that results in the formation of a power-centered personality at maturity—that is, one who prefers to impose rather than to persuade even when persuasion would accomplish every desired outcome (except the opportunity to coerce). And the matter is further complicated by the changing patterns of development as different modes of conduct are treated indulgently or deprivationally in the home circle, the school, the community at large. The relevant configuration is continually shifting through time as political rôles change their relationship to personality systems; and the developmental history of personality systems is a perpetual flux. Finally, insight and understanding—knowledge of the self by the self, intelligence concerning past decisions in the decision process—enter into the vast and continual redefinition of rôle, personality, and development.

14

Very likely the *Psychopathology* performed a positive part in pointing toward the configurative study of man in context. But it is obvious that a gigantic intellectual enterprise, itself an act of institution building, is essential if we are to move nearer to what we *can* know. A major part of the task is to make the theory of political personality explicit for each important observational standpoint. (The operational indexes vary from standpoint to standpoint.)

Without attempting to make an exhaustive classification of observational standpoints we may indicate some criteria by which intensiveness may be graded. The most intensive procedures are those in which (1) the subjects are aware of the observer and of the fact of being studied,

(2) the methods of recording and processing data require specialized training, and (3) the time relations are prolonged. The prolonged psychoanalytic interview is a highly intensive standpoint since the subjects are acutely aware of being studied by a specialist who may take many hours (and possibly years) to complete the observation. The standpoint is also intensive, though not psychoanalytic, when an observer uses a battery of tests at periodic intervals under experimental conditions, or acts as a participant in ordinary life situations (while recording the data —a standard technique of social anthropologists). The standpoint is much less intensive when the subject matter is restricted to reporting and commenting upon the professional career, for instance (as when a judge tells his story to a legally trained person). The standpoint is even less intensive when tests are administered that bring out only a few preferences and expectations of the subjects; or when a qualified observer—such as a psychoanalyst—is unable to apply his distinctive method to the subject but makes inferences about him based on data obtained in other circumstances (as when interpretations are given of the conduct of a witness in litigation, or a prisoner awaiting trial or serving a sentence).

Besides distinguishing among standpoints according to intensiveness it is useful to add such criteria as the objectives of participants (therapy or training, for example), and the degree to which the objective is accomplished (in the judgment of the observer who relies exclusively upon the data obtained in the situation). Schematically:

OBSERVATIONAL STANDPOINTS

A. Intensiveness—extensiveness
   1. Hours consumed

  2. Specialization of recording and processing (including experimentation)
  3. Subjects' awareness, unawareness
    a. Of observer
    b. Of being studied
B. Objectives—results
  1. Therapy, training, research objectives
  2. Degree to which objectives are obtained

By "collector" we mean an observer who has no immediate relationship to the subject and cannot affect the result (as in the case of the historian who studies Julius Caesar today). The "interviewer" is known by his subject to be studying him. The "participant" is known by his subject but is not recognized to be studying him. The "spectator" observes persons who are unaware of the observer or of being observed for study purposes. The procedures of interviewers, participants, or spectators may be experimental or non-experimental. The objectives may be research, training, or therapy.[19]

[19] One of the most important movements of recent years has been the multiplication of attempts to quantify the psychoanalytic interview situation as a step toward experimentation. Many modifications of the orthodox model crystalized by Freud are now in use, of which the most novel is perhaps the therapeutic group. It may be of historical interest to note that although I spoke with many psychiatrists and psychoanalysts in Europe in 1928 and 1929 no one could see any merit in trying to obtain verbatim interviews, or of extending the record to include physiological changes or notes on visible body movements. Another American (E. Zinn) was posing the same "weirdly American" ideas independently at about the same time. I returned in 1929 fully confident of the importance of "objectifying" the interview situation. Among American psychiatrists, Harry Stack Sullivan was among several who were fully committed to objectification and who had recorded some of his work with schizophrenic patients at the Sheppard and Enoch Pratt Hospital at Towson, Maryland. The new Social Science Research Building at the University of Chicago made it possible to begin an objectification program. Dr. William A. White, Superintendent of St. Elizabeth's Hospital, Washington, D. C., was most encouraging about the project. With the assistance of Chester Darrow and others apparatus was devised which made it possible to correlate variations in electrical skin conductivity with the verbatim record, and also to obtain

15

A comprehensive approach to the study of political personalities would relate every general concept to specific indexes obtainable in each standpoint of observation. For working purposes let us define a political personality as "power-centered," as emphasizing the power value (*relative* to the group of which the subject is representative; relative emphasis is important since we know that power occupies a low conscious position in various cultures, social classes, interest groups, personalities, and intercrisis periods).

Suppose we relate this brief definition to one of the less complex observational standpoints (call it standpoint A) appropriate to the study of such politicians as judges, administrators, party leaders. Standpoint A is that of an

continuous tracings of pulse rate and respiration. The interviewer kept notes of all observed body movements. Blood-pressure readings and blood samples were taken before and after interviews. The following articles report some of the results: Lasswell, "Verbal References and Physiological Changes During the Psychoanalytic Interview: A Preliminary Communication," *Psychoanalytic Review*, 22, 1935, 10-24; "Certain Prognostic Changes During Trial (Psychoanalytic) Interviews," *Psychoanalytic Review*, 23, 1936, 241-247; "Veränderungen an einer Versuchsperson während einer kurzen Folge von psychoanalytischen Interviews," *Imago* (Vienna), 23, 1937, 375-80.

When I left the University of Chicago in 1938 the trucks that were transporting the research records had an accident. The driver of the first truck went to sleep and ran off the road, and the second truck ran into the first, and sprayed the papers and sprung files with gasoline. Since my chief concern was collective political processes the coming of the war led me to concentrate upon problems of communication. Content analysis methods, originally tried out on psychoanalytic interviews, were adapted to the surveillance of printed and recorded material. Since the war several major projects have proceeded with the objectification of the interview. See F. Auld, Jr., and E. J. Murphy, "Content-Analysis Studies of Psychotherapy," *Psychological Bulletin*, 52, 1955, 377-95. See, for instance, J. Dollard and O. H. Mowrer, "A Method of Measuring Tension in Written Documents," *Journal of Abnormal and Social Psychology*, 43, 1947, 3-32. Also, Lasswell, "A Provisional Classification of Symbol Data," *Psychiatry*, 1, 1938, 197-204; Lasswell, Leites, and Associates, *Language of Politics, Studies in Quantitative Semantics* (1948).

interviewer who is legally trained and who is asking not for a total history—which would include information about the sex life of the subject, for instance—but for a strictly professional autobiography. Assume that in standpoint A no use is made of free association, analytic interpretation, or tests. We now specify some of the operational indices by which "political personalities" are to be recognized. In general our indexes include all statements articulating a "demand to impose." We sub-classify according to whether the statements are "by the self" "about the self," or "about others" (than the interviewer); or "about the interviewer." (In the classification of the data obtained we may adopt the convention of authorizing the use of the term "political personality" in reference to subjects in the upper quartile of each group.)

The categories:

"Pro-self": Direct expressions of satisfaction by the statement maker at having imposed his will upon others in any situations of any kind any time in his life; accounts of such situations; declarations of intention to impose himself in the future; predictions of success and elaboration of plans and forecasts.

"Anti-self": Condemnations of the self for having permitted someone to impose his will upon him and get away with it; accounts of the alleged occasions; pessimistic forecasts of the outcome of future efforts at "emancipating" himself or in imposing his will on others.

"Anti-other" (than interviewer): Condemnation of others for having tried to impose their will, whether successfully or not; accounts of alleged occasions; imputation of plans by the other to dominate; elaboration of such plans.

"Pro-other" (than interviewer): Praise of others for having tried to dominate others—including the statement maker—and for having gotten away with it; elaboration of circumstances; approving forecasts of future efforts at imposition; elaboration of the forecasts.

"Pro-interviewer": Praise of interviewer for having tried to impose his will, with or without success; elaboration; approving forecast of future efforts; elaboration.

"Anti-interviewer": Condemnation of interviewer for having tried to impose his will with or without success; elaboration; accusing forecasts; elaboration.

Is it entirely satisfactory to say that all persons (and groups) obtaining a low score during a "professional-interviews-professional" interview (standpoint A) are *not* political personalities? No. Experience suggests that in some cultures it is regarded as inadmissible to make such statements to a fellow professional (even in the name of "science"—if that term has any meaning in the culture). We also know that members of different social classes are likely to differ in uttering statements of the kind. And we know—or at least strongly suspect—that some personality systems do not tolerate such admissions.

We must therefore take the results obtained in standpoint A as provisional, and give higher priority to the results in more intensive standpoints (as when the subjects agree to discuss their entire lives, intimate or professional, and accept the interviewer as professionally qualified to receive such revelations). In our culture such a standpoint (call it B) is most likely to be taken by a physician, social worker, or psychologist; but it can also be occupied by a person who has little training in these professions, but has a reputation for broad experience and personal maturity. Even today we do not have enough systematic experience with the gathering of data by procedures of type B to know how to relate them to the results obtained in comparable contexts by procedure A.

16

Standpoints A and B have been discussed as means of ascertaining the conscious perspectives of the persons studied. But the *Psychopathology* obviously did not restrict the definition of political personality to conscious perspective. It examined the results of various observational standpoints in order to bring out unconscious as well as conscious structure. Data concerning unconscious orientation are important in arriving at a final classification of political rôles as nuclear or peripheral to a given personality system. The significant question appears to be whether denials of opportunity to play a political role—even a humble one—will destroy the integration of the person. Sometimes the environment performs an "experiment" for us and imposes such deprivations upon the individual— by forcing him out of office, for instance. As a result the person may attempt an extreme internalization (suicide) or display somatic conversion symptoms of a severely incapacitating nature, or become mentally disordered. Some of the cases reported in the *Psychopathology* came to the attention of the therapists precisely because of political reverses. They were power-oriented persons in the fullest sense of our definition, since their capacity to continue as integrated members of society depended upon a social situation in which they pursued and exercised power with some success. These personality systems were so rigidly oriented toward the playing of a particular set of rôles that they were unable to maintain their integrity when these opportunities were shut off.

By examining the unconscious dimensions of the personality of a person who has not yet been rebuffed we may be able to predict his response to political deprivation. However, if the exploration of the unconscious is carried on in a manner that enables the subject to increase his insight a prediction may appear to be falsified. (We should point out that it is possible to assess the unconscious orientation of a subject without contributing to his insight, as in the use of narcosynthesis or certain methods of projective testing.)

Besides enabling us to diagnose the nuclear or peripheral significance of a specific political rôle or of the power value within a personality system, the study of unconscious factors makes it possible to investigate "developmental" sequences. That is to say, the technique by which unconscious dimensions are made manifest is a technique by which past events are currently represented. In the psychoanalytic interview the representation may be by the reporting of events alleged to have occurred in the past. The representation also takes the form of repetition in the present of acts of the past. This occurs, for instance, when the subject "acts out" an early response, even to the extent of weeping, employing childhood intonations and vocabulary, or resuming early body postures. It is to be noted that many acts when initiated in the current interview situation do not obtain direct access to full waking awareness. Anxieties are too acute. However, these acts may achieve indirect expression obtained by "historicizing" in the form of "recall" or "repetition."

The spreading upon the current record of "past reference events" or "past repetition events" enables the scientific observer to obtain data pertinent to the reconstruction of the sequences that typically lie behind selective stress upon political rôles. As indicated before, we must be meticulous in distinguishing between events that occur in the interview context and in pre-interview, co-interview, or post-interview contexts, since it is important to keep the operational indexes of each standpoint separate. The story of a past seduction, for instance, is a datum in the interview situation because it is a story told in the situation, not because it has any truth value about the alleged seduction.[20] It enables the analytic theory to be formulated in operational terms such as these:

When seduction stories are told in interviews, the interviewee will presently change the story from a statement of fact about an overt occurrence to a statement of fact about a past subjective demand on his part (e.g., to be seduced by the individual referred to). Or: The probability that a seduction story will be told is increased if the interviewee has been accusing the interviewer and other authority figures of intending to assault him. (And so on.)

Ideally it should be possible at any given time to report the frequency with which these hypotheses have been confirmed or disconfirmed up to date. It is apparent that if the frequency of actual seductions involving adults and children is to be established, other observational standpoints must be utilized. The developmental theory formulated in the psychoanalytic situation and operationally defined within it can be applied—with different operational definitions—in the other standpoints. In general our scientific knowledge is complete to the extent that we can reliably predict the results that will be obtained in *all* standpoints from the data obtained in *any* standpoint. Thus it may turn out that psychoanalytically interviewed politicians are largely recruited (95 per cent) from persons

[20] Freud learned the significance of this distinction the hard way. Ernest Jones puts the pertinent incidents in proper perspective in the first volume of his biography of Freud.

who allege that they were exposed as children to a certain set of experiences. Data may confirm the prediction that a lower percentage (90 per cent) among those taking projective tests allege similar experiences (or give evidence of having had them). Further research may confirm the prediction that a smaller percentage (75 per cent) will testify to experiences of the type when interviewed by less intensive methods (as in standpoint A above). The broad hypothesis about inter-standpoint predictions is that *predictability varies directly with the intensive-extensive distance of the standpoints*. More intensive positions predict the lesser.

17

The figures given above are hypothetical, since little systematic work has been done along such lines. However, we have enough accumulated experience to justify the formulation of hypotheses concerning developmentally significant experiences. In the present discussion I shall not go further than to say that the most comprehensive proposition is that *power-centered personalities are developed by individuals who come to rely upon power practices (rôles) as the preferred means of maximizing their value position. This comes about in response to deprivations received from persons who are also regarded as sources of great indulgence. Strong rage and persistence responses find outlets that are successful in mitigating deprivations though not in reinstating full indulgence.* To be fully meaningful each proposition must be specified operationally for each cross-section along the career line for each standpoint of observation (from least to most intensive). The hypothesis can be restricted as desired to bring into the focus of consideration political formations of various degrees of complexity. For instance, a minimum skill requirement can be added to make sure that persons who live only in fantasy and who have no modicum of success will be excluded.[21]

18

One advantage of distinguishing between conventional and functional politics is that it promises to bring into focus the location of the men of power in bodies politic of different kinds. In a huge industrial nation like the United States where the tradition of popular government is lively the "ladder up" probably appeals to a great variety of personality types. At the precinct level in many solid residential districts the politically active corps is often composed of people whose motivations are far removed from the inner agonies of power.[22] We often see housewives who are bored or depressed with the routine and welcome a chance to engage in active citizenship, which they have been educated to regard as a moral responsibility. They enjoy the congeniality of association with other precinct workers, and welcome the increment of respect that comes from being accepted by friends and neighbors as a "wheel." There is a flow of interesting gossip about City Hall or the State Capitol and Washington— gossip that gratifies several motivations, not excluding the demand for enlightenment about the forces that affect

[21] See Lasswell, *Power and Personality* (1948) (Thomas W. Salmon Memorial Lectures, New York Academy of Medicine, 1947) ; "Democratic Character," in *The Political Writings of Harold D. Lasswell* (1951), 465-525; H. J. Eysenck, *Political Personality* (1954).

[22] Scraps of evidence are being gathered by the behavioral scientists who focus on political process. Among others consult the work of V. O. Key, A. Heard, A. Leiserson, A. de Grazia, H. F. Gosnell, S. Forthal.

one's destiny. Some precinct workers take pride in the skill with which their operations are conducted, and glory in the fact that a new "party" family has been won over by calculated friendship and advice on what to do about a storm sewer. Modest economic advantages may accrue to the precinct committeeman whose insurance or legal firm benefits from his wide circle of contacts. In many precincts not a single worker is ambitious to get ahead up the ladder of conventional politics. The "Catonian strength of conviction" that characterized the youthful Lenin or the insatiable sly ambition of Stalin appear to be phenomena of a different order.

Yet it is not to be overlooked that even in times of security at home and abroad the demand to coerce, and the ambition to work one's way into a position where it is possible to impose one's will upon others, is far from dead even in conventional party politics. The situation is most obvious where it is the crudest; and this applies to some precincts located in high-mobility regions in great metropolitan areas. To the outsider the stakes may seem trivial, but the political organization may appear to offer one of the few means of escape from the oblivion of the city jungle to a place "up there." Physical violence and intimidation may be the norm, not the exception, among juveniles and in the relations between husband and wife, parent and child, neighbor and neighbor. Some boys do what they can to master the hostile forces around them. The police or the military provide the "way up"; and the new recruit is determined to get everything he can whenever he can.

In a society that affords an outlet for "middle-class" ambition there are many conventional paths to top positions in governmental and party organizations. We see bright young men and women moving into law and journalism, and more recently into economics, political science, and the social sciences, in the hope of advancement. Almost all these young people, though ambitious, are far from power-centered; and this, from the standpoint of the public order, is a great source of strength to the common-wealth. Those who move up to the top spots are likely to be friendly though rivalrous men and women for whom a complex pattern of gratification (in terms of affection, respect, enlightenment, and skill, for instance) is more to be sought than power in the functional sense of the word. In American politics the escalator to the top is not a regi-mented, orderly lift, but a tangle of ladders, ropes, and runways that attract people from other activities at various stages of the process, and lead others to a dead end or a blind drop.

The recruitment process in industrialized and demo-cratic nations probably tends to transform power-centered persons into multi-valued individuals, or to reject them entirely. The rejected seekers of power have outlets avail-able in business, trade unionism, organized crime, and other institutions where they can hope to consolidate a monopolistic position and domineer over others. But the world of business, like the world of labor and related activities, has a structure that is controlled only in part by monopolistic elements. Up to the present at least the oc-currence of monopoly control has set counter-monopoly movements in action, which have presented obstacles to the rise of effective dictatorship.

In venerable autocratic and aristocratic systems of pub-lic order human relations are channeled according to "station" in life. The degree of participation in politics is set according to this principle. The elites of recent des-potisms have been carried to power on the shoulders of mass movements which they have instigated and more or less successfully managed or navigated. Fearful of letting go the reins of power, the key elements in the new ruling classes have sought to substitute the principle of professional party service for the older principle of rank, and to use the party to perpetuate ideologically sound elements at the key decision spots. Because of the *ambiance* of terror in which despotisms operate, the process by which elites are recruited puts a premium upon persons who are able to endure uncertainty without losing the ability to identify individuals with whom they can in fact cooperate. If they survive at all, power-centered persons rise rather directly from level to level within the party; and in the long climb they must retain their drive without allowing ambition to darken their appraisal of realistic factors.

The complex division of labor in modern society has been transforming large-scale organizations into large bureaucracies. In a bureaucratic system indirect rather than direct manifestations of power are rewarded; indulgences are given to professional competence, personal affability, sensitiveness to the opinion of others, ethical conduct within the understood code of officialdom, unostentatious consumption, and similar traits. Power motivations are not encouraged to find expression in mass leadership or in open leadership of any kind. In particular, spontaneity is not encouraged; and spontaneity is one of the apparent, and often genuine, characteristics of the "charismatic" figure with whom crowds and fanatics can identify.

The standardization of "position" in modern industrial societies is equivalent to the assignment of "rank" in the feudal-agrarian systems. It is likely to increase the vulnerability of the great administrative machine to seizure at the top by adventurous bands. Under emergency conditions modern armies and weapons lose much of their potential from fear of their own destructiveness. Hence they are almost certain to lose time in checking and re-checking messages that on the surface at least provide them with an opportunity to trigger a counterattack. Given the potential paralysis of the vast organization, remarkable opportunities are created for small bands of disciplined and competent men, not only to disrupt, but to take over. Power-centered personalities will undoubtedly continue to probe the soft spots in the dinosaurian structures of the modern globe.

19

One of the main thrusts of the social and psychological sciences in recent years has been to uncover the degree to which human predispositions to behave in specific ways can be influenced by the impact of small group or neighborhood environments. By means of experiment it has been possible to show that the nature of the response varies, to a spectacular extent, according to the layout of the situation irrespective of the personalities of the participants. That is to say, the participants could exchange rôles and the rôle, not the personality, would account for resulting shifts in behavior.[23]

To what extent can any response be elicited from any person irrespective of the predispositions with which he enters a situation? It is obvious that some responses cannot be obtained directly (at least, not without confronting the participants with overwhelmingly drastic threats of deprivation or opportunities for indulgence). For instance, prisoners of war cannot in general be expected to denounce their country and beg for citizenship in the country of the

[23] Consult E. Shils, "The Study of the Primary Group," and A. Bavelas, "Communication in Task Oriented Groups," in Lerner and Lasswell, eds., *The Policy Sciences: Research Developments in Scope and Method* (1951), Chapter 10; Guetzkow, "Building Models about Small Groups" in R. A. Young, ed., *Approaches to the Study of Politics* (1958).

enemy immediately after capture, if the inducement is nothing more substantial than a promise to receive better living conditions. However, the terminal behavior (rejection of citizenship) may be brought about at the end of a series of sub-situations in which the participant (or participants) expect to be so much better off that a small concession seems to be no more significant than a temporary cost. The indulgences or deprivations may be subtly balanced, so that in one context "being better off" may be the gaining of better food, or the removal of a threat to have worse food. The values at stake—no matter how minute or grand —range through all that we have identified. In particular the conscience of a participant may be split so that while part of the personality continues to inflict guilt feelings or shame upon him (— rectitude, — respect) another part projects his guilt to the "Wall Street" interests who got him into the mess in the first place "to save their investments in the arms industries" and who are alleged to have the utmost contempt for patriotism save as an "opiate" of the people. By treating others as guilty and dishonorable, one increases the image of the self as have suffered deprivation; but the deprivation is now perceived as originating in the world outside, so that the responsibility for immoral and dishonorable behavior lies elsewhere than upon the primary ego.

Education and therapy proceed according to the fundamental pattern that we have been describing. Scholars and students are not expected to live up to various norms of conduct all at once, but to approximate the norm at various times and places on the basis of exposure to indulgences and deprivations of values. Bodily pain or discomfort, and the manipulation of affection and respect presumably play diminishing rôles as children grow older and internalize the commands of past environments. They may become more responsive to opportunities relating to skill and enlightenment, rectitude, and more complex practices related to wealth or politics. Societies regard its members as adult in the rôle-playing sense when they have internalized enough rôles to keep the use of external coercion at a minimum.

Therapy, too, proceeds by stages when the patient suffers from disorders which are rooted in unconscious processes. "Communication therapy" puts the accent upon sending signs back and forth between therapist and patient (and between other participants in the therapeutic community) which directly affect all the values of all concerned. "Chemical and related therapies" rely upon the use of non-sign events to affect the patient, seeking to operate only upon the well-being variables. It often happens that the repair of some physical events will profoundly influence symbolic events, and vice versa. The interdependence of physical and symbolic events is such that combined communicative and noncommunicative means are employed to obtain optimum results.

20

What is the significance of the new—or at least perfected—strategy of controlling conduct by "micro-slicing" the social process into more and more cross-sections, each of which can become the site of deliberate manipulative intervention?[24] To the extent that this strategy is applied to every social interaction during every twenty-four hours of life from birth to death, every interaction becomes

[24] See the methods developed by F. F. Skinner, *The Behavior of Organisms* (1938); "Teaching Methods," *Scie ce*, 128 (1958), 969-71; note also his imaginative novel *Walden Two* (1948).

amenable to planned change. Two sub-strategies are always applicable which we call the strategies of "sanction" and of "correction."[25]

Consider first the strategy of sanction. This consists in the management of value indulgences and deprivations on the assumption that the participant or participants can influence their conduct by taking indulgences or deprivations into account. For instance, we adjust fines for speeding or the recognitions given to good drivers on the assumption that most people are capable of perceiving the probable results of the driving alternatives open to them, and are therefore to be regarded as people who take calculated risks when they violate a prescribed norm.

The strategy of correction comes into play when it cannot be assumed that people are equipped to take the advertised consequences of policy into account. We do not, for instance, regard children as measuring up to the minimum level of knowledge and self-control of a "standard" adult. Similarly, we do not look upon physically incapacitated individuals as equipped to conform to certain norms.

In dealing with children the distinction between sanction and correction is applicable. We believe that by being reproved or slapped one child can learn to take the danger of deprivation into account in considering future conduct. But another child is "still too young"; it is a waste of time (and more) to reprove or slap him for a specific act. Corrective action may be devised to keep the child away from temptation.

Unconscious factors often have enough influence upon conduct to interfere with the freedom with which individuals can evaluate the policies available to them in a given

[25] For a special case see H. D. Lasswell and R. L. Donnelly, "The Continuing Debate over Responsibility: An Introduction to Isolating the Condemnation Sanction," *Yale Law Journal*, 68, 1959, 869-99.

context. One of the earliest and most impressive demonstrations of the rôle of the unconscious was the person who performs a criminal act in order to provoke the community into punishing him, thus relieving him—at least for the time being—from a chronic sense of guilt which had been generated within his personality system by incompatible drives. To the extent that unconscious factors affect his conduct, the individual who violates a norm poses a problem not of sanction but of correction.

If unconscious factors are as pervasive as psychoanalytic findings suggest, are we justified in assuming that sanction problems exist at all? Is freedom of choice an illusion fostered by unliquidated residues of the infant's omnipotence of thought? In short, can anybody be trusted to be free enough to play the rôle of judge, therapist, or teacher?

We know that to some extent unconscious and conscious dimensions of human personality can be molded by exposure to the sequence of situations comprising the culture of a civilized society, a social class, an interest group, or a group of personalities; and that the results are modified according to high, middle, and low levels of crisis. We also know that every member of some groups will respond about the same way to certain policy problems. However, although we can foretell how group members will be distributed among alternatives on many matters, we cannot always say *who* will choose *which*. If we choose to postulate that all responses are "completely determined," we can draw a distinction between responses whose "determination is known" at a given time, and responses whose determination at the time is "incompletely known." This amounts to saying that in so far as available knowledge enables us to predict the response of an individual in a group situation we can regard his conduct as "highly determined";

hence if his conduct violates a norm, he becomes a target of corrective strategy. To the extent that an individual's response cannot be predicted he may be regarded as open to sanction in that context. The conception of "incompletely known" determination can be used as a working definition of "incomplete freedom"; and "completely determined" as a definition of "complete unfreedom." The postulate may be changed to read that "complete determination is ultimately impossible"; and the shift does not affect the state of knowledge at a given moment. Fundamental postulates cannot be proved or disproved; thus their postulational character, and the formal equivalency of all ultimate postulates.

The inference is that in a democratic society those judges, therapists, and teachers can be trusted who as adults are no longer free to abandon the ideal demand for the realization of human dignity. They are no longer free, not because they are coerced from outside, but because they have incorporated the demand to act as responsible instruments of a society characterized by widespread rather than narrow participation in value shaping and sharing. However, they exercise "incomplete freedom" by examining the alternatives open to them for the furthering of the ideal commonwealth.

Attention can now be shifted to the sequence of situations in which judges, teachers, and therapists, for example, become totally committed. As we understand it the democratic ideal endorses an ultimate public order in which coercion is at a minimum and reliance is upon persuasion. In applying a micro-slicing technique to the social process of any democratic body politic, the aim is manipulative in the sense that the purpose is to increase the harmony between the overriding goal and the situations which comprise the culture, and especially the pre-adult socialization

sequences of the culture. The aim is to make it possible
for human beings to develop into adult personalities whose
unconscious processes support rather than frustrate the
achievement of a mature level of democratic participation.
It is thinkable that the cultural sequences of any society
can be modified in this direction, and that a character type
can emerge who is multiple-valued, and hence capable of
according to others all the respect and love that he is
capable of directing toward his own ego.

Persons who are competently trained in this orientation
will be acutely sensitive to the fact that all men are born
helpless, weak, and barbarous; and that during the early
months and years of life each one is almost wholly dependent upon the values contributed by the human beings
in their immediate circle. Unless bathed in indulgence
from outside—especially of affection—the primary ego
cannot develop a self which is able to love either itself or
another.[26] Gradually, in the course of socialization, the biological unit becomes a social unit and moves toward the
time when it is capable of passing on to others the support
that it originally received from the environment.

Such a person will perceive that he does not know the
true boundaries of the "self" with which his primary ego
is identified. The self is not to be confused with the physical body of any one individual—least of all with the
somatic site of the primary ego.[27] The patterns of interaction which are the true units of the social process may
seem narrowly focused around family members or the
neighborhood; but with advancing enlightenment it is evi-

[26] The infant's smile is a built-in grantor of indulgence. See R. A. Spitz
and K. M. Wolf, "The Smiling Response. A Contribution to the Ontogenesis
of Social Relations," *Genetic Psychological Monographs*, 34, 1946, 57-125.

[27] Consult P. Schilder, "The Image and Appearance of the Body," *Psyche
Monographs*, No. 4 (1935) ; also L. C. Kolb, "Disturbances of the Body-Image,"
Ch. 39 in Silvano Arieti, ed., *American Handbook of Psychiatry* (1959), Vol. 1.

dent that the primary ego interacts with a vast scientific, technical, religious, philosophical, and aesthetic inheritance.

Unconscious components of personality can become allies in the process whereby the human potential of a given social context is brought to a high level of realization. Persons on good terms with their entire personality structure can benefit from "partial regressions" that bring new form-potentialities to completion.[28]

21

We have had little to say directly about targets outside the body which are objects of reference or movement as impulses pass through or from an unconscious phase. Since the figures immediately present in the environment do not always indulge the developing infant or child fully (from the point of view of the child), fantasy events are used which refer to figures beyond the immediate circle. The fantasy objects provide magic mountains of indulgence. It is true, also, that the world beyond the immediate circle may be populated by non-indulgent, highly threatening figures. This comes about as the child struggles against inner impulses to kill or damage a figure who is also loved. The conflict can be in part resolved by projecting the hostile impulse upon a fantasied ogre.

Since every child acquires schematic representations of indulgent and deprivational images, predispositions are

---

[28] See E. Kris, *Explorations in Art* (1952) ; L. Kubie, *Neurotic Distortion the Creative Process* (1958) : K. Horney, *Self-Analysis* (1942). "Brainstorming" is a group situation adapted from psychoanalysis in which individuals are encouraged to make any suggestion whatever irrespective of plausibility; also Hilgard, "Creativity and Problem Solving," and Lasswell, "The Social Setting of Creativity," in H. H. Anderson, ed., *Creativity and Its Cultivation* (1959).

early available for the creation of maps of supposed reality beyond the primary circle. The socialization process
in any society is consciously or unconsciously directed
toward the capture of these predispositions in order to
consolidate them around culturally standard conceptions.
The technique of capture is to provide value indulgences
for the transfer of early "plus" fantasies to the "plus"
symbols of the adult myth, and early "minus" fantasies to
the "minus" fantasies of the adult symbiology. (In the latter case the transfer is, for example, to the names of
"enemies" or "immoral beliefs.")[29]

A principal question in regard to a political myth is how
"realistic" it can be. The child's world of fantasy is complete; it can occupy the whole focus of attention. It is

[29] Students of politics are particularly concerned with the process by which
persons are incorporated into the ideological or counter-ideological systems in
a body politic. Sample studies: E. H. Erickson, "Hitler's Imagery and German
Youth," *Psychiatry*, 5, 1942, 573-96; Bingham Dai, "Divided Loyalty in War,"
Psychiatry, 7, 1944, 327-40; E. Jones, "The Psychology of Quislingism" in
Essays in Applied Psychoanalysis (1951); G. Almond, *The Appeals of Com-
munism* (1954); N. W. Ackerman and M. Jahoda, *Anti-Semitism and Emo-
tional Disorder* (1950); N. Leites and E. Bernaut, *Ritual of Liquidation*
(1954); R. E. Lane, "How Are Unconscious Needs Expressed in Politics?"
Chapter 9 in *Political Life: Why People Get Involved in Politics* (1959);
E. Burdick and A. J. Brodbeck, eds., *American Voting Behavior* (1959), chap-
ters on "The Problem of Irrationality and Neuroticism Underlying Political
Choice," "The Relations between Primary and Secondary Identifications:
Psychiatry and the Group Sciences," "Emotional Factors in Voting Behavior,"
"The Principles of Permanence and Change: Electioneering and Psychother-
apy Compared"; N. Leites, *A Study of Bolshevism* (1953); E. H. Schein,
"The Chinese Indoctrination Program for Prisoners of War; A Study of At-
tempted 'Brain Washing,'" *Psychiatry*, 19, 1952, 149-72; R. J. Lifton, "Thought
Reform of Western Civilians in Chinese Communist Prisons," *Psychiatry*, 19,
1952, 173-95; J. A. Meerloo, *Rape of the Mind* (1956); Lasswell, "Collective
Autism as a Consequence of Culture Contact: Notes on Religious Training
and the Peyote Cult at Taos," *Zeitschrift für Sozialforschung*, 4, 1935, 232-46;
"The Triple Appeal Principle," *American Journal of Sociology*, 37, 1932;
"Propaganda and Mass Insecurity," *Psychiatry*, 13, 1950, 283-300; "Selective
Effects of Personality on Political Participation," in R. Christie and J. Jahoda,
eds., *Studies in the Scope and Method of "The Authoritarian Personality"*
(1954), 197-225; S. de Grazia has published two volumes of a projected trilogy
with great relevance to the problems dealt with here.

evident that an infant or child is exposed to a limited reality, and does little rejection of fantasy as incompatible
with reality. Images, of course, are compounded of expectations, demands, and identifications; "reality" does eventually succeed in modifying all matter-of-fact assumptions
(expectations) and identifications. Sentimentalized symbols—especially the preferences and volitions (demands)
—are capable of great continuity. Similarly, the boundaries of the self can fluctuate around the primary ego
without necessarily undergoing drastic change.

That symbol events resist the discipline of external
events ("reality") is well known. When resistance is overcome and an interpretation of the "world outside" does
crystallize, it is clutched as an asset for which a price has
been paid. Thus an interpretation of reality provides
stabilizing criteria for the symbol system. Hence the rigidity displayed by established perceptual patterns.[30]

The perceptual rigidity of ego systems helps to explain
the lack of realism so often found at the intelligence phase
of a decision process. The complex slots that have been
worked out for perceiving "Chinese," "upper-class families," "machine-tool interests," or "outgoing personalities," for instance, influence the way that a reporter sees
a happening and the signs that he chooses in order to
evoke a comprehending symbol in an audience. Stereotypes, as Walter Lippmann felicitously named them years
ago, are standardized modes of enlightenment which typically are regarded as damaged if new experiences fail
to fall into pattern. The response to contradiction may take
the form not of revision but of reiteration, accompanied

---

[30] On contemporary studies of perception see especially the publications of
E. Brunkswik and of J. Bruner and collaborators. Also J. T. Marsh and F. G.
Worden, "Perceptual Approaches to Personality," in *Psychiatric Research
Reports*, No. 6, American Psychiatric Association (January 1956), 171-77.

by the diverting of attention from the source of unwelcome images.

By concentrating scientific activity upon *mis*conception we are becoming more alert to the task of improving the intelligence phase of the political process. The unconscious fear of being taken by surprise, which is a component of distrust, plays a prominent rôle in this connection; and, as is true of unconscious activities generally, the fear is often self-defeating. By substituting pretense for the results of re-inquiry an individual or a group often endangers its own security.

By the systematic study of intelligence and appraisal functions we can hope to devise methods that increase the realism of perception in the decision process.[31] Unconscious components, for example, are vulnerable to direct attack by means of free association and interpretation, and also by such noncommunicative techniques as brain chemicals.

The point has often been made that the chief strategy of democracy has traditionally been "negative," that is, trust in competitive practice rather than an explicit positive goal. The body politic is assumed to be in sound health if political parties, businesses, and mass media are in competition. No one would seriously deny that a very considerable degree of power dispersal is likely to be more favorable to freedom than hyper-concentration of power. But competition is not enough. The plain fact is that the best information and the most competent interpretations may *not* appear even in the competitive press.

[31] Lasswell, "The Intelligence Function: Built In Error," *Prod*, 3 (1959), 3-7; *The Decision Process; Seven Categories of Functional Analysis* (1956); A. B. Szalito, "Some Comments on Psychological Aspects of Evasion and Disarmament," in S. Melman, ed., *Inspection for Disarmament* (1958), 251-60; G. Ichheiser, "Misunderstandings in Human Relations: A Study in False Social Perception," *American Journal of Sociology* (August 1949, supplement).

Something more is needed than simple faith in an unseen hand. Granted that we need competition, and that we need anti-monopoly policies; we also need quality competition. Quality competition is still competition: it means the joining in the competitive fray of persons who report and recommend the best facts and the most thoughtful interpretations available in the body politic at a given moment in history. The strategy is not to supplant but rather to supplement the practice of democratic statecraft.

The practice of quality competition is especially essential in connection with the media of general and special communication in modern industrial democracies. We are well aware of the fact that there are vested and sentimental interests in diminishing the enlightenment and skill functions of the public media. The most immediate explanation appears to be that businessmen who advertise their products bring pressure to bear upon the media to alienate as few potential customers as possible. Hence the steady dilution of quality.

However, the obvious factor is not always the most important one. Why do business interests not see that by destroying the press as an instrument of free government they are destroying two of the institutions without which a free economic system cannot endure? It is not enough to assert that businessmen are conniving at suicide because they are dull-witted, or because they are more grasping than other members of the community. Nor is it strictly accurate to plead ignorance and to claim that "they have never been told" about the fragile character of private business. On the contrary, the spokesmen of many business associations have "said the right things."

There are many indications that the critical factor is deeper and less spectacular than stupidity or ignorance. Judging from the intimate histories of some businessmen,

I think there is ground for suggesting that key factors are unconscious fear of admitting the vulnerability of the self in so far as the self is identified with the business system, and the resulting failure to perceive the meaning of messages that provide a realistic picture of the true state of affairs.

These defense mechanisms can be and often are overcome by members of the business community, but are not successfully penetrated by the business group as a whole. Evidently our society's technique of handling communication channels is so inept that it has been unable to break through the unconscious defenses and to liberate businessmen to the discovery of their own best interests.[32]

No one denies that other groups in the community are as opaque as businessmen. They are, however, less admired and less directly influential in supplying the advertising funds which presently work the corruption of the public media. One might expect the businessmen who run the presses to resist corruption; and some of them do. But they appear to be among the more timid members of the community in their dealing with other businessmen.

We can look with some hope to the technique of microslicing when we apply it to the whole sequence of events through which individuals pass in learning the social myth. At every stage of the exposure—to the images of culture, class, interest, personality—a procedure for the appraising of reality must be built in. The implication is that all early fantasy elements will be open to test. Realistic revisions can be encouraged by managing value indulgences and deprivations in harmony with combined strategies of sanction and correction.

---

[32] See the conclusions and recommendations of the Commission on Freedom of the Press (Chairman, Robert M. Hutchins), *A Free and Responsible Press* (1947).

As it is today we are on the threshold of the task of reorganizing our modes of acquiring skill, or of assessing the realism of the intelligence maps upon which people base their choices. As an aid in this huge enterprise it will be essential to improve the coverage and the depth of the current flow of information that appraises unconscious as well as conscious factors throughout the world social process. For the United States the following questions suggest some of the major points to be covered in a continuing survey of unconscious trends:

Is the weight of the super-ego becoming less severe upon Americans than it was a generation ago?[33] Can we say, for example, that the conscience is less punitive, and that it is peremptory in regard to a much narrower range of conduct than formerly? Is the rate of change different in New England, the Middle Atlantic States, and other regions? Are there different rates among metropolitan and sub-metropolitan areas? Do the rates vary according to upper-, middle-, or lower-class position in terms of each major value? Are there some interest groups—such as those connected with the communications industry—where the rates are rapid or stabilized at a certain high (or low) level? Are the rates responsive to crisis (and intercrisis) situations?

Are the images that one group of Americans have of other Americans becoming more or less realistic? The images of themselves? What of the images that Americans entertain of non-Americans? To what extent do unconscious misperceptions occur in face-to-face relations? In mass audience contexts?

[33] D. Riesman, *The Lonely Crowd* (1950); *Faces in the Crowd* (1952); M. Rosenberg, "The Meaning of Politics in Mass Society," *Public Opinion Quarterly*, 15, 1951; E. Kris and N. Leites, "Trends in Twentieth Century Propaganda," in G. Roheim, ed., *Psychoanalysis and the Social Sciences* (1947); L. Trilling, *Freud and the Crisis of Our Culture* (1955).

What are the most economical noncoercive means of modifying the propensities of a given group to misperceive themselves and others? At what cost—calculated in terms of all values—can there be a ten-per-cent shift within a year toward realistic perception in primary situations? In secondary situations? Under various levels of crisis?

22

In concluding I offer this comment: We are in the early stages of an explosive development in every field of scientific knowledge, including knowledge of men's changing value predispositions and gratifications through time. The tempo has risen markedly, though not as rapidly in the knowledge of mastery of self as in the command of nature. As the discrepancy grows, our tenure of life as a species grows more precarious. It is obvious that we can live and kill and die. We also have excellent ground for the belief that we can live and nurture and create. The psychopathology of "individuals," which is becoming the psychopathology of society, calls attention to the formidable factors that stand in the way of a world commonwealth of human dignity. The discovery and scrutiny of such factors pre-condition policies that reduce the discrepancy between ideal aspirations and levels of effective participation in government, politics, and law.

APPENDIX A

SELECT BIBLIOGRAPHY

Reprinted from the 1930 Edition

The literature of psychoanalysis from its inception to 1926 is conveniently available in John Rickman's *Index Psychoanalyticus, 1893–1926*. The *Gesammelte Schriften* of Sigmund Freud have been published by the Internationaler Psychoanalytischer Verlag, Vienna, in eleven volumes. This publishing house puts out most of the literature of the circle around Freud. Of Freud's books the beginner may be referred to his *General Introduction to Psychoanalysis*, *The Interpretation of Dreams*, and *Three Contributions to Sexual Theory*. An English edition of Freud's collected papers is in process of publication. The most important technical journal is the *Internationale Zeitschrift für ärztliche Psychoanalyse*. There is an English journal, *the International Journal of Psycho-Analysis*, and an American one, *The Psychoanalytic Review*. (A French periodical has recently appeared.) Among the "orthodox" psychoanalytical treatises the following are of particular importance:

FERENCZI, S. *Bausteine zur Psychoanalyse*. Leipzig, 1926.

———. *Versuch einer Genitaltheorie*. Leipzig, 1924.

FERENCZI, S., and HOLLOS, S. *Psychoanalysis and the Psychic Disorder of General Paresis*, "Nervous and Mental Disease Monograph Series," No. 42. New York and Washington, 1925.

The psychological manifestations of a physical disease are predicted on the basis of the psychoanalytical theory of personality development. Of great methodological importance.

ABRAHAM, K. *Klinische Beitrage zur Psychoanalyse aus den Jahren 1907–20*. Leipzig, etc., 1921.

———. *Psychoanalytische Studien zur Charakterbildung*. Leipzig, etc., 1925.

The most influential approach to the problem of character formation. Amplified in many directions by Jones, Glover, etc.

ALEXANDER, F. *Psychoanalyse der Gesamtpersönlichkeit.* Leipzig, etc., 1927.

A notably lucid presentation of the general theory. Recently translated as *The Psychoanalysis of the Total Personality* and published in the "Nervous and Mental Disease Monograph Series."

HARTMANN, H. *Die Gründlagen der Psychoanalyse.* Leipzig, 1927.

A very important book which views analytical concepts in relation to the data of experimental psychology.

DEUTSCH, FELIX. "Experimentelle Studien zur Psychoanalyse," *Internationale Zeitschrift,* IX (1923), 484–96.

Reports the demonstration of the mechanism of repression by the use of post-hypnotic suggestion.

KEMPF, E. *Psychopathology.* St. Louis, 1921.

Stresses the function of the autonomic functions, and undertakes to amplify psychoanalytical theory in this direction.

Among those who have broken off from Freud, after having been associated with him, are Stekel, Jung, and Adler. Stekel has published ten volumes of case histories which are valuable for the beginner who needs to acquire a sense of what sort of thing the human mind is capable. The other two are of more theoretical importance. Jung's *Psychological Types* is of the most immediate interest to social scientists, although his speculations about the "racial unconscious" are suggestive. Alfred Adler's standpoint is set out in his *Individual Psychology.* His circle in Vienna publishes a journal.

An excellent manual is *The Structure and Meaning of Psychoanalysis* (New York, 1930), by William Healy, Augusta F. Bronner, and Anna Mae Bowers.

The psychoanalytical movement can be placed in the general perspective of medical psychology by referring to such a manual as William A. White's *Outlines of Psychiatry* or Bernard Hart's *Psychopathology.* There are excellent books in German on medical psychology by Kronfeld, Birnbaum, Schilder, Kretschmer, and many others. The general movements in the field can be followed in the *American Journal of Psychiatry* or the *Journal of Nervous and Mental Diseases,* the latter of which is edited by William A. White and Smith Ely Jelliffe, who also supervise the well-known series of books, usually translations, called the "Nervous and Mental Disease Monograph Series." Pierre Janet's *Psychological Healing* reviews the general history of psychopathology. Among the innumerable articles and books which undertake to appraise the clinical and normal implications of psychoanalysis, the symposium edited by Hans Prinzhorn may be chosen, *Krisis der Psychoanalyse* (Leipzig, 1928), Band I (the projected second volume will not appear). Otto Rank, who has likewise broken with Freud, is publishing a series of books on the psychoanalytical interview which promises to serve as a bridge between the general theory and the objective studies of the interview situation which are in progress in America.

On the special problem of personality and character types, the volume by A. A. Roback, *The Psychology of Character*, may be instanced as a very comprehensive guide to the literature. His *A Bibliography on Personality* is also available. An acute analysis of typologies was offered by O. Selz before the German experimental psychologists in 1923. See the following:

SELZ, O. "Über die Personlichkeitstypen und die Methoden ihrer Bestimmung," *Bericht über den VIII. Kongress für experimentelle Psychologie.* Jena, 1924.

KLÜVER, H. "An Analysis of Recent Work on the Problem of Psychological Types," *Journal of Nervous and Mental Diseases*, LXII, No. 6 (December, 1925).

The current output is reviewed from time to time in relation to tests by Mark A. May, Gordon W. Allport, and certain other psychologists who are especially interested in the field. The *Psychological Index* can be consulted for the purpose of keeping abreast of the large quantity of published material.

The most influential recent book is Kretschmer's *Physique and Character*. The somatic factors in personality are stated with charm and brevity by E. Miller, *Types of Mind and Body*. Useful summary and critical volumes are by William I. Thomas and Dorothy S. Thomas, *The Child in America* (New York, 1928), chapters viii–xiii inclusive, and by R. G. Gordon, *Personality* (New York, 1926).

The psychoanalytical literature which has undertaken to deal with politics or politicians explicitly may be appended here:

PFISTER, OSKAR. "Analytische Untersuchungen über die Psychologie des Hasses und der Versöhnung," *Jahrbuch der Psychoanalyse,* II (1910), 134–78.

———. "Die Bedeutung der Psychoanalyse für die Staats- und Gesellschaftslehre" (Vortrag an VI. Int. Psa. Kong., Hague, September 8–11, 1920), abstract in *Internationale Zeitschrift,* VI, 400.

———. "Die menschlichen Einigungsbestrebungen im Lichte der Psychoanalyse," *Imago,* XII (1926), 126–35.

The *Imago* is the psychoanalytical journal which is devoted to applications of psychoanalytical theory to the interpretation of culture.

SACHS, HANNS. "Die Bedeutung der Psychoanalyse für Probleme der Soziologie" (Vortrag), abstract in *Centralblatt für Psychoanalyse,* II (1911), 464–69.

———. "Ein Traum Bismarcks," *Internationale Zeitschrift,* I (1913), 80–83.

SACHS, HANNS, and RANK, OTTO. *Die Bedeutung der Psychoanalyse für die Geisteswissenschaften.* Wiesbaden, 1913.

This was published in the "Grenzfragen des Nerven und Seelenlebens," No. 93, a series which contains many volumes of great interest to social scientists. Kretschmer now is the responsible editor. The book also appears as No. 23 in the "Nervous and Mental Disease Monograph Series."

RANK, OTTO. "Der 'Familienroman' in der Psychologie des Attentaters," *Der Künstler* (virte vermehrte Auflage; Leipzig, etc., 1925), pp. 142–48.

This fragment first appeared in 1911.

STORFER, A. J. "Zur Sonderstellung des Vatermordes." Leipzig, etc., 1911.

Parricide and regicide are punished with unusual severity in different legal systems.

ABRAHAM, KARL. "Amenhotep IV (Echnaton)," *Imago,* I (1912), 334–60.

One of the earliest applications of analytical concepts to a historical personage.

FREUD, SIGMUND. *Totem und Taboo.* Leipzig, etc., 1913.

Outlines his hypothesis of the origin of culture in an original parricide by a band of revolting brothers, who resented the monopoly of the females by the old man of the tribe, and who undertook to repress memories of the crime. See the discussion by Malinowski of this hypothesis in *Sex and Repression in Savage Society* (New York, 1927).

———. "Zeitgemasses über Krieg und Tod," *Imago*, IV (1915–16), 1–21.

———. *Massenpsychologie und Ich-Analyse.* Leipzig, etc., 1921.

An application of Freud's theories to the psychology of crowds and social institutions. See William McDougall, "Professor Freud's Group Psychology and His Theory of Suggestion," chapter xvii of *Problems of Personality* (ed. Campbell and others; New York, 1925).

———. *Unbehagen der Kultur.* Leipzig, etc., 1929.

JEKELS, LUDWIG. "Der Wendepunkt im Leben Napoleons I," *Imago*, III (1914), 313–81.

KAPLAN, LEO. "Der tragische Held und der Verbrecher," *ibid.*, IV (1915), 96–124.

JONES, ERNEST. "War and Sublimation." Read before the British Association for the Advancement of Science, Section of Physiology, September 10, 1915; published in *Reports* of the Association, LXXXV, 699 ff.

———. (ed.). *The Social Aspects of Psychoanalysis.* London, 1923.

TAUSK, VIKTOR. "Zur Psychologie des Deserteurs," *Zeitschrift*, IV (1916–17), 193–204, 228–40.

BLÜHER, HANS. *Die Rolle der Erotik in der männlichen Gesellschaft.* 2 vols. Jena, 1917.

BERNFELD, SIEGFRIED. "Die Psychoanalyse in der Jugendbewegung," *Imago*, V (1919), 283–89.

———. "Über eine typische Form der männlichen Pubertät," *ibid.*, IX (1923), 169–188.

FEDERN, PAUL. *Die Vaterlose Gesellschaft.* Leipzig, etc., 1919.

CLARK, L. PIERCE. "A Psychologic Study of Abraham Lincoln," *ibid.*, VIII (1921), 1–21.

————. "A Psycho-historical Study of the Epileptic Personality in the Genius," *ibid.*, IX (1922), 367–401.

————. "The Narcism of Alexander the Great," *Ibid.*, X (1923), 156–69.

————. *Napoleon: Self-Destroyed.* New York, 1929.

KOLNAI, AUREL. *Psychoanalyse und Soziologie.* Leipzig, etc., 1920.

LAZELL, EDWARD W. "Psychology of War and Schizophrenia," *Psychoanalytic Review*, VII (1920), 224–45.

RINALDO, JOEL. *The Psychoanalysis of the Reformer.* New York, 1921.

WHITE, WILLIAM A. *Thoughts of a Psychiatrist on the War and After.* New York, 1919.

LOW, BARBARA. "Civic Ideals: Some Psycho-analytical Considerations," *Sociological Review*, 1922.

BOVEN, WILLIAM. "Alexander der Grosse," *Imago*, VIII (1922), 418–39.

BERGER, G. "Zur Theorie der menschlichen Feindseligkeit," *ibid.*, IX (1923), 344–67.

LORENZ, EMIL. *Der politische mythus, Beitrage zur mythologie der Kultur.* Leipzig, etc., 1923.

Illustrates the state-father relationship from the lore and literature of many cultures.

REIK, THEODOR. *Geständniszwang und Strafbedürfnis: Probleme der Psychoanalyse und der Kriminologie.* Leipzig, etc., 1925.

Outlines in masterly fashion the implications of the need for punishment and the compulsion to confess for criminology. Reik has also published extensively on religion from the psychoanalytical standpoint.

KOHN, ERWIN, *Lasalle der Führer.* Leipzig, etc., 1926.

ALEXANDER, FRANZ, and STAUB, HUGO. *Der Verbrecher und seine Richter.* Vienna, 1929.

A sketch of criminology from the psychoanalytical standpoint, drawing heavily on Alexander's conception of the neurotic character, as distinguished from the neurotics who show hysteric or compulsive symptoms.

FRIEDJUNG, JOSEF K. "Zur Psychologie des kleinen Politikers," *Imago*, XIV (1928), 498–501.

Among those who have undertaken from allied fields to apply psychoanalytic viewpoints may be mentioned William F. Ogburn, who read a paper before the economists in 1918; Thomas D. Eliot, sociologist; Harry Elmer Barnes, historical sociologist; E. D. Martin, social psychologist; Preserved Smith, historian; R. V. Harlow, historian; W. H. R. Rivers, ethnologist; and Theodore Schroeder, lawyer. See especially:

BARNES, HARRY ELMER. *The New History and the Social Studies*, chap. iii. New York, 1925.

Discusses the bibliography in English.

SWOBODA, HERMANN. "Zur Psychologie des Parlamentarismus," *Oesterreichische Rundschau*, Band XIV, Heft 1, January 1, 1908.

———. "Die Kunst des Regierens," *ibid.*, Band XVII, December 15, 1908.

———. "Der Volksvertreter," *ibid.*, Band XXXII, Heft 3, August 1, 1912.

These articles of Swoboda are the first well-considered applications of psychoanalysis to politics by a non-specialist. The first article treats the rôle of parliamentarism as "catharsis," and specifically refers to the work of Breuer and Freud.

Aside from specifically psychoanalytical efforts to interpret individuals and collective trends, there have been many efforts on the part of other psychiatrists and physicians, or their followers, to offer such interpretations. The whole literature of "pathography" is abstracted and discussed here:

LANGE-EICHBAUM, WILHELM. *Genie-Irrsinn, und Ruhm*. Leipzig, 1928.

Students of politics will be most interested in the references and abstracts concerning Rousseau, Alexander the Great, Amenhotep IV, Bismarck, Blücher, emperors and princes, Frederick the Great, Lincoln, Loyola, Ludwig II of Bavaria, Napoleon, and

Robespierre. Möbius put "pathography" on a scientific basis.
The following is one of the best of the "pathographies," since it
stresses the diseased aspects of the personality in the perspective
of the total development of the subject's career:

HEIDENHAIN, ADOLF, *J.-J. Rousseau, Persönlichkeit, Philosophie
und Psychose* "Grenzfragen des Nerven- und Seelenlebens,"
Heft 117. Munich, 1924.

The study of the effect of individual pathology on culture, and
of culture upon individual pathology, is envisaged as a program
in the following:

BIRNBAUM, KARL. *Grundzüge der Kulturpsychopathologie,*
"Grenzfragen des Nerven- und Seelenlebens," Heft 116. Munich, 1924.

The reckless extension of individual pathological terms to the
state of society as a whole has caused much confusion, but a case
can be made out for a valid use of the concept of the pathological.
Thus:

SCHNEERSOHN, F. "Zur Grundlegung einer Völker-und Massen-
psychopathologie (Soziopsychopathologie)," *Ethos,* I (1925–
26), 81–120.

This includes an exhaustive bibliography of the efforts of psychiatrists
to extend their conceptions to society, and a detailed consideration of the
methodological issues involved.

Special attention should be called to the forthcoming volume
by Harry Stack Sullivan on *Personal Psychopathology* in which a
systematic treatment of the whole field of psychiatry and sociology
is presented. Dr. Sullivan has vastly stimulated a *rapprochement*
between physician and social scientist in the United States. See
the *Proceedings* of the two colloquiums on personality investigation, held under the auspices of the American Psychiatric Association, first published in the *American Journal of Psychiatry* for
May, 1929, and May, 1930, and separately obtainable.

APPENDIX B
QUESTION LIST ON POLITICAL PRACTICES
Reprinted from the 1930 Edition

This question list refers directly to the organized political life of the subject. Questions which are designed to elicit preferences are not included. For general personality questions and trait lists, the usual sources may be consulted for suggestions.[1]

The question list here must, of course, be modified if used orally or with naïve subjects. An effort is always to be made to elicit specific incidents which arise in the mind. "Reminiscences" and not theories about the self are desired.

1. List the various associations and organizations of which you have been a member and in which you enjoyed rights which were approximately equal to those exercised by everyone else. Specify in each case whether you were almost inactive, moderately active, quite active. State when you became a

---

[1] More specifically, Kretschmer's *Psychobiogramm*, published in H. Hoffmann, *Das Problem des Charakteraufbaus*, as an appendix; Heyman's trait list (republished in *Gesammelte Kleinere Schriften*, Dritter Teil); the psychograms of W. Stern (in *Die differentielle Psychologie in ihren methodischen Grundlagen*), of Baade, Lipman, and Stern (*Zeitschrift für angewandete Psychologie*, Band III), of P. Margis (Breslau dissertation, 1911, *Das Problem und die Methoden der Psychographie mit einer Individualanalyse von E. T. A. Hoffmann*), of L. Lewin (*Friedrich Hebbel: Beitrag zu einem Psychogramm* [Berlin, 1913]), of E. Stern ("Patho-psychographische Untersuchungen," *Archiv für Psychiatrie und Nervenkrankheiten*, Band LXI), of F. Kehrer and S. Fischer, ("Modell einer klinisch-experimentellen Pathographie," *Zeitschrift für die gesamte Neurologie und Psychiatrie*, Band LXXXV) ; the outlines of Dr. Paul Federn (*Schema der Libidoaufnahme*, MSS in my possession), of F. L. Wells (MSS in my possession), of G. V. Hamilton, of Adolf Meyer (mimeographed MSS in my possession), of Amsden and Hoch, of Floyd Allport, and the lists of Woodworth, Laird, House, Freyd and Thurstone.

member and how your subsequent activity fluctuated. Give
dates when possible. Remember that you have been a member of various democratically organized political units. Mention also the prep-school class organizations, school and college organizations, alumni associations, profession organizations, civic associations, parties, and elective public offices. Organizations which were autocratically organized
(that is, which exercised authority over those who had no
formal right to choose the officials) should not be included.
Do not omit associations of war veterans, Daughters or Sons
of the Revolution, pacifists, anarchists, reform agitators, constitutional defense leagues, etc.

2. List the various organizations with which you have been associated either as one in autocratic authority or as one subject to autocratic authority. This should include schools
which you have attended, appointive offices in the government, most business connections, trusteeships, etc.

3. List your various free-lance activities which have involved
scarcely any organization but which have been a source of
income. Partnerships which have involved practically no
staff, private secretaryships, and such are meant to be listed
here.

The following questions are intended to bring out the
salient facts in connection with your relationship to each
democratically organized and autocratically organized association or institution with which you were affiliated.
Answer for each organization which you have listed in so
far as applicable.

4. Just how did you become a member of this organization?
What steps did you take? Who helped you? Why were
you taken in? If you organized this body, why did you do
it? When did you first entertain the idea? How did your
plans develop? What assistance did you get and by what
means? What was your reputation inside the organization
when you first came in? Were you, for instance, ignored or

regarded as promising or accepted and given responsibility immediately?

5. What friends or enemies did you have inside the organization when you first came into it?

6. To what offices or positions of authority in the organization were you elected or appointed?

7. In each case explain how it came about. When did you first entertain the idea that selection was possible? How much did you hesitate and ponder before deciding to try for the position or before accepting it if it was thrust upon you? What alternatives did you consider? With whom did you talk over the matter? What was urged on you? What were the disadvantages which deterred you or the advantages which lured you? Just what did you do to get the office or position? Who were your chief aids? Who were your chief competitors? What were the points in your favor and in favor of the others? How did the various cliques, groups, and other components of the organization line up? Sketch your strategy and practices in dealing with each one before selection. Did any issues of policy figure and how?

8. What were the cases in which you ran or were considered at one stage or another for selection? Answer the questions as before for each instance.

9. What appointive power or influence did you exercise in office? Whom did you consult in making or influencing these appointments? To what extent did you consider competence? The rewarding of friends? The division or elimination of your opponents?

10. What objectives, if any, had you thought out when you assumed responsibility?

11. What were the chief issues on which you took a position? How did your influence make itself felt in each instance (in public speaking, interviewing, appointive pressure, etc.)? How did each major issue happen to emerge? How did you arrive at your position? Whom did you consult? What considerations were balanced on both sides of the question? To what extent did you make issues by interjecting specific proposals into the situation? How did you happen to do this? What were the elements in the organization which were lined up on either side of the question? What concessions

did you make in order to achieve your ends? Do you regard your concessions as too cheaply bought as you look back upon them? What results did you secure which satisfy you?

12. During your tenure were there personal misunderstandings, quarrels, and hatreds between you and anybody? How did they come about? What did you do and what was the relation of what you did to what happened?

13. Were there personal misunderstandings, quarrels, and antipathies among others inside the organization which you were asked to settle or which you tried to settle? What did you do and what relation did it bear to what finally happened?

14. Were there personal misunderstandings, quarrels, and antipathies between members of your own organization and people in other organizations which you were asked to settle or which you tried to settle? What did you do and what relation did it bear to what finally happened?

15. Did your organization have any ill feelings as a body for other organizations or groups when you came into office? What did you do to inflame or reduce it? What effect? Why?

16. Did your organization have any friendly feelings as a body for other organizations or groups? What did you do to cement or to disrupt these relations? Why? With what effect on the course of events?

17. Did your organization develop any friendly or unfriendly relations with organizations or groups to which they had been previously indifferent during your term in office? What did you do that had anything to do with this result? Why?

18. Did your organization use physical, legal, or other forms of pressure upon any other organization or group during your term? What was your rôle in suggesting, supporting, directing, or obstructing the adoption of these tactics? Why? What resulted?

19. Did your organization use physical, legal, economic, or other forms of pressure upon any of its own members during your term? What was your rôle in suggesting, supporting, directing, or obstructing the adoption of these tactics? Why? With what effect?

20. By whom were you praised during and after your term of office for your record? How were you praised or recognized and honored and for what? Effect on you?

21. By whom were you adversely criticized during and after your term in office for your record? How were you censured and for what? Effect on you?

22. Were you re-elected or reappointed, promoted or demoted, after serving your term or before? Why?

23. How did you get along with your immediate superiors, collaborators, and assistants? To what extent did you manipulate them? What different tactics did you employ with each? What success?

24. What were your formal and ceremonial duties in the organization as an officer? Did you enjoy them?

25. How did you enjoy your other official activities?

26. As a non-official, or non-position-holding member of the organization, what did you enjoy about it? The ceremonies? The routine operations? The uncertain features?

27. As a member of the rank and file, what policies and activities did you initiate, support, or oppose? Why? How much did you do and to what effect? How did the elements of the organization line up? Were you usually in the minority or the majority? What elements were usually with you?

28. How did your reputation change during your years in the organizations?

29. What particular friends and enemies did you acquire?

30. As a member of the rank and file, did you have personal misunderstandings, quarrels, and hatreds between you and other members? Why? What did you do? Results?

31. Did you arbitrate any grievances or try to smooth them out? Success? Why?

32. What was your attitude toward other organizations or groups with which your organization either competed or had some relations? As a member of the rank and file, what did you do to change or intensify prevailing attitudes? Influence?

33. Did your organization use physical or other means of pressure against outside organizations and other members of your organization? As a member of the rank and file, what did you do and with what effect? Did you think your organization was the best of its kind?

34. Have you severed your connection or become inactive? Why?

35. If you are still active, what are your plans and hopes?

36. How did this particular organization touch the administrative, legislative, and judicial branches of the government? The political parties? How? What methods were used to bring pressure to bear? What was your part in them?

37. As you look back on your life in the organization do you think of practices which you indulged in or tolerated which you regard as perhaps questionable? Instances? Did you so regard them at the time? What would have happened if you had not indulged in them? Should an organization be run on a different basis now?

38. What effect did life in the organization have upon your activity in the politics of the community at large? Did you have impulses to express yourself publicly or privately upon matters which you felt it expedient to follow? Or were you driven to such expression and activity?

39. If you were to judge entirely in terms of your experience as a member of this organization, what would be your judgment of the honesty and efficiency of the public service and the party machine?

40. What political prejudices or philosophies were current among various elements inside the organization?

41. Think of various members of this organization who were rather typical. How did you act toward them when you met them? What topics of conversation, of anecdote, etc., did you indulge in? What activities in common were there?

42. Did you think that you were imposed upon by any members as you look back upon it now? Did you estimate some of them too highly? Who? Why?

43. Did you underestimate some? Who? Why?

44. Were you estimated too high or too low? By whom? Why?

45. What things apart from common dishonesty would have caused you to lose standing in the organization? What opinions and activities would have compromised you?

46. Did you risk loss of standing at any time by word or deed? Were you tempted to? Why did you refrain?

47. When you tried to add others to the organization, whom did you seek? What type of people, in general, were you interested in?

48. Did the organization live up to your ideal? Why?
49. Who were the most powerful ones in the organization at different periods? What were your relations with them? What did you do consciously to win them? Success? What did you do to antagonize them? How did they take it? What, in short, was the attitude of the leaders toward you?
50. Did you ever have a sense of frustration arising from your failure to participate in discussions of policy, either because you hesitated to express yourself or because you expressed yourself badly?
51. What is your matured judgment of the utility of this organization in society?
52. How did your organization connections help or hurt you socially or any other way?
53. How did your outside connections help or hurt you in the organization?
54. What, generally speaking, were your advantages and disadvantages with reference to securing and holding a prominent position in the organization?
55. In general, what place did this organization play in your life?
56. With respect to each one of your so-called free-lance or very personal activities, answer such questions as these: How did you happen to take it up? Upon what factors would your success and failure depend? What did you do to manage the persons upon whom success or failure depended? With what result? What reaction did your experience have upon your outlook upon political life generally?

INDEX

Abraham, Karl, 103, 150 n.
Adjustive thinking, 226
Adler, Alfred, 71 ff.
Administrators: definition and histories of, 127 ff., general theory of, 151 ff.
Adolescence and politics, 187
Agitators: definition and histories of, 78 ff., general theory of, 124 ff.
Aichhorn, August, 230
Alexander, Franz, 139, 178, 182, 199, 220 n., 254
Allport, Floyd, 58
Anderson, John, 232
Apfelbach, Hans, 61, 62, 64
Aristotle, 39
Attitudes, 234 ff.
Autistic reveries, 226

Bernfeld, S., 177
Bernheim, 20
Biography, political, uses and limitations of, 3
Birnbaum, K., 200 n.
Bjerre, 239
Blackstone, 175
Bleuler, 71
Blondel, 11
Blüher, Hans, 178 n.
Boas, 13
Bodin, 54
Boss, 48
Breuer, 19
Bridgman, P. W., 251 n.
Brücke, 18
Bryce, 252
Bühler, Charlotte, 230
Burrow, Trigant, 201 n.

Carlyle, 42
Case histories, 3 ff., 78 ff.
Catharsis, 195
Catlin, G. E. G., 46
Charcot, 18
Chave, 59 n.
Chicago, University of, 13, 201 n., 207 n.
Christensen, 39, 53 n.

Composite types, 53
Comte, 10
Consensus, 192
Convictions, political, 153 fl.
Conway, 52, 53 n.
Co-relational types, 55
Cowley, W. H., 59
Crises, political, 179 ff.
Croner, Else, 232 n.
Crowd, 193 n.

Debate, zone of, 192
De Grange, 10 n.
Democracy, 194 ff.
Despot, 46
Deutsch, Helene, 123 n.
Developmental types, 60
Dicey, 1
Dictator, 197
Dilthey, 11, 49
Discussion, 194 ff.
Dream, 26
Durkheim, 10

Eder, 173, 181, 190
Education, 201
Ellis, Havelock, 83 n., 199
Emotional bonds, 185, 192
Energy of developed personality, 65
Events, subjective and external, 240 ff.
Exhortation, 196

Fabian Society, 186
Familiarization, a purpose of the study, 14
Federn, Paul, 180, 234
Ferenczi, S., 71, 97, 103 n., 105 n., 150 n., 213, 220 n., 255
Fliess, 62, 69
Follett, Mary L., 48
Forms of expression, thought and interest, 235 ff.
Formula for development of political man, 75
Frazer, 73
Free-fantasy, 32